This Book Comes With Lots of
FREE Online Resources

Nolo's award-winning website has a page dedicated just to this book. Here you can:

KEEP UP TO DATE. When there are important changes to the information in this book, we'll post updates.

GET DISCOUNTS ON NOLO PRODUCTS. Get discounts on hundreds of books, forms, and software.

READ BLOGS. Get the latest info from Nolo authors' blogs.

LISTEN TO PODCASTS. Listen to authors discuss timely issues on topics that interest you.

WATCH VIDEOS. Get a quick introduction to a legal topic with our short videos.

And that's not all.
Nolo.com contains thousands of articles on everyday legal and business issues, plus a plain-English law dictionary, all written by Nolo experts and available for free. You'll also find more useful **books, software, online apps, downloadable forms,** plus a **lawyer directory.**

Get updates and more at
www.nolo.com/back-of-book/FIFO.html

6th Edition

The Foreclosure Survival Guide

Keep Your House or Walk Away With Money in Your Pocket

Attorney Amy Loftsgordon

with bankruptcy updates by Attorney Cara O'Neill

SIXTH EDITION	SEPTEMBER 2017
Editor	CARA O'NEILL
Book Production	SUSAN PUTNEY
Proofreading	IRENE BARNARD
Index	VICTORIA BAKER
Printing	BANG PRINTING

Names: Loftsgordon, Amy, author.
Title: The foreclosure survival guide : keep your house or walk away with
    money in your pocket / Attorney Amy Loftsgordon.
Description: 6th Edition. | Berkeley, CA : Nolo, 2017. | Includes index.
Identifiers: LCCN 2017012253 (print) | LCCN 2017014240 (ebook) | ISBN
    9781413324396 (ebook) | ISBN 9781413324389 (pbk.)
Subjects: LCSH: Foreclosure--United States--Popular works.
Classification: LCC KF697.F6 (ebook) | LCC KF697.F6 E43 2017 (print) | DDC
    346.7304/364--dc23
LC record available at https://lccn.loc.gov/2017012253

Please note

We believe accurate, plain-English legal information should help you solve many of
your own legal problems. But this text is not a substitute for personalized advice from
a knowledgeable lawyer. If you want the help of a trained professional—and we'll
always point out situations in which we think that's a good idea—consult an attorney
licensed to practice in your state.

About the Author and Updater

Amy Loftsgordon has worked in the area of foreclosure for over ten years, on the sides of both borrowers and lenders. She has also worked on legal process outsourcing initiatives, developed customized foreclosure-related training programs, and audited completed foreclosures to determine if they were processed in accordance with applicable laws. She received a B.A. from the University of Southern California and a law degree from the University of Denver Sturm College of Law. She is licensed to practice law in Colorado. Amy has authored numerous foreclosure articles on Nolo.com.

Cara O'Neill (Chapters 5 and 6) is a legal editor and writer at Nolo, focusing on bankruptcy, consumer credit, and debt. She edits and authors several Nolo book titles. Prior to joining Nolo, Cara practiced for over 20 years in civil litigation and bankruptcy. During that time, she served as an Administrative Law Judge mediating disputes in the automotive industry, taught undergraduate and graduate law courses, and served as house counsel for a large insurance company. She earned her law degree in 1994 from the University of the Pacific, McGeorge School of Law, where she served as a law review editor and graduated a member of the Order of the Barristers—an honor society recognizing excellence in courtroom advocacy. Cara maintains a bankruptcy practice in Roseville, California at the Law Office of Cara O'Neill.

Table of Contents

Appendix

Your Foreclosure Companion

No word strikes greater fear in a homeowner's heart than "foreclosure." This book deals with how to think about foreclosure and provides a number of pathways and options that you can choose according to your individual circumstances and where you live.

If you want to keep your home, your best option is to work something out with your mortgage lender in a way that will satisfy both of you. If, on the other hand, you are ready and willing to leave your home, there are ways to follow that path that will leave you relatively flush rather than destitute.

Many people want to stay in their homes but need to change some aspects of their mortgages—the amount of principal, the interest rate, the monthly payment. Although many homeowners used to qualify for a mortgage modification under the federal government's Home Affordable Modification Program (HAMP), the program is no longer available. To replace HAMP, Fannie Mae and Freddie Mac (the government-supported enterprises that own or back many mortgages) developed the Flex Modification program. Lenders are also free to provide programs for settling mortgage issues. Many offer in-house ("proprietary") modifications, forbearance agreements, or repayment plans. Chapter 4 of this book explains how homeowners can ask for relief under these programs.

For other homeowners, the best strategy is to walk away from their homes rather than pour money into what may be a hopeless cause. If you take this approach, it often makes sense to stay in your home throughout the foreclosure process—the longer you can live in your home without making mortgage payments, the better off you'll be financially. However, if you are contemplating walking away, you should be aware of, and take into consideration, the consequences (such as a possible deficiency judgment). A short sale or deed in lieu of foreclosure might work better in your circumstances, by allowing you to transfer title to the property without going through a foreclosure.

The goal of this book is to help you choose and implement the best strategy for your particular situation.

Changes in the Sixth Edition

In 2008, when the first edition of this book was published, home values were in free fall and foreclosures were becoming all too common. Since then, there have been millions of completed foreclosures across the United States. Now, nine years later, foreclosure rates have fallen. According to Black Knight Financial Services lenders are foreclosing on fewer homes. However, approximately a half million homeowners continue to face the prospect of losing their homes despite the lower foreclosure numbers. The foreclosure rate remains high in places such as New Jersey, Illinois, Delaware, Nevada, and Florida.

Fortunately, federal and state laws protect homeowners facing foreclosure. This edition discusses these new laws and trends, including:

New federal mortgage servicing rules. New rules implemented by the Consumer Financial Protection Bureau (CFPB) require servicers to provide certain borrowers with foreclosure protections more than once over the life of the loan. The rules also expand protections to surviving family members who inherit the home after the mortgage borrower dies. The new CFPB rules will go into effect on October 19, 2017.

State foreclosure laws. Since the last edition of this book, some states have changed existing laws. For example, important aspects of foreclosure law changed in several states, including Alabama, Illinois, and Wisconsin.

Better foreclosure avoidance options in some states. Some states enhanced existing foreclosure avoidance initiatives, such as the existing Hardest Hit Fund programs.

The availability of these programs (offered in 18 states and the District of Columbia) has been extended to 2020, and new foreclosure avoidance options have been added. This edition provides details about those programs.

Revised Fannie and Freddie modification programs. While HAMP and most other options to avoid foreclosure under the government's Making Home Affordable program are no longer available, this edition covers the programs likely to replace them. For instance, Fannie Mae and Freddie Mac developed a new program, the Flex Modification Program, as a replacement for HAMP. The new program should reduce an eligible borrower's mortgage payment by 20%. Also, almost all lenders offer "proprietary" (in-house) modifications to qualified borrowers who are having difficulty making mortgage payments.

How soon you can get another mortgage after a foreclosure, deed in lieu, or short sale. Homeowners who are losing their home to a foreclosure, deed in lieu, or short sale often wonder if they'll ever qualify for another mortgage. This edition covers home loan eligibility after one of these events.

What You'll Find in This Book

In addition to explaining changes that have occurred in the past several years, this book explains:

- the ins and outs of foreclosure procedures, with state-by-state information
- how to decide whether or not you should try to keep your house
- how you can get free help with a mortgage modification
- how filing for bankruptcy can help you keep your house, and
- how to avoid foreclosure "rescue" scams.

The book also explains ways to make the most of your situation if your income and mortgage payments preclude keeping your house, such as:

- how long you'll likely be able to stay in your house—and save up money—if the foreclosure goes ahead
- how to do a short sale or deed in lieu of foreclosure if either strategy would be useful in your situation
- how to use bankruptcy to put a temporary wrench in the foreclosure gears, and
- how bankruptcy can eliminate debts and tax liabilities typically associated with foreclosure.

For many people who feel swamped with debt and are considering filing for bankruptcy, it makes absolutely no sense to keep pouring money into houses they are destined to lose. For others, it's completely sensible to do everything they can to keep ownership. Sometimes the reasons for these decisions are personal; sometimes they are economic.

In the end, you must make this decision for yourself—this book provides some useful guidance in helping you decide, and then helps you succeed in whichever strategy you choose to follow. If it's not in the cards for you to keep your house, the book shows you how to derive the greatest possible benefit from the situation—how to make really good lemonade from the lemons life has handed you, if you will.

The book also tries to provide some perspective on home ownership. To sum it up, your house is not your home. Owning the house where you live may feel like the American dream, and losing it might seem like the end of that dream. Believe us when we say that it's not. If you are eventually forced to give up the house you are living in, painful as it may be, it's a loss that you will recover from over time, both emotionally and financially.

But in the meantime, there is a lot you can do to restore your financial health and take control of the situation. Good luck!

Get Legal Updates and More at Nolo.com

You can find the online companion page to this book at:

www.nolo.com/back-of-book/FIFO.html

There you will find important updates to the law (federal and state foreclosure laws are changing rapidly), podcasts, links to online articles on foreclosure (including many articles on state-specific foreclosure procedures, state mediation programs, and other foreclosure articles tailored to the law in your state), links to helpful calculators regarding mortgage refinancing and loans, and more.

Foreclosure: The Big Picture

Foreclosure doesn't usually come as a big surprise to homeowners. You'll probably know, well before it happens, that you're going to have trouble making your mortgage payments. Maybe you've become unemployed or face unexpected medical bills, or maybe that adjustable-rate mortgage you took out a few of years ago is scheduled to reset at a much higher rate, making payments out of reach.

Once you do fall behind, you'll have a few months before your lender even starts the foreclosure process thanks to federal mortgage servicing rules. The fact that foreclosure is a process—sometimes a long one—is good news for you. You don't need to panic. You'll have time to plan, negotiate, and evaluate your options—*if* you act as soon as you smell trouble coming. The more time you have, the better.

If your only problem is a few missed payments, your lender will probably be willing to let you get current over time or even add the missed payments to the end of the loan. If you've missed four or five payments, your lender may not be flexible—but you still may be able to work something out.

Indecisiveness May Cost You Big Time

If you're likely to lose your house sooner or later, your failure to immediately face this reality may cost you thousands of dollars. Here's why: Any mortgage payments you make now will do you no good if you end up losing your house in foreclosure. Assume your mortgage payment is $2,000 a month and you scrape together enough money each month to pay your mortgage because you don't want to lose your house. If $2,000 is way more than you can afford even in the short term, it's inevitable that you'll start missing payments. If you start missing payments six months down the road and you end up in foreclosure, the payments you scraped together during that six-month period will have been for naught unless you somehow find a way to get current on your mortgage payments or you file and complete a Chapter 13 bankruptcy. On the other hand, if you stopped paying your mortgage six months ago when you first realized that holding on to your house was a lost cause, you would now be $12,000 in the black.

> CAUTION
>
> **Check for updates.** Federal and state foreclosure laws change rapidly. Check this book's companion page on www.nolo.com for recent changes in the law. (See the introductory chapter, "Your Foreclosure Companion" for the link.)

Don't wait for the lender to contact you. As soon as you realize you're going to have trouble making your mortgage payments, you should start working on the problem. This chapter will show you how.

You're Not Alone

Houses are expensive—that's why most homeowners pay for them over 30 years, one monthly payment at a time. And it's not uncommon for people to find they just can't afford to keep making the payments. If you lose your job, get divorced, or face unexpected medical bills, keeping current on your house payments may be next to impossible.

While the brunt of the foreclosure crisis is behind us, foreclosures could very well spike again. According to the U.S. Department of Housing and Urban Development, homeowners took advantage of nearly 11.1 million mortgage modifications (and other forms of mortgage assistance arrangements) between April 2009 and the end of November 2016. More than 1.6 million modifications were through the government's popular Home Affordable Modification Program (HAMP).

While HAMP provided a lower monthly mortgage payment for many homeowners, the interest rate on most will start to climb after five years, rising about 1% each year for several years. For instance, a modification with an initial rate as low as 2% could eventually peak at 6%.

This isn't a worst-case scenario—the majority of HAMP homeowners will experience this type of rate increase. Also, because many proprietary (in-house) modifications used the HAMP structure, the interest rate on many private modifications will increase, too. As a result, thousands of homeowners who received a modification through HAMP or a similarly-structured proprietary mortgage modification might not be able to afford the payment after the interest rate increase. If those homeowners find themselves in default, the foreclosure rate could, once again, go up dramatically.

> (!) **CAUTION**
>
> **Don't panic—and don't get scammed.** Foreclosure rescue scams have popped up all over the country. Almost without exception, you will be worse off with these scams than if you let the foreclosure go through. (To find out how scammers work and what to look for, see "Don't Get Scammed by a Foreclosure 'Rescue' Company," below.)

What to Expect

What happens next depends on whether you are trying to stay in your home or are resigned to moving on. (More about that choice later.)

If you want to keep your home. Your first move is to find a HUD-approved housing counselor to help you figure out what options are best for you, whether it be a modification, a refinance, or another mortgage solution. These folks are there to help you stay in your home and won't charge you a penny for their help. Go to www.consumerfinance.gov and search for "Finding a housing counselor" or call 888-995-HOPE and ask for a HUD-approved counselor in your area.

Your HUD-approved housing counselor will help you determine which option is best for you, explain what documents you will need to provide to your mortgage company, and may be able to contact the mortgage company on your behalf.

If a modification or another workout is not in the cards, and depending on the procedure required by your state, you'll receive some sort of notice (usually a formal written notice) that foreclosure is coming unless you make things right. Foreclosure procedures differ greatly depending on where you live and the nature of the loan. (Ch. 2 explains these procedures and highlights the variables you'll want to know about when planning your strategy.)

Unless you use one of the remedies explained briefly below (and in detail in later chapters), the foreclosure will end, usually after a few months, with the sale of the property, typically at a public auction. The foreclosure process is explained in detail in Ch. 2.

Your Options: An Overview

Here's a look at your main alternatives when you think foreclosure is on the horizon. We'll talk about these scenarios in detail later. For now, just try to get an idea of what you're dealing with.

Your Options If You Are Facing Foreclosure

- Reinstate the existing loan by making up the missed payments, plus costs and interest.
- Negotiate a workout (such as a loan modification, forbearance, or repayment plan) with the lender with the help of a free HUD-approved housing counselor.
- Refinance the entire loan.
- Arrange a short sale or deed in lieu of foreclosure.
- Arrange a reverse mortgage, if you qualify.
- Delay the foreclosure sale by filing for Chapter 7 or Chapter 13 bankruptcy.
- Fight the foreclosure in court and either stop or delay it.
- Give up your house.

Reinstate Your Mortgage

If you have enough cash (or access to another loan), you can "reinstate" your mortgage by making up all the missed payments plus fees, costs, and interest the lender charges you. Your state's law will probably give you a certain amount of time to get this done, after the lender gives you notice that the foreclosure is beginning. (You can check your state's rule in the appendix.)

For example, in California you have the right to reinstate your loan for a period of three months after the lender mails you a "notice of default," or NOD. After that period ends, if you haven't negotiated a workout, the lender can and usually does accelerate the loan (notify you that it is declaring the entire amount due immediately) and send you a notice of trustee's sale, telling you that the house will be put up for sale in 20 days. California state law provides a further right to reinstate the loan up to five days before the foreclosure sale.

Also, many mortgage contracts have a clause giving the borrower the ability to reinstate the loan by a certain deadline. Even if the mortgage contract doesn't provide this right, lenders often prefer to work something out rather than accelerate the loan.

If you have enough resources to consider reinstatement, you can probably also work something out with the lender.

Negotiate a Workout

As mentioned, you should start with a HUD-approved housing counselor. (See Ch. 4 for more on this topic.) With this assistance, you may be able to get:

- temporary relief from having to make your monthly payments or reduced monthly payments (forbearance)
- a plan to make up your missed payments (at the end of your mortgage or on top of your current payments within a specified period of time)
- a lower interest rate—and as a result, lower monthly payments, or
- a reduction in your principal loan balance.

HUD-Approved Housing Counselors Might Be Overwhelmed

Providing effective counseling in the foreclosure arena is a labor-intensive activity, which means that using a counselor may require patience and persistence on your part. If you are in the midst of a foreclosure, you may not be able to put up with the delays and inevitable glitches that seem to accompany the mortgage modification process. If you cannot get the service you need from your HUD-approved counselor, you might be tempted to pay someone to get the job done for you. Because scams abound, it's best to hire a lawyer. It's not that a lawyer will necessarily do a better job than a nonlawyer, but in most states you will have some type of recourse if the lawyer turns out to be just another scam artist.

Refinance

If you can refinance at a better rate and pay off your old loan, you can start fresh. Unfortunately, refinancing can be tough unless you have good credit, equity in your house and the home value curve in your community is trending up rather than down. Of course, if your mortgage is owned by Fannie Mae or Freddie Mac and you qualify for a refinance under the Home Affordable Refinance Program (HARP), your refinancing worries may be over—the program is designed to help those who are unable to get traditional refinancing because the value of their homes has declined. (HARP is discussed in Ch. 4.) Unfortunately, the program is scheduled to end in 2017, but there's a chance that it might get extended (as has already happened several times). You can check for updates on this book's companion page on www.nolo.com. (See the introductory chapter, "Your Foreclosure Companion" for the link.)

File for Chapter 13 Bankruptcy

In this kind of bankruptcy, you come up with a plan for making your regular monthly payments and paying off the arrears. If the bankruptcy court approves your plan, you'll have three to five years to make the payments. Chapter 13 bankruptcy also reduces or eliminates your total debt load, making your mortgage more affordable in terms of your overall budget. In some situations (and depending on where you file the bankruptcy), you can get rid of a second or third mortgage entirely, reduce a first mortgage on a vacation or rental home to the market value of the house, and even reduce the interest rate on your first mortgage to 1.5 points above prime rate. If you live in one of the nonjudicial foreclosure states—where foreclosures regularly take place without the review of a judge or the benefits of a court hearing—Chapter 13 bankruptcy may be your best opportunity to challenge the legality of your mortgage and any threatened foreclosure. (See the appendix to find out whether your state is a nonjudicial foreclosure state.) Chapter 13 bankruptcy is discussed in Ch. 5.

File for Chapter 7 Bankruptcy

If you are current on your mortgage (or can get current in a hurry) but have no room in your budget to continue making your payments, filing for Chapter 7 bankruptcy can make your mortgage more affordable by reducing your total debt load—and so help to prevent foreclosure in the long run. Chapter 7 bankruptcy is quick (it takes about three or four months). It's also inexpensive if you represent yourself, which many people do. (Although if you're worried about losing your home, it's wise to at least consult with a lawyer.) Chapter 7 bankruptcy typically will wipe out your unsecured debt—for example, credit card debt, personal loans, medical debts, and most money judgments. This will free up whatever income you were using to pay down those debts so you can put it toward your mortgage payments.

Even if you have decided to leave your house, bankruptcy can be of great assistance in keeping you in your home for a few extra months free of charge, as well as giving you a fresh start by wiping out liabilities arising from your mortgage or the foreclosure itself.

Despite these benefits, Chapter 7 bankruptcy may not be appropriate for you. For example, you may have more equity in your house than you can protect (exempt) in your bankruptcy, which means the bankruptcy would trigger an involuntary sale of your home. Also, unlike Chapter 13 bankruptcy, Chapter 7 bankruptcy provides little opportunity to mount a legal challenge to the validity of your mortgage or foreclosure proceedings. (Chapter 7 bankruptcy is discussed in Ch. 6.)

Take Out a Reverse Mortgage

A reverse mortgage is a way to tap into the equity of your home without selling the house. You get money from a lender and generally don't need to pay it back as long as you live in the house. The loan must be repaid if you sell your house, permanently move out, or die.

To qualify for a reverse mortgage (also called a home equity conversion mortgage or HECM), you must have substantial equity and be over age 62. The Department of Housing and Urban Development (HUD) administers the HECM program and almost all reverse mortgages are currently made under this program. A reverse mortgage can prevent foreclosure and preserve your equity for your own needs. However, a reverse mortgage, because it takes part or all of your equity, leaves less value for you to pass on to your heirs at your death or less money if you decide to sell the home.

Even though you don't have to make payments on the reverse mortgage, you are responsible for paying the property taxes and insurance, as well as maintaining the property. Since 2015, lenders must complete a financial assessment before making a HECM loan to make sure that the borrower can afford to keep up with the property taxes and insurance payments. If the assessment reveals that the borrower is likely to fall behind in these expenses, the lender must establish a set-aside account. A set-aside is an amount drawn under the HECM that is reserved for payment of these expenses. The account reduces the amount of money the borrower will receive.

FHA is also currently considering requiring lenders to evaluate the borrower's ability to cover utilities in addition to taxes and insurance as part of the financial assessment. Reverse mortgages are discussed further in Ch. 3.

 RESOURCE
More information about reverse mortgages. Learn more at www. consumerfinance.gov/askcfpb/224/what-is-a-reverse-mortgage.html.

Fight the Foreclosure in Court

If you can show that the foreclosing party violated your state's procedural rules for foreclosures or the terms of your mortgage agreement, you might be able to derail the foreclosure, at least temporarily.

Some courts require foreclosing parties to present documentary evidence of ownership and authority for bringing the foreclosure action before letting the foreclosure proceed. And because of the way mortgages were sold and resold during the real estate bubble, sometimes this evidence is missing.

Chapter 7 or Chapter 13 Bankruptcy: A Quick Comparison		
	Chapter 7	Chapter 13
Who qualifies	Anyone whose household income is below the state median OR who passes a "means test"	Anyone who has enough income to propose a reasonable repayment plan
Effect on foreclosure	Delayed two to three months	Delayed; possibly avoided
What happens to your property	You keep everything that is legally exempt; the rest is sold to repay your creditors.	You keep your property, but you must pay your unsecured creditors the value of your nonexempt property.
What happens to your mortgage	The amount you owe is discharged, but the lien created by the mortgage remains, and you must make payments to avoid foreclosure.	Your first mortgage will probably remain intact; second and third mortgages can be eliminated if they are not at least partially secured by the house's value.
What happens to your debts	Most debts are wiped out (discharged); some (such as child support and back taxes) survive.	You repay a percentage of debt over three to five years, under a repayment plan you propose to the court; if you finish the plan, the rest of the debt is wiped out.
How long it takes	Three to four months	Three to five years
Will you need a lawyer?	Probably not	Almost always

Foreclosure defense attorneys have also uncovered instances of lenders violating laws governing the recording, notarization, and assignment of mortgages. In some cases, major mortgage lenders temporarily ceased foreclosure activities pending internal investigations of their foreclosure practices.

Finally, violations of federal fair lending rules and other federal and state laws regarding consumer transactions may also provide a defense against foreclosure. (Fighting foreclosures in court is discussed in Ch. 7.)

TIP
Extra protections for service members. If you are on active duty in the military, or have been on active duty within the previous year, you can delay the foreclosure lawsuit—and get other help as well. (See Ch. 4.)

Give Up Your House

For some people, it makes good economic sense to give up their houses and move on. If you arrive at this decision, there are several ways to say goodbye to your house. You'll want to choose the method that causes the least financial and emotional upset to you and your family. (There's much more about making this decision in Ch. 3.)

Walk Away

Although this book covers several basic approaches to giving up your home, sometimes the best approach is to simply stop all further mortgage payments. When you walk away, you will almost certainly lose your house in foreclosure. However, while the foreclosure process chugs along, which can take months, you don't have to make mortgage payments to anyone but yourself. This can result in a sizable nest egg, which you can then use when searching for new shelter. The subject of "walking away" is discussed throughout this book, most specifically in Ch. 8. Here we give you a brief overview of the subject.

People walk away for two main reasons. The most common reason is that the mortgage has become unaffordable due to an increase in interest rates, the loss of employment, or some other unexpected occurrence. Even after a mortgage modification, circumstances may still render the mortgage unaffordable.

The second reason for walking away is that your home has turned into a lousy investment. Even if you can afford your mortgage payments, you may be better off walking away if your mortgage is deeply underwater and you bought the house as an investment rather than a place to live. While it's impossible to predict what will happen to home values in the future, many homes have moved out of negative territory as the economy and housing market continue to recover. Though there are still millions of homeowners who are underwater, things are looking up in many areas of the country. Even if your situation isn't improving, there may be a better option available to you, such as a short sale or a deed in lieu of foreclosure. You might even get some money to help with your relocation costs if you complete one of these options. (For more on this topic, see Ch. 8.)

Strategic Defaults

Walking away from a home when you can afford to pay the mortgage has been labeled a "strategic default." The default is strategic because the homeowner voluntarily chooses to default after completing a cost–benefit analysis. There are several risks involved for those who choose this route. If you strategically default, you probably won't be eligible for a Fannie Mae-backed mortgage for seven years from the date of the foreclosure. Fannie Mae has also stated that it will take legal action to recoup the outstanding mortgage debt from borrowers who strategically default on their loans in jurisdictions that allow for deficiency judgments.

Rather than strategically defaulting, you may be able to give up the home through a short sale or deed in lieu of foreclosure. Fannie Mae and Freddie Mac will let some borrowers who are delinquent or current on their payments give up their properties under special deed in lieu of foreclosure programs, if the borrowers meet certain criteria. These programs could provide an alternative to strategic default for some borrowers. (For more on this topic, see Ch. 8.)

Aside from not being able to acquire a new home loan after a strategic default, walking away can lead to other negative consequences:

- Sooner or later you will lose ownership of your home through foreclosure—unless you are able to successfully challenge the legality of the mortgage in state court or in bankruptcy.

- In most states, you can be sued for the difference between the amount your house was sold for at foreclosure and the amount you owed at the time of the foreclosure sale. Your liability for this difference, called a "deficiency," can be discharged in bankruptcy, but if bankruptcy is not for you, for one reason or another, you may be stuck with a large debt.

- The mortgage lender may write off the deficiency as a loss. The amount of the deficiency would then turn into taxable income for you. This tax liability can be avoided in several ways—including declaring insolvency or bankruptcy—but if you don't qualify for one of the exceptions, you can be nicked for a lot of money. More information about the potential tax liabilities related to foreclosure is provided in Ch. 8.

Arrange a "Short Sale" Without Foreclosure

You can negotiate with your lender to sell your house, without a foreclosure, for less than the amount you owe on your mortgage. This is called a short sale. If you live in a state that allows your lender to sue you for the deficiency (the difference between the amount you owe on the mortgage and the sale price of your home), a short sale can be a good idea, but only if you get your lender to agree (in writing) to let you off the hook for the deficiency.

If you have a second or third mortgage, you'll also need to get those lenders to sign off on the short sale. This is usually difficult (if not impossible) to accomplish because, by definition, a short sale produces less than is owed on the first mortgage and the holder of the second or third mortgage stands to get little or nothing from the deal. If you can talk the first mortgage lender into giving some of the proceeds from the sale to the second and third mortgage lender, you'll have a better chance of getting the deal done.

How Will Your Choice Affect Your Credit?

Foreclosures, short sales, and deeds in lieu of foreclosure are all bad for your credit. (Only a bankruptcy is worse.) If you avoid owing a deficiency with a short sale or deed in lieu, your credit score probably won't fall as much; but, overall, these events are pretty similar when it comes to how they affect your credit.

It's virtually impossible to predict how much damage a foreclosure, short sale, or deed in lieu of foreclosure will do to your credit. For one thing, credit scoring systems change over time. For another, credit scoring agencies do not make their formulas public, and your score will vary based on your prior and future credit practices and those of others with whom you are compared.

But it also depends, in large part, on your credit before you lose your home. Most people who resort to foreclosure, short sale, or a deed in lieu of foreclosure have already fallen far behind on mortgage payments. According to experts, late payments cause a huge dip in your credit score, which means a subsequent foreclosure will not matter as much since your credit is already seriously damaged. If you are one of the rare homeowners who hasn't missed a payment before doing a short sale or deed in lieu of foreclosure, those events will cause more damage to your credit.

For more information on the subject of consumer credit, and how to rebuild it, see *Credit Repair* by Amy Loftsgordon (Nolo).

Another pitfall of short sales is that the buyer of your home will probably want you to leave immediately after the sale closes. This won't be a problem if you don't mind leaving, but you'll miss out on the opportunity to build a healthy nest egg by living in the house without paying your mortgage.

Hand Over the House Without Foreclosure

You may be able to get your lender to let you deed the property over so that no foreclosure is necessary; this is called signing a "deed in lieu of foreclosure." But before you go this route, you'll want to have an agreement (in writing) that the lender won't go after you for any deficiency. With a deed in lieu of foreclosure, the deficiency amount is the difference between the total debt and the fair market value of the property. This remedy probably won't be available if there are second or third mortgages since those lenders won't get anything out of the deal.

How You Can Stay in Your House Payment Free

If, early on, you decide that you don't want to keep the house and will ultimately be moving on, you'll be able to skip payments for several months before the foreclosure process finally begins. If you apply for a modification once the foreclosure starts, the proceedings are put on hold pending an assessment by the mortgage servicer as to whether you qualify for a payment reduction or some other mortgage workout plan (see Ch. 4). During this time, you don't have to make any payments. After the foreclosure sale, chances are great that you can keep living in the house for a while longer free of charge. You may be able to live in the home during the redemption period (if there is one). And, in some states, you can stay in your house until the new owner gives you a formal written notice demanding that you leave, and a court orders you out after you receive notice and a hearing is held. Though, generally, it is best to vacate your home after you get the notice demanding that you leave and thereby avoid a formal eviction. (See the information for your state in the appendix.)

Having payment-free shelter for many months—before the foreclosure action is brought, during the foreclosure, and after the sale—gives you a golden opportunity to save some money. And that will make things easier when you do have to find a new place to live. (See Ch. 9 for more on how to come out of foreclosure with some cash in your pocket.)

Why Foreclosure Doesn't Have to Be So Bad

Home ownership can be overrated. Americans take for granted that owning a home is superior to renting one, especially if you have a family. We accept the phrase "American dream" without question when applied to home ownership. And politicians are wringing their hands over the prospect of the American dream being lost for the thousands of homeowners who face foreclosure.

However, ownership is not an automatic key to happiness. (We go into this in more detail in Ch. 3.) For now, just try to open your mind to the possibility that renting rather than owning is not always a bad way to go, and that your particular dream need not include home ownership. And, even if you go through a foreclosure, you'll likely be able to buy another home at some point if you decide you want one.

TIP

Getting a mortgage after foreclosure. To be eligible for another mortgage loan following a significant derogatory credit event, such as a foreclosure, short sale, or deed in lieu of foreclosure, Fannie Mae requires a waiting period and re-established credit. In general, the waiting period is seven years after a foreclosure. However, if you have gone through a job layoff, divorce, or have incurred significant medical bills (and you can document the event impact on your finances) the waiting period is three years. With a short sale or deed in lieu of foreclosure, the waiting period is four years or two years with extenuating circumstances.

Don't Get Scammed by a Foreclosure "Rescue" Company

A large "foreclosure rescue" industry, much of which is a scam, has mushroomed as a result of the mortgage crisis. If you are close to losing your home to foreclosure, you may receive an offer of help from a foreclosure rescue company. Companies scour public records and call homeowners who've received foreclosure notices.

The con artists who run these companies will tell you that they have resources that are unavailable to HUD-approved housing counselors and that they care about you and will find a way for you to save your "American dream." But unlike HUD-approved housing counselors, these companies aren't really trying keep you in your house. They're trying to make money. If you have equity in your house, they go after it. And if you've only got money in the bank, they'll go after that, instead.

Scams That Target Home Equity

If you have significant equity in your home, you are a prime target for the mortgage rescue scams aimed at getting ownership of your house away from you.

One common trick sounds especially good because the mortgage gets quickly reinstated, at least temporarily.

What you'll hear: "We'll buy your house right now—just temporarily, of course. We'll make the mortgage payments. You can stay right where you are, lease the house from us, and buy the house back when the loan is paid off."

How to Protect Yourself

- Never rely on an oral promise, such as, "Don't worry; you'll get the deed back in no time." Get everything in writing.
- Never sign an agreement unless you understand every word and phrase in it, even if you've had help from a HUD-approved housing counseling agency.
- Never sign anything that has blank lines or spaces. Representations and information you had no knowledge of can be inserted and appear to be part of the signed agreement.
- Never transfer ownership of your property to the "rescuer" or a proposed third-party lender.
- Never accept a loan that you can't afford or that must be paid back quickly at a high interest rate as a condition of staying in your house.

What really happens: The foreclosure rescue company is confident that you won't be able to buy the house back, especially if it involves a big balloon payment, which is common. Ultimately, you lose your home and are quickly evicted. Eviction comes quickly because you have only the status of a tenant under the lease or rental agreement that was supposed to be temporary. By contrast, if the house had gone through foreclosure, you would have been able to stay there for months payment-free as the foreclosure process wore on.

Another scam involves wresting ownership away from the homeowner without the homeowner's knowledge.

What you'll hear: "We'll get a workout with the lender. We'll handle everything—just send your mortgage payments to us and we'll pass them on to the lender."

What really happens: The papers you sign actually transfer ownership to the company. (This can easily be accomplished because people expect legal documents to be full of gibberish they don't understand or don't notice that the documents they sign have blank lines that can be filled in later with terms they never agreed to.) Instead of sending your mortgage payments to the lender, the scammer uses them to refinance the property. Then it sells the house to an innocent third party and disappears, leaving you without equity or a workout.

If You Don't Have Much Equity

If you have little or no equity in your home, you probably won't be approached by anyone who wants title; what would be the point? But if you are close to a foreclosure sale, there are plenty of other snake-oil peddlers out there.

For a stiff up-front fee—often in the thousands of dollars—they offer to help you fight your foreclosure by finding affordable loans or by negotiating with your lender for a mortgage modification, an interest rate freeze, or an arrangement in which your missed payments get added to the end of your loan. But not only will you not get results, there's a good chance that these people will disappear once your money is in their hands.

When the foreclosure crisis began, hundreds of brand-new "modification specialists" hit the street, many "certified" by schools set up to train former mortgage brokers for this new bonanza. These people take money for services that can be obtained for free from HUD-approved housing counselors or the Making Home Affordable website at www.makinghomeaffordable.gov. (Although the majority of programs under the Making Home Affordable program have expired, the website still contains useful information for homeowners facing foreclosure.)

> **EXAMPLE:** Frieda and Ted are in foreclosure. They wake up one morning to find a flyer on their doorstep advertising the Compassionate Care Foreclosure Rescue Service, which seems tailor-made for their difficulties. The flyer asks, "Is your home about to be sold at a foreclosure sale? Do you want help negotiating a loan modification with your mortgage servicing company? Want to refinance your mortgage at a low interest rate? We can help!"
>
> They call the number on the flyer and are referred to a "foreclosure rescue specialist," Nick, who tells them in a soothing voice that Compassionate Care has helped "thousands of people just like you" work out their mortgage difficulties and stay in their homes. After Frieda and Ted give him information about their plight, Nick tells them that he can negotiate a loan modification with the servicer on their behalf and get an extension of the foreclosure sale date. The fee: $1,500—up front.
>
> Frieda and Ted borrow the $1,500 from Frieda's son and send a cashier's check to Nick at a post office box, along with a signed power of attorney form that Nick says he needs so he can negotiate with the servicer. A few days later Nick tells them that he has gotten the foreclosure sale postponed. Two weeks later, though, the home is to sold at a foreclosure auction. Frieda and Ted get a call from someone they've never heard of telling them that he bought their home at the foreclosure sale and wants to make arrangements for them to move out. Frieda and Ted call Nick in a panic. The number has been disconnected. Frieda and Ted have lost their home—and paid $1,500 for the privilege.

Mass Joinder Lawsuit Scams

In a mass joinder scam, a group claiming to be a law firm (often it's not a law firm at all or they use unqualified attorneys) sends out unsolicited mailings inviting distressed homeowners to participate in a lawsuit. The mailing informs you that you can join together with other homeowners to sue your lender and force it into providing loan modifications or stopping foreclosure. You then call the number listed on the mailing and talk to a sales representative who provides false information or makes misleading claims about the success of such a suit. To join in the mass joinder lawsuit, you must pay up-front legal fees that can range from $5,000 to over $10,000. Typically, once the scammers have taken your money, they either do nothing (and disappear with the funds) or file the lawsuits and neglect them, leading to dismissals.

Forensic Loan Audit Scams

In a forensic loan audit scam, you pay a company an up-front fee of several hundred dollars for a so-called forensic loan auditor to review your mortgage loan documents to determine if your lender complied with mortgage lending laws. Companies offering this type of service often claim that the audits find lender violations 90% of the time. They further claim that, if a forensic loan audit finds violations of the law, you can use the results to stop a foreclosure, force the lender to give you a loan modification, or rescind (cancel) your loan.

In fact, there's no evidence that forensic loan audits are effective in accomplishing any of these things. First of all, the "audit" is typically completed by a processor who simply plugs information from your loan origination documentation into loan compliance software, which then supposedly identifies violations and compiles them into an automated report. Secondly, often only minor violations are found. Even if the audit does find fraud, predatory lending, or other significant violations of state or federal law, you would need to file a lawsuit against the lender (either as an answer to the lender's judicial foreclosure complaint or as your own lawsuit in a nonjudicial foreclosure) to stop a foreclosure. Sending a copy of the audit report to the lender or telling it that you had a forensic loan audit done will have no effect on your foreclosure.

Profile of a Scammer: What to Look For

The people who prey upon homeowners in foreclosure use many tactics to gain your trust. Be wary of anyone who:

- contacts you by phone or mail or knocks on your door (legitimate foreclosure consultants don't seek you out; you must go to them)
- provides little or no information about the foreclosure process
- claims government affiliation
- uses "affinity marketing"—Spanish speakers marketing to Spanish speakers, Christians to Christians, senior citizens to senior citizens, and so on
- offers "testimonials" from other customers
- claims the process will be quick and easy (dealing with foreclosure is never quick and easy) and uses messages such as "Stop foreclosure with just one phone call" or "I'd like to $ buy $ your house" or "Do you need instant debt relief and CASH?" or
- tells you to cease all contact with the mortgage lender.

State and Federal Laws Governing Foreclosure Consultants

If a company approaches you using the above tactics, it very well may be breaking the law. Many states have laws governing the activity of foreclosure consultants. In addition, in 2010, the Federal Trade Commission (FTC) promulgated rules regulating "mortgage assistance relief services" (MARS) in an effort to protect homeowners from foreclosure consultant scams. Among other things, the MARS rule (now known as Regulation O) requires MARS providers to make certain disclosures about their services, prohibits advance fees, and bans certain misleading advertising claims. The FTC and the Consumer Financial Protection Bureau (CFPB) enforces the MARS regulation. To lodge a complaint with the FTC about a MARS company (in English or Spanish), call 877-FTC-HELP (877-382-4357), or go to www.ftc.gov. You can also submit a complaint with the CFPB at www.consumerfinance.gov.

To learn more about the MARS regulation, go to www.ftc.gov and search for "Mortgage Assistance Relief Services Rule" and follow the link.

Beware of Property Preservation Companies

Mortgage servicers hire property preservation companies to secure homes when homeowners move out before the foreclosures are complete. Recently, however, there have been reports of property preservation companies illegally changing locks, removing belongings, or taking other actions while homeowners are still living in their homes.

The Lender May "Secure" Your Home If Vacant

While you have the right to occupy the home during foreclosure, if you abandon (move out of) the home during the process, most mortgages give the lender the right to do whatever is reasonable or appropriate to protect its interest in the property. For example, the lender may do the following things to secure the property if it is vacant:

- enter the property to make repairs
- change the locks or padlock the entrance
- replace or board up doors and windows
- remove debris or trash
- have utilities turned on or off, and
- eliminate building or other code violations or dangerous conditions.

Generally, the task of securing the home falls on the mortgage servicer (on behalf of the lender), which typically farms out these services (called field services) to property management firms, which are called field service companies or property preservation companies.

Property preservations companies are hired to inspect, clean, and secure abandoned homes. Unfortunately, however, these contractors can get it wrong and clear out homes people are still living in. They can prematurely change your locks, remove your belongings, or take other actions even though you are still living in your house.

How the Process Works

When you fall behind in your home mortgage payments or go into foreclosure, the servicer will usually hire someone to do a drive-by inspection to figure out if the home is occupied or vacant. If the inspector determines that the home is vacant (sometimes mistakenly), the servicer might take steps to secure and maintain the home, such as making sure that trash is picked up and that the home is protected against the weather. In too many instances though, property preservation companies have been known to let themselves into currently occupied homes, causing damage and illegally taking the homeowners' personal property.

Tips to Keep the Lender From Treating Your Occupied Home as Vacant

If you are in the midst of the foreclosure process, you want to make sure your home and your belongings are protected. There are several steps you can take to ensure that your mortgage lender or servicer (or the field services company that it hires) doesn't treat your occupied home as vacant.

Call your lender/servicer when you are late in payments. If you are behind in your payments, call the mortgage lender or servicer (the company you make your payments to) and let it know you still live in the property. (To figure out who your loan servicer is, look at your monthly mortgage payment coupon.) All loan servicers keep communication logs that note each time you call and include information about the conversation. While the communication logs are not especially detailed, if later on there is a dispute about occupancy, at the very least there should be a note in the servicer's records that you said you are still living in the property. This is also a good opportunity to ask about mortgage workout options.

Inform your loan servicer in writing that you're still living in the property. You can also send a letter to the lender or servicer informing it in writing that you are still occupying the property. Send the letter by certified mail, return receipt requested, so you can prove that you sent it and that the lender or servicer received it.

If the field service company leaves a notice, call it too. A field service company may post a notice that it has deemed your property vacant before locking you out. If so, be sure to call the company and let it know that you are still living in the property. It is also a good idea to send a letter (via certified mail, return receipt requested) to prove that you have notified it of your occupancy.

Even if you do all these things, a property preservation company may still lock you out or illegally take your belongings. If this happens, you should consult with an attorney to figure out your next steps.

Foreclosure Nuts and Bolts

This chapter paints a general picture of how foreclosures work in your state. You might feel like skipping this information and getting on with deciding what to *do*—get right with your lender, fight the foreclosure, or walk away with the help of a short sale or the bankruptcy court. But you can't make smart decisions without some knowledge of how a foreclosure proceeds.

At the very least, you need to know what's coming if foreclosure looms. Here are the big issues:

- **How much time you'll have before your house is sold.** If you know that your house can be sold at auction in just 30 days after you first get official notice of the foreclosure, you'll need to act differently than if you can count on three or four months in which to work out an arrangement with the lender or try other strategies. Fortunately, even in short-notice states, you can pretty much count on learning about the intended sale in time to use one of the strategies explained in later chapters.

- **Whether or not your foreclosure will go through court.** In a little fewer than half the states, foreclosures are judicial, meaning they go through court; in the others, your house can be sold without a judge's approval in what is called a power of sale (nonjudicial) foreclosure. If you know that you won't lose your house unless a judge gives an official go-ahead, your strategy will likely be different than if your foreclosure will be proceeding without judicial oversight. This is because court foreclosures usually take longer than nonjudicial ones and it's easier to raise the common defenses to foreclosure when you automatically get face time with a judge.

- **Whether you'll be liable for a "deficiency judgment" if the foreclosure goes through.** If the house sells for less than you owe on it, in many states the lender can sue you for at least some of the difference. Homestead laws (state laws that protect your home equity from creditors) don't help you, because mortgage debt has priority over any homestead rights your state's law provides. One reason many people file for bankruptcy when faced with foreclosure is that bankruptcy eliminates liability for deficiencies.

Understanding Foreclosure Terminology

Here are a few terms you may run into. There are lots more definitions in the glossary. As with any system, getting the words right is half the battle.

Promissory note. A promissory note is a written promise by one party (a borrower) to pay a specific amount of money (called principal) to another party (such as a home loan lender), which often includes a specified amount of interest on the unpaid principal amount and penalties for failure to pay according to its terms. Homebuyers usually think of the mortgage or deed of trust as the contract they are signing with the lender to borrow money to purchase a house, but it is actually the promissory note that contains the promise to repay the amount borrowed. (The mortgage or deed of trust pledges the home as security for the loan.) A promissory note is basically an IOU that contains the promise to repay the loan, as well as the terms for repayment.

Mortgages and deeds of trust. When you got a loan to buy your house, you agreed that the loan would be secured by the house. That meant that if you defaulted on your payments, the owner of the loan could foreclose— that is, sell the house to repay the debt. Security agreements such as these are filed (recorded) in the local land records office. In some states, this security agreement is termed a mortgage, while in others it's called a deed of trust. With a few exceptions, mortgages can only be foreclosed in court, while deeds of trust can be foreclosed without going through court.

In this book, except when it makes a difference, we use the term mortgage to refer to either an actual mortgage or a deed of trust.

First, second, and third mortgages. The first loan you took out to buy your home is called the first mortgage. If you also borrowed a lesser amount for the down payment, or if you later took out a loan against your equity, this later loan is called a second mortgage. And finally, if you took out a third loan or arranged a line of credit to be secured by your home, you have a third mortgage.

Assignments and indorsements. An assignment is the document that is the legal record of the transfer of the mortgage or deed of trust from one bank (or holder) to another. Assignments are typically recorded in the county

Understanding Foreclosure Terminology (continued)

land records. When the loan changes hands, the promissory note is indorsed (signed over) to the new owner of the loan. In some cases, the note is indorsed in blank, which makes it a bearer instrument under Article 3 of the Uniform Commercial Code. This means that any party that possesses the note has the legal authority to enforce it. Assignments and indorsements prove which bank owns the debt and may start a foreclosure.

Lenders, investors, and mortgage servicers. Chances are, the bank or other lender you got your mortgage from (the mortgage originator) quickly sold the mortgage to another entity (called an investor), which in turn resold it, and so on. You are supposed to be notified of these transactions, but these notices are not written in plain English so you may not know who really owns your mortgage or who is entitled to foreclose if you default. (In this book, we use the term lender to refer to the investor as well unless the distinction is important.)

Whether or not you know who your lender or investor is, you've probably been dealing with a company termed a mortgage servicer. (The servicer could be the bank who made the loan or some other entity. Servicers purchase and sell servicer rights independent of the loan.) The servicer receives your payments and passes them on to whoever is entitled to receive them—perhaps an overseas bank or a trustee for a mortgage trust.

If you default on your payments but want to keep your house, your mortgage servicer will represent the lender in the loss mitigation (workout) process. If you aren't able to work out an alternative, the servicer will begin the foreclosure proceeding.

In the past, servicers were almost always banks. Now, servicing rights are often sold to "nonbank" servicers such as Ocwen Loan Servicing, Nationstar, and Select Portfolio Servicing. As of 2015, nonbank servicers hold roughly one-fourth (out of a nearly $10 trillion mortgage-servicing market) of the mortgage servicing rights. The CFPB has received thousands of complaints about these nonbank servicers. Ocwen, for example, has had serious issues with its servicing practices, including backdating letters it sent to borrowers who were trying to save their homes from foreclosure.

> TIP
>
> **Read the law.** All of these foreclosure issues are discussed here, and the laws of each state are summarized in the appendix. Nonetheless, you may be curious to find out for yourself what the statutes actually say, word for word. Reading the law will give you a better understanding than the brief summaries in the appendix. So if you have access to a law library or the Internet and some patience, use the citations on your state's page to look up the law for yourself. (Ch. 10 provides help on finding your state's laws online.)

How Much Time You'll Have to Respond

Under federal mortgage servicing rules that went into effect January 10, 2014, in most cases, the servicer cannot officially start a foreclosure (that is, make the first notice or filing required by state law) until you are more than 120 days (four months) delinquent on payments. This means that in judicial foreclosures, the servicer cannot file a court document (such as a complaint, petition, order to docket, or notice of hearing) until after you're more than 120 days late. If the foreclosure is nonjudicial (such as under a power of sale in a deed of trust), the lender cannot begin the foreclosure by recording or publishing the first notice until after you're 120 days behind. (If state foreclosure law doesn't require a court filing or a document to be recorded or published, the first notice is the earliest document that establishes, sets, or schedules a date for the foreclosure sale.) This 120-day time frame is supposed to give you time to work out a way to avoid foreclosure.

The servicer is allowed to send you other early notices during this time, such as those that provide information about housing counseling, preforeclosure mediation, or other helpful information. For example, in most situations the mortgage servicer may send a letter informing you that you are late in your payments, that your loan is in default, and how to cure the default. The exact type and timing of the notice will depend on your mortgage documents and state law. For example, most home mortgages and deeds of trust contain a clause that requires the lender to send a notice, typically called a breach letter or demand letter, that informs you that you get 30 days to cure the default. And all states require that you get at least some form of notice before your house is sold because of foreclosure. See your state's page in the appendix for information on what kind of notice you can expect to receive.

Depending on your state and your circumstances, the foreclosure will be either judicial or nonjudicial. If it's a judicial foreclosure (one that goes through court), you'll be given some time, typically between 15 and 30 days, to respond to the court complaint that starts the foreclosure lawsuit. In some states, the court, when it approves the foreclosure, orders the lender to publish a "notice of sale," which gives you even more time before you have to move.

You also get some presale notice for nonjudicial foreclosures. Some states require 20 or 30 days (30 days in Georgia, for example) or as much as four months (in Oregon). In some states, including California, you get two notices: one giving you a period of time to make up the missed payments (cure the default) and a second one (called a notice of sale) giving you the date of sale in the event you haven't caught up on the payments.

Early Intervention Requirements

Under a 2014 federal law, the servicer must attempt to make contact with you to a discuss workout option (called "loss mitigation") no later than 36 days after the loan becomes delinquent. The servicer must also send you a written notice that describes any options not later than the 45th day of the delinquency. Also, the mortgage servicer is required to assign personnel to help you by the time you fall 45 days delinquent. The personnel must be available by phone and able to advise you about loss mitigation options, how to apply for a mortgage workout, the status of any loss mitigation application, and applicable deadlines. Starting in 2017, the servicer must continue to do these things at certain times while you remain delinquent on the loan. (See Ch. 4 for further information.)

In most states, in addition to mailing you a notice by certified or first-class mail, the foreclosing entity must publish a notice in the "legal notices" section of a local newspaper of general circulation. (This is an admittedly weird concept that assumes you read the legal notices section.) Sometimes posting a notice on the property is required as well.

CAUTION

Scammers do read the legal notices. Once a formal notice of foreclosure is published, recorded at the local land records office, or filed in court, it's public knowledge that the homeowner is in financial trouble. Con artists may prey upon you, knowing that you're under stress. Don't fall for a foreclosure "rescue" scam. (How to spot risky deals and outright crooks is discussed in Ch. 1.)

It is also a common requirement that the foreclosing party post notices on the courthouse door and in other public places. In fact, in Mississippi, this is the only notice you may get (along with publication). This is a little less weird than the legal notices publication, at least in small communities. One of your neighbors (if not you) may see a notice posted in a public place and let you know.

Many people facing foreclosure are like the proverbial deer in the headlights: stunned and unable to react quickly. Don't be one of them. This notice period gives you precious time to plan a strategy that is most advantageous to you.

If you or a family member is on active military duty, you have extra protections, including the right that a judge evaluate the merits of the foreclosure even if you are living in a state where nonjudicial foreclosures are the norm (so long as you took out the mortgage before your period of military service began). (The Servicemembers Civil Relief Act is discussed in Ch. 4.)

Extra Protections If You Have a High-Cost Mortgage

The states listed below have special rules for foreclosures when you have a high-cost mortgage. Each state defines high-cost mortgages differently, but typically they are mortgages where interest and prepayment penalties are significantly higher than those being charged for standard mortgages.

Generally, these laws require lenders to give you more notice before foreclosure, and there may be more lenient reinstatement rules (discussed in Ch. 1). If you are in one of these states, check your state's page in the appendix. You'll find a brief summary of the protections you're entitled to, and a citation that will help you find the statute if you want to look it up.

Arkansas	Kentucky	New Mexico
California	Massachusetts	New York
Georgia	Nevada	South Carolina
Illinois	New Jersey	Tennessee
Indiana		

In or Out of Court?

Foreclosures take one of two major paths: judicial (in court) or nonjudicial (out of court). If your home loan is secured by a mortgage, chances are you'll have a judicial foreclosure. If your loan is secured by a deed of trust, you'll probably have a nonjudicial foreclosure. The real estate industry in a particular state—and the laws that industry's lobbyists have pushed through that state's legislature—pretty much determine whether mortgages or deeds of trust are used there.

A judicial foreclosure often takes a lot longer than a nonjudicial one. A judicial foreclosure also gives you a ready-made opportunity to oppose the foreclosure and assures that your home won't be lost to foreclosure unless a judge signs off on it. Judicial oversight is an important protection against illegal tactics by the foreclosing party.

> ### Foreclosure by Possession
>
> In Massachusetts, New Hampshire, and Rhode Island, an arcane procedure called foreclosure by possession lets the lender take possession of a house by "peaceful entry." Because of legal uncertainties regarding title and what constitutes peaceful entry, these laws are not used very often, if ever. If you live in one of these states, you should ask a HUD-approved housing counselor (see Ch. 4) whether this method of foreclosure is used in your area.

Do You Have a Mortgage or a Deed of Trust?

As you'll see, it isn't always clear what the foreclosure process will be. Even in a state that typically requires foreclosures to go through court, nonjudicial foreclosure may be permitted if the loan is secured by a deed of trust rather than by a mortgage and if allowed by state law. On the other hand, even if your home loan is secured by a deed of trust, your lender may decide to foreclose judicially if there is a problem that a court needs to resolve, such as issues with title, or if it wants to obtain a deficiency judgment. For example, in Alaska, the lender cannot obtain a deficiency judgment after a nonjudicial foreclosure, but a deficiency judgment is allowed if the foreclosure goes through the courts.

Not sure which document was used to secure your home loan? You can find out by:

- reviewing your original paperwork (that pile of documents you got when you closed escrow on your house)
- calling your mortgage servicer (the company to whom you make your payments)
- visiting your local land records office and pulling up the recorded document (under your name or address) on the public-access computer, or
- checking your local county clerk and recorder's website. Sometimes there is an online search tool you can use to find out which documents have been recorded (such as a mortgage or deed of trust) on your property.

In some states, the borrower has a right to request a judicial foreclosure even if a deed of trust authorizes a nonjudicial foreclosure. See your state's page in the appendix for more information on whether you've got this option.

Judicial Foreclosures

If you live in one of the states listed in the table below, and your home loan is secured by a mortgage, the foreclosure will probably take place in court.

In judicial foreclosures, your lender gets things started by filing a foreclosure lawsuit in the local court. You will receive official notice of the lawsuit when a sheriff or process server personally serves you with (or posts on your door, leaves a copy at your home with a person of suitable age and discretion, and/or mails you, in some cases):

- a summons explaining your right to file a written response to the lawsuit and telling you how long you have to do so, and
- a copy of the document (called a petition or complaint) that requests the foreclosure and sets out the reasons the judge should issue a foreclosure order.

States Where Judicial Foreclosure Is Customary	
Connecticut	New Jersey
Delaware	New Mexico
District of Columbia (sometimes)	New York
Florida	North Dakota
Hawaii	Ohio
Illinois	Oklahoma
Indiana	(if the homeowner requests it)
Iowa	Pennsylvania
Kansas	South Carolina
Kentucky	South Dakota
Louisiana	(if the homeowner requests it)
(executory proceeding)	Vermont
Maine	Wisconsin

You can contest the foreclosure or let it proceed. If you don't respond, the lender will most likely get a default judgment authorizing the sale of the home. (A default judgment means that you automatically lose the case since you didn't respond to the suit.) If you do respond by filing an answer with the court, the foreclosing party can't get a default judgment. Instead, it will likely file a motion of summary judgment. You must respond to the motion or else the lender will win automatically. Even if you respond, the court may grant summary judgment in favor of the foreclosing party if there is no dispute as to the important facts of the case. However, if you have a valid defense and the court denies summary judgment, the case will proceed toward a trial, at which you and the lender will present your evidence and arguments. The judge will then either:

- order the foreclosure to go ahead (and in many states, set the sale date), or
- dismiss the case, sending the lender back to the drawing board.

In two states, Connecticut and Vermont, a judge who approves the foreclosure can order ownership (title) to be transferred then and there. This is called a strict foreclosure.

Judicial foreclosures are seldom if ever permanently derailed, but they can be significantly delayed. If you have grounds to fight the foreclosure, either because the foreclosing party can't prove its case or because you offer proof that casts doubt on the foreclosure's legality, such as evidence that the party seeking to foreclose doesn't own the loan, it can take many months before the case is resolved one way or the other.

Eventually, if the foreclosure is legally appropriate, the judge authorizes your house to be sold at auction or, in the strict foreclosure states, transferred directly to the lender.

Here's how a typical judicial foreclosure might proceed:

Peter and Mary bought their house several years ago at the price of $400,000. They made a 10% down payment and borrowed the other $360,000. The house now has a market value of just $325,000. Peter was laid off from his $60,000-a-year job and now earns $10 an hour. He and Mary can no longer afford their payments.

Shift Between Judicial and Nonjudicial Foreclosures in Oregon

Prior to 2012, most Oregon foreclosures were typically nonjudicial. In 2012, however, most lenders in Oregon filed judicial foreclosures. There were two main causes for this shift. In July 2012, the state implemented a Foreclosure Avoidance Mediation Program law, which only applied to nonjudicial foreclosures. In order to avoid the mediation program, many lenders proceeded judicially instead.

Also in 2012, an Oregon appellate court ruled that lenders must record loan ownership changes (when the lender or servicer transfers your mortgage to another company) with the county before starting a nonjudicial foreclosure. (*Niday v. GMAC Mortgage LLC*, 251 Or. App. 278 (2012).) This ruling meant that foreclosure cases involving Mortgage Electronic Registration Systems (MERS) had to go through the courts. (For more on MERS, see Ch. 7.)

This changed again mid-2013. The Oregon Supreme Court overruled the appellate court in *Niday*, so that MERS cases no longer have to go through court. And the Oregon legislature expanded the foreclosure mediation program to include judicial foreclosures. Because of these changes, many lenders have shifted back to using the nonjudicial foreclosure process in most cases. However, depending on the particular case, the lender might choose judicial foreclosure.

They live in Ohio, a judicial foreclosure state. Once they miss four payments, the lender sends them a written notice that foreclosure proceedings won't start for 30 days and that the proceedings can be avoided if they make up the missed payments plus costs and interest. Peter and Mary decide to let the foreclosure happen, given that they have no equity in the house, they won't be able to make the payments (even if modified downward), and the prospects for future appreciation of the property are bleak. They let the 30 days expire without paying the amount needed to cure the default.

Two weeks later, Peter and Mary are served with a copy of a summons and foreclosure complaint that the lender has filed in the local court. They have 28 days to respond. They visit a lawyer, who tells them they may be able to put off the foreclosure sale by filing a response contesting the allegations in the complaint and demanding a trial. Unfortunately, the lawyer wants too much money. Peter and Mary could do some research into possible defenses and represent themselves, but they decide they really can't afford the house any longer and will have to move anyway. They let the 28 days go by without responding.

The court issues a default judgment (that's what happens when you don't respond to a suit filed against you) that authorizes sale of the property. After the judgment, the property is appraised (because in their state the home can't be sold for less than two-thirds of its appraised value at the foreclosure sale) and then notice of the date, time, and place of sale is published for three consecutive weeks in a newspaper of general circulation in the county where the property is located. The lender files the notice of sale with the court at least seven days prior to the sale and sends a copy to Peter and Mary, as well as to the other parties that have appeared in the case. Then, on the specified date, the property is put up for sale at auction. But because no buyer comes forward to pay the asking price, ownership goes to the lender.

The entire process, from the time Peter and Mary first missed a payment until the auction, takes about ten months. Had Peter and Mary contested the foreclosure, the process might have dragged on for many more months.

After the auction, the court must confirm the sale and the new owner gets title to the property. In Peter and Mary's case, this happens 30 days after the sale. If they haven't left the property by this time, the new owner (the lender) will take steps to remove them from the home.

The lender asks the court for a writ of possession, which orders the sheriff to remove Peter and Mary from the property. (The lender does not have to file a separate lawsuit to evict them.) At this point, a representative from the sheriff's office will notify Peter and Mary of the date by which they must vacate the premises, typically between ten days and two weeks later.

Nonjudicial Foreclosures

If you live in one of the states listed below, the foreclosure will probably be nonjudicial. This means a court will not oversee the procedure (except in a few states, where a court signs off on the foreclosure). The foreclosure could be judicial though, for a variety of other reasons (for example, because of a title issue). Also, see your state's page in the appendix for information about your possible right to choose a judicial foreclosure.

Generally, a deed of trust authorizes the entity named as trustee in the deed of trust to foreclose on the property if you ever default. The deed of trust typically allows the foreclosure to proceed outside of court.

Your state's law sets out the specifics of the foreclosure procedure, including how much notice you get, how the property will be sold (typically at a public auction), and what rights (if any) you have to reinstate the loan before the foreclosure date or recover title to the property after it's sold.

States Where Nonjudicial Foreclosure Is Customary	
Alabama	Nevada
Alaska	New Hampshire
Arizona	New Mexico (sometimes)
Arkansas	North Carolina
California	Oklahoma (unless homeowner
Colorado	requests judicial)
District of Columbia (sometimes)	Oregon
Georgia	Rhode Island
Idaho	South Dakota (unless homeowner
Maryland	requests judicial)
Massachusetts	Tennessee
Michigan	Texas
Minnesota	Utah
Mississippi	Virginia
Missouri	Washington
Montana	West Virginia
Nebraska	Wyoming

CAUTION

Time may be short. You have to be on your toes when a foreclosure looms in a nonjudicial state. That's because you may get little notice of the foreclosure sale, and once it happens you may be permanently out of luck.

Here's how a typical nonjudicial foreclosure might proceed:

When Jason and Emilia bought their home for $400,000, it seemed like a great deal—but now it's worth only about $350,000, less than they owe on their loan. Jason and Emilia live in California, where nonjudicial foreclosures are the norm. Like most California homebuyers, they signed a promissory note and a deed of trust.

The deed of trust authorizes the lender to "accelerate" the entire loan (declare the whole enchilada due immediately) and states that the trustee (a California title insurance company) can sell the property at a public auction if Jason and Emilia default on their monthly payments or fail to maintain the insurance and pay property taxes. However, the terms of the deed of trust and California law require the lender to first give the homeowner some time to get current on the loan—this is called reinstating the loan—by making up the missed payments plus costs and interest. (See Ch. 1.)

After they miss four payments, Jason and Emilia receive (by mail) a 30-day notice notifying them that if they do not catch up on all of the payments, a foreclosure will be initiated. They decide to avoid responding. A month later, they receive (by certified mail) a notice of default. It gives them 90 days to cure the default by making up the missed payments, plus interest and costs. (See your state's page in the appendix to find out whether you'll receive a notice of default or similar notice and, if so, how much time it gives you to cure the default.) Jason and Emilia don't have the cash to make up the payments, and they are unable to work out a repayment plan with their lender. After the 90 days pass, they receive another document: a 20-day notice of intent to sell the property at an auction on the courthouse steps at a specific time.

At the auction, the property ends up with the lender because no one else makes a bid. Because the lender doesn't take immediate action to have Jason and Emilia evicted, they continue living there payment-free for another month. The lender then tries to negotiate a move-out date with Jason and Emilia, but that doesn't work. So the lender follows the California eviction laws for taking possession from former homeowners, and serves Jason and Emilia with a three-day notice to quit.

Although Jason and Emilia are legally entitled to stay until the lender goes to court and gets an eviction order (about a two-month process), they decide to move out to avoid having the eviction case on their credit record. Even so, Jason and Emilia have remained in their home for about nine months without making a payment, and have managed to save most of the money they would have paid for shelter during that period—which will make it easier for them to move out and find a new place to live. (See Ch. 9 for more on coming out of a foreclosure with some serious cash in your pocket.)

Deficiency Judgments: Will You Still Owe Money After the Foreclosure?

When deciding whether to fight a foreclosure, take steps to avoid it, or just walk away, you'll want to know whether you'll be stuck for the money that the lender loses because of your default. This is usually measured as the difference between the foreclosure sale price and the amount of your loan. It's called a deficiency, and it can be many thousands of dollars.

> **EXAMPLE:** Jonas owes $350,000 on a house he bought for $400,000 but that is now worth $300,000, according to a recent appraisal. He is no longer able to earn overtime at his job and falls behind on his payments. The lender threatens foreclosure and Jonas doesn't qualify for a workout. Not wanting to fight the foreclosure or file for bankruptcy, Jonas hands the keys to the lender and walks away.
>
> The lender forecloses on the property and schedules it for auction at a minimum bid of $300,000. No bids are made, so the property reverts to the lender. In Jonas's state, the lender can sue for the difference between the property's value and the amount owed on the loan—in this case, $50,000. Unless Jonas files for bankruptcy to wipe out this debt, the lender (or more likely, a collection firm) will sue to obtain a judgment, then use the judgment to go after his paycheck and bank account.

You may not have to worry about a deficiency judgment. A few states prohibit lenders from suing for deficiencies under certain circumstances. (Loans that fit in this category are called non-recourse loans, because the lender has no recourse if you default.)

In almost every nonjudicial foreclosure state, the lender cannot recover a deficiency without bringing a separate lawsuit and getting a money judgment. In a judicial foreclosure, on the other hand, most states allow the lender to seek a deficiency judgment as part of the underlying foreclosure lawsuit; a few states require a separate lawsuit.

Many states limit the amount of the deficiency to the difference between the loan and the property's fair market value. For instance, if the loan is for $400,000, the fair market value is $350,000, and the property is sold for $300,000, the deficiency judgment is limited to $50,000. This is so even though the lender technically lost $100,000— the difference between the loan amount and the sales price. Fair market value typically is determined by a fairly complex statutory appraisal process set out in state statutes.

You can wipe out a deficiency judgment by filing for Chapter 7 or Chapter 13 bankruptcy. Check the appendix to find your state's rules on deficiency judgments.

Taxes

Unsurprisingly, how you deal with foreclosures can have tax consequences.

Income Taxes

Essentially, if there's a deficiency in the course of a foreclosure, short sale, or deed in lieu of foreclosure, and the lender later cancels or forgives the debt, the amount is considered your taxable income, unless the deficiency arose from a loan used for the acquisition or improvement of your principal home. This exclusion also applies to refinances to the extent the refinance paid off the loan you used to buy or improve the home. (This issue is discussed in more detail in Ch. 8.)

Capital Gains Tax

If your adjusted tax basis on your house is less than the sale price of the house, you may incur a capital gains tax. For example, if you bought your house for $200,000 and it sells for $300,000, you have a $100,000 capital gain, minus the cost of any improvements you added to the property. This gain will be taxed at the capital gains tax rate, subject to your one-time exclusion ($250,000 for one person, $500,000 for a married couple). Check with a tax expert to see whether you'll face a capital gains issue at the sale or foreclosure of your house. If you will, consult a bankruptcy lawyer for advice on how filing for bankruptcy might help.

Can You Keep Your House? Should You?

If foreclosure looms because you've missed some payments, or you think you will soon, it's time to face what's probably the toughest question of the whole process: whether or not you should try to hang on to your house.

Of course, you must take a good look at whether it's financially feasible to try to keep your house. But the decision isn't always a simple matter of finances and cash flow. You'll need to sort through emotional factors, too. Would the loss of your residence be so catastrophic that you would do anything to keep it, or might you be better off letting go and moving on? Could you accept it as an economic setback rather than a personal failing?

This chapter will help you figure these things out. Then you can move forward, either to take steps to keep your house or to start planning how to give it up in the most emotionally and economically advantageous way. The next chapters discuss how to take these next steps after you decide what direction you want to go in.

The Emotional Part of Foreclosure

It's important to acknowledge that the prospect of losing your house can be a psychological blow as well as a financial and practical one. You can't avoid these emotional realities—you're not a machine—but facing them can help you approach the situation in as calm and rational manner as possible.

Dealing With Fear

If you're like many homeowners, the thought of foreclosure triggers fears of ending up on the street. So let me reassure you: It just doesn't happen like that.

Foreclosure is an orderly process. You'll get notice before the process starts and before the house is eventually sold, if it comes to that (see Ch. 2). You may also have the right to live in the home during the redemption period, if there is one, after the sale. (See Ch. 9 for a more detailed explanation of how this works.)

Even when the property ends up in the hands of a new owner at the foreclosure sale, in many states, the new owner will have to give you a formal written notice to leave. Typically, you'll have from three to 30 days. And if you don't leave at the end of that period, the new owner will have to go to court and get an eviction order. In other words, you'll almost certainly have enough time to make new housing arrangements.

Were You Nesting or Investing When You Bought Your House?

Much of this chapter—and the book, for that matter—assumes that you have an emotional attachment to your house. But maybe you don't, or at least not much of one. Maybe you bought your house primarily as a way to build some wealth. Some of the people we've worked with lived in rental apartments and rented out the houses they owned. Others, while living in their houses, were ready to move on, if necessary, in the same way any other small business owner would move on when the economics of the business dictate.

If you bought your house primarily as an investment, your decision-making process should be based on the economics of your situation. If you are way upside down, get out the best way you can. If you are close to the line, decide whether or not to hang in there and hope things get better. If you are living in your house but aren't particularly attached to it, stay as long as legally possible without making a payment. (See Ch. 9.)

Grieving for Your Loss

You may not have thought of it in these terms, but you are likely to go through a grieving process when faced with the loss of your house. It's something like what you might experience if you were contemplating the loss of your marriage or career.

In her seminal book, *On Death and Dying*, psychiatrist Elisabeth Kübler-Ross identified five stages that patients commonly experience when given a terminal prognosis. To a lesser extent, people facing the possibility of foreclosure often go through similar stages, which are:

- denial (This isn't happening to me!)
- anger (Why is this happening to me?)
- bargaining (I promise I'll make every mortgage payment on time from now on!)
- depression (I don't *care* anymore.)
- acceptance (I'm ready to make lemonade out of lemons.)

Denial. People commonly ignore the first warning signs of impending foreclosure—the missed payment, the call from the lender, even the formal notice that is the prelude to a foreclosure. Envelopes are unopened, notices go unread, and phone messages are quickly erased. Homeowners know something bad is happening but cling to the hope that something—anything—will come along to bail them out or that they can ride out the current situation.

Anger. When it finally dawns on them that they might actually lose their house, they become angry—with themselves, their spouse, the lender, or maybe the president of the United States.

Bargaining. Anger gives way to negotiation. They tell themselves that if somehow they can avoid losing their home, they will make all their mortgage payments on time, hew to a strict budget, and even get a second job, if necessary.

Depression. As the foreclosure sale draws nearer, the reality of the possible loss of their home sets in and they may become physically ill and unable to deal with the daily grind. Each day begins and ends in fear.

Acceptance. The state of depression turns into a state of acceptance that the foreclosure is coming and must be dealt with—which results in:

- a search for new quarters
- a plan to fight the foreclosure
- a visit to a bankruptcy attorney, or
- a resolve to remain in the home as long as possible, payment free.

Avoiding the "American Dream" Trap

Owning real estate—as opposed to leasing or renting it—is commonly equated with achieving the American dream. We take for granted that owning a home is superior to renting one, especially if you have a family.

To a large extent, we have been sold on this idea by industries that stand to benefit from a robust housing market and governments that depend on property taxes. There are, however, many more important aspects to the American dream than owning a house. Democracy, freedom, public education, and equal economic opportunity come to mind.

Your House Is Not Your Home

You will likely have an easier time dealing with foreclosure if you understand (and remind yourself regularly) that your house and your home are not necessarily the same thing. A home is where you and your loved ones live. It's about your neighbors, your memories, and shelter from the storm. Your home is where you sit down to a family meal, entertain friends, and get in touch with your creative side by arranging furniture, hanging art and family portraits, or changing the wallpaper. A home is where you can relax after work or return after a trip.

In essence, home is a concept you can take with you whether you buy another house or end up renting. Sure, you would probably rather stay where you are, but the fact that you may have to move should be seen for what it is: a temporary interruption in your life from which you are certain to recover. In fact, finding a new place to live can lead you to new opportunities, new friends and neighbors, new community activities, and a different perspective on life.

You Are Not Your House

In the same way your house is not your home, you are not your house. It's deeply ingrained in our culture that the size and location of the house we live in indicates our value as human beings. For example, given the opportunity, most of us would prefer to live in a large house with a stunning view. It's not because we need a large house—average household size has gone down just as average house size has gone up. But for most of us, a large fancy house provides the status and self-esteem we crave.

Renting Has Advantages

Renting has definite advantages. It offers freedom from the economic burdens and stress every homeowner feels when faced with the need to pay for rodent control, a new paint job, a new roof or furnace, an expensive city assessment for road improvements, increasing property tax, broken water pipes, and a variety of other problems that homeowners are naturally heir to. It can be a real luxury to be able to call the landlord when a big-ticket maintenance problem—for example the water heater—rears its ugly head.

If you need to relocate, get away from neighbors, or travel over long periods of time, renting gives you flexibility that you lack with home ownership. And if you want to stay put, a long-term lease is a good hedge against having to move before you are ready.

If you're putting an inordinate amount of money into your mortgage, you quite likely are making sacrifices in other important areas of your life, such as your family's health, your children's education, charitable contributions, or visits to far-flung relatives, to name but a few common expenses. Living in poverty-like conditions just to remain in your house doesn't make a whole lot of sense.

The Economics of Foreclosure: What You Need to Know

Apart from the emotional considerations that surface whenever a foreclosure is threatened, there are economic factors you just can't ignore. Before you can decide whether or not to try to keep your house, you need to answer a few questions about your financial situation—which has no doubt changed since you bought your house.

Do You Have Equity in Your House?

To a large degree, your options depend on whether or not you have equity in your house. When you bought your house, presumably it was worth more than the amount you borrowed to buy it. If your house is still worth at least as much as you owe on it, it may make sense to oppose the foreclosure (see Chs. 5, 6, and 7) or sell it and get out from under the loan.

Estimates of real estate values are traditionally based on the amounts that similar houses in the neighborhood have recently sold for. To find out that information, you can use www.zillow.com, www.housevalues. com, or similar websites (search for "home value calculators"). Local real estate brokers and agents can also give you an estimate by looking at similar sales in your neighborhood.

If there are other foreclosures going on in your community, a house similar to yours may have sold for far less than you could get for your house if you could afford to be patient. Also, buyers will pay substantially more for a well-kept home than for one that has been trashed, as many foreclosed homes are.

Take the best estimate you can come up with and use the simple worksheet below to help you determine what, if any, equity you have in your house.

Homeowners' Equity Worksheet

1. Market value of your home $ _____

2. Costs of sale (if unsure, put 5% of market value) $ _____

3. Amount owed on all mortgages $ _____

4. Amount of all other liens on the property $ _____

5. Total of Lines 2, 3, and 4 $ _____

6. Your equity (Line 1 minus Line 5) $ _____

Where the Housing Market Stands Today

At the time of this writing, it is now roughly nine years since the start of the housing collapse. Homes have regained their value (and then some) in many parts of the country. Other areas, however, haven't fared as well. At the end of 2016, around six million homeowners were still underwater. Nevada and Illinois, for example, still have a substantial number of underwater homes. And, while foreclosures have been declining overall since their peak in 2010, some states are still experiencing heavy volumes. For example, foreclosure rates in Florida, New York, and New Jersey remain high as lenders try to get through the lingering inventory of delinquent loans.

The bottom line is that while, overall, the housing market is considerably better than it was a few years ago, there are still many homeowners across the United States who have to figure out what to do with their underwater home or a looming foreclosure.

Can You Keep Making Your Monthly Payments?

There is no point in putting time and effort (not to mention emotional energy) into trying to hang on to your house if you really, truly can't afford it. If, for example, you were one of the many homebuyers who were counting on your house's value going up so you could refinance your way out of an unfavorable mortgage, you may have no choice but to move. People who have lost their jobs are in the same boat.

Many people are current on their mortgages but just about to go under. It's not uncommon for people to pay upwards of 50% of their gross (not take-home) income toward their overall mortgage debt. That leaves little or nothing left for food, utilities, transportation, out-of-pocket medical costs, and the like. Quite simply, their economic position is untenable.

Here's how to think about whether or not you can really afford your current loan.

Use the Standard Ratios

For decades, the conventional wisdom was that you shouldn't pay more than 25% of your gross income for shelter. Slowly that figure crept up as lenders relaxed their rules to underwrite ever-increasing numbers of mortgages. After the government established HAMP (Tier 1) of the Making Home Affordable program, this percentage has settled in at 31%. Under this thinking, if you are paying more than 31% of your gross income on your first mortgage, you are at serious risk of default. So, for example, if you are paying $3,100 a month on your first mortgage (including tax and insurance), your annual gross income should be in the neighborhood of $120,000. If your income is $75,000 a year, your first mortgage payment (including tax and insurance) shouldn't exceed about $1,938 a month. This is obviously a cookie-cutter approach—especially because second mortgages and home equity lines of credit aren't included in that 31%.

In terms of deciding whether your home is affordable as a factual matter, there may be times when the 31% figure can be thrown out the window. If, for example, you have a child with special needs or two kids in college, your mortgage payment might not be affordable even if it's below the 31% threshold. And if you have few other expenses (for example, you live simply, don't own a car, and grow some of your own food), you might be able to afford a mortgage payment that is a higher percentage of your income.

How Much of Your Income Should Go to Your Mortgage?		
	Maximum Mortgage Payment	
Annual Gross Income	**25% of monthly income**	**31% of monthly income**
$50,000	$1,042	$1,292
$75,000	$1,562	$1,938
$100,000	$2,083	$2,583
$125,000	$2,604	$3,229

Use an Online Calculator

The Internet is chock full of calculators that purport to tell you how much house you can afford. They're very easy to use, but they make some assumptions that might not quite work for you.

A good one is the Nolo mortgage affordability calculator. To use it, go to www.nolo.com/legal-calculators/index.html, then click "How much mortgage might I qualify for?"

You can find another calculator at www.bankrate.com. Click on "Mortgages" and then "Mortgage Calculator." For other calculators, do an online search for "home affordability calculators."

These formulas tell you how much you can borrow, according to the general opinion of the housing finance industry.

Do a Budget

You can take a no-nonsense look at your income and expenses and see whether there is room in your budget for your current or projected mortgage payments. If the numbers don't add up the first time around, see what expenses you can trim.

Don't know where to start? As you might guess, lots of websites offer budgeting software and spreadsheets. One that offers a combination of free and low-cost services is www.debtsteps.com/budget-calculators. html. Or just search for "online budget planning" to come up with a list.

RESOURCE

Get budgeting help. For more information about how to create a budget and control your spending, get *Solve Your Money Troubles*, by Cara O'Neill and Amy Loftsgordon (Nolo).

Ask a Budget-Counseling Agency

Everyone who files for bankruptcy must, by law, take a budgeting class in order to receive a discharge of their debts. To meet this demand, hundreds of companies, for-profit and nonprofit alike, have set up shop to deliver debtor education classes. These organizations can also help you with budgeting, even if you're not planning to file for bankruptcy.

The courses are taught online or by telephone and mail. The fee averages about $50.

For a list of agencies that have been approved by the Department of Justice for bankruptcy purposes—although you don't have to file for bankruptcy to use them—go to www.justice.gov/ust/eo/bapcpa/ccde/de_approved.htm. Because budgeting is pretty much the same everywhere, and because you don't need to show up in person, you can use a service even if it's far from where you live.

Last but certainly not least, HUD-approved housing counselors can also provide budgeting help to people trying to save their homes from foreclosure. (See Ch. 4.)

Could You Reduce Your Debt Load?

If you don't have enough cash each month to keep making your existing mortgage payments, there are a few ways that you might be able to make them affordable. Basically, you need to either get the mortgage payments reduced or get your hands on more cash.

Here are the main ways to go about this (all of which are discussed elsewhere in the book):

- **Modify your mortgage.** When the Home Affordable Modification Program (HAMP) expired at the end of 2016, Fannie Mae and Freddie Mac developed the Flex Modification program to replace it. If you have an FHA-insured loan, you're entitled to a special loss mitigation process that might help you qualify for a modification. Also, almost all lenders offer modifications to borrowers who are struggling to make mortgage payments. (You can get details in Ch. 4.)
- **File for Chapter 13 bankruptcy** and come up with a repayment plan that will let you reduce the amount of your monthly payments on your other debts and get rid of them altogether in three to five years.

- **File for Chapter 7 bankruptcy** to get rid of your unsecured debts, such as those from credit cards, medical services, or signature (personal, unsecured) loans, so you'll have a greater share of your income to devote to your mortgage.

When It Makes Sense to Keep Your House

Your answers to the questions discussed above, about your equity and your budget, will largely determine whether or not you should try to keep your house.

You Have at Least Some Equity in Your House

If you have equity in your house and are facing foreclosure because of missed payments or a rapid increase in your mortgage interest rate, it may make sense to hold on to the house if for no other reason than to protect your equity. Needless to say, the more equity you have, the stronger this reasoning.

You Can Afford Future Monthly Loan Payments

If you have some equity in your house and think you can afford future monthly mortgage payments, it's probably worth it to try to hang on to your house.

If you don't think you can afford your monthly payments, see "Could You Reduce Your Debt Load?" above for ideas on how to free up more of your income or change the payments themselves.

You Have Equity and Can Get a Reverse Mortgage

It's not uncommon for people with fixed or limited incomes (disability or retirement income, or low-paying jobs) to own homes with affordable mortgage payments and with substantial equity ($50,000 or more). But they can't borrow against this equity because their income level won't support repayment of the loan, so the only way to benefit from the equity is to sell the house. However, for whatever reason, selling may not be an option.

Even people with higher incomes may not be able to borrow against their equity, either because credit has dried up, they have bad credit, or because other debts and their lifestyle won't support repayment of a new loan.

If you are 62 or older, you might benefit from taking out a reverse mortgage. The most widely available reverse mortgage is the FHA's Home Equity Conversion Mortgage (HECM). With a reverse mortgage, a homeowner can tap into the equity in his or her home to provide cash. A reverse mortgage is different from a traditional mortgage in that it does not require you to make monthly payments to the lender to repay the loan. Instead, loan proceeds are paid out to you according to a plan, which consists of a lump sum, monthly payment, or line of credit (or a combination of monthly payments and a line of credit).

In the past, many reverse mortgage borrowers immediately took out the full amount of the loan in a lump sum, leaving them with less money in later years to pay for taxes, insurance, and home maintenance costs. This led to a large number of defaults and foreclosures, and caused HUD to change its reverse mortgage policies. HECM rules, which went into effect in 2013, limit the amount can you take out in a lump sum or during the first year. You can only take out 60% of the total amount (called the "principal limit") in the first year. (If there are mandatory obligations, such as an existing mortgage, the initial disbursement is limited to the amount needed to pay off the mandatory obligations plus 10% of the principal limit.) The goal of this change is to encourage people to access their home equity slowly and steadily over the years, rather than all at once. It also allows borrowers to keep some equity in their homes.

In addition, as of late April 2015, a lender must complete a financial assessment and credit analysis when making a reverse mortgage loan to ensure that homeowners can afford the future taxes and insurance payments. If a lender determines that a homeowner may not be able to keep up with these payments, the lender must also establish a set-aside account. (The set-aside is an amount drawn under the HECM that is then reserved to pay property taxes and insurance.) In the future, FHA might require lenders to evaluate the borrower's ability to cover utility costs in addition to taxes and insurance as part of the financial assessment.

If the lender does not require a set-aside, you can pay the taxes and insurance with a voluntary set-aside or, in some cases, by having the lender withhold sufficient amounts from the monthly disbursements, or by charging funds to the line of credit. You could also choose to pay the taxes and insurance on your own.

The reverse mortgage loan becomes due and payable when you:

- sell the property
- permanently move out (for example, to a nursing home)
- do not meet the obligations of the mortgage (such as paying taxes and insurance), or
- die.

Because reverse mortgages are premised on stable real estate values, you are unlikely to qualify for one unless you have a lot of equity in your house—at least enough to convince the lender that it'll recoup its investment.

Reverse mortgages can be risky and aren't a good idea for everybody. If you fall behind on property taxes or homeowners' insurance, leave your home for longer than allowed under the mortgage contract, or fail to comply with other requirements, you could default and trigger a foreclosure. Be sure to consider all options before you take out this type of loan.

When It Makes Sense to Give Up Your House

It's never an easy decision, but if you are behind on house payments and find yourself upside-down on your mortgage, there's not much point, from an economic perspective, in trying to keep the house unless you can get your mortgage payment reduced with a modification or by working something out with your lender (and many lenders do want to keep you in your house; see Ch. 4).

Keep in mind, though, that even if you wouldn't lose any equity by walking away from your mortgage, you could end up liable for some or all of your mortgage or home equity loan debt if you don't file for bankruptcy. And you might be taxed on the amount of the mortgage debt lost by the lender (although there are several ways to avoid this tax liability). (See Ch. 8.)

If you decide that the smartest course is to give up the house, how you choose to proceed can make a very big difference to your financial future.

Your options (all of which are discussed later in the book) include:

- a short sale—that is, getting the lender's permission to sell the house for less than you owe
- a deed in lieu of foreclosure (getting your lender to accept the deed back in exchange for an agreement to call off the foreclosure)
- letting the foreclosure happen, staying in your house payment-free for months until you get a notice to leave, and building up your cash reserves, or
- filing for Chapter 13 or Chapter 7 bankruptcy to eliminate foreclosure-related liabilities and delay the foreclosure sale for at least several months, thereby extending the time you can remain in the house payment-free.

Although for many it's painful to give up a house, try to keep in mind that doing so may make things much easier for you and your family in the long run. You will probably be able to stay in the house for months without making any more mortgage payments—giving you time to save some money, which will make moving easier.

Working Out a Way to Avoid Foreclosure

W hen you are at risk of defaulting on your mortgage, or have already fallen behind on your payments, you may have a number of options for keeping your house.

Refinance your mortgage under the federal Home Affordable Refinance Program. Usually, refinancing is available only if you have equity in your home. However, under the government-sponsored refinance program known as the Home Affordable Refinance Program (HARP), you may be able to refinance your current mortgage into a 15- or 30-year fixed-rate mortgage. This may not reduce your payment much in the short term, but it will help avoid nasty interest rate resets that might be in your future under your current mortgage. HARP is discussed later in this chapter.

Lower your monthly mortgage payment with a modification. It might be possible to get a modification from your mortgage lender if, like many, it would rather have you stay in your house than foreclose on it. You would do well to use a HUD-approved housing counselor to help you head off the foreclosure. The counselor can explain your options, work with your lender, and do a lot for your peace of mind. (See "Using a HUD-Approved Housing Counselor," below.)

File for bankruptcy. If you can't work out an agreement that will let you stay in your house under certain conditions—and you don't have the wherewithal to reinstate your mortgage under your state's law (see Ch. 1)— your next step is to explore filing for Chapter 13 or Chapter 7 bankruptcy. Chapter 13 can give you time to make up your missed payments and might lower your other secured debt payments (your car note or a short-term home equity loan, for example). Chapter 7 bankruptcy can quickly do away with credit card and other unsecured debt and free up income to use toward your mortgage payments, thereby allowing you to keep your home.

Challenge the foreclosure in court. Finally, you may be able to successfully challenge the foreclosure in court because of irregularities in the paperwork or the procedures followed by the foreclosing party. Courts throughout the country have disapproved of foreclosures in circumstances where the record of mortgage ownership is incomplete or where court documents have been fraudulently prepared. You will likely take this route only if you can't work out a way to avoid a foreclosure with the lender.

This chapter concentrates on the various ways you can change the terms of your mortgage or the amount of your monthly payment as a strategy to keep your home. Later chapters cover filing for bankruptcy and fighting foreclosure in court.

How Bankruptcy Can Help

Filing for bankruptcy can be a marvelous way either to save your house or at least to stay in it payment free for longer than you would otherwise.

It's important to understand that Chapter 7 bankruptcy will keep you in your home long-term only if you file while you are still current on your mortgage. It will help you by wiping out (discharging) your other debts, freeing up your income to make your house payments. Chapter 13 bankruptcy, however, can keep you in your home long-term even if you are behind on your payments. (See Chs. 5 and 6.)

Do You Have Enough Time to Work Out an Alternative to Foreclosure?

It can take a while to work things out with your lender (typically through its representative, a mortgage servicing company). If you're not sure how much time you've got left before your house is sold in foreclosure, find the page for your state in the appendix and see how much notice you're entitled to. Also, remember that federal law gives you 120 days before foreclosure can start so that you can begin exploring options. Your failure to keep track of time constraints can sink your attempt to keep your house.

During the mortgage crisis it was common for homeowners to negotiate with their servicers right up to the moment of the scheduled foreclosure sale. Then, when the negotiations fell through—as they frequently did—there wasn't enough time to stop the sale from going through.

Because of this practice (called "dual tracking"—that is, proceeding with foreclosure while simultaneously working with the homeowner on a loan modification or other form of loss mitigation)—many homeowners who were sure that a loan modification was forthcoming were shocked to ultimately lose their homes to foreclosure. Now, there are federal and various state laws in place to prevent dual tracking and provide other protections to homeowners trying to save their home.

In particular, the Dodd-Frank Wall Street Reform and Consumer Protection Act of 2010 imposed new requirements on servicers and gave the Consumer Financial Protection Bureau (CFPB) the authority to both implement the new requirements, as well as adopt new rules. On January 10, 2014, the CFPB's final mortgage servicing rules under the Real Estate Settlement Procedures Act (RESPA), also known as Regulation X, and the Truth in Lending Act (TILA) known as Regulation Z, went into effect. These rules establish national mortgage servicing standards and impose new requirements on lenders and servicers (subject to some exceptions).

Many of the new rules are designed to ensure that homeowners get a fair shot at getting a mortgage modification or other foreclosure relief. For example:

The servicer can't start a foreclosure for 120 days. A servicer cannot make the "first notice or filing" under state law unless the loan is more than 120 days delinquent. (This is a relatively new industry standard. It used to be that the lender would typically start a foreclosure when the loan was 90 days delinquent—sometimes even sooner.) This means that, in a judicial foreclosure, the foreclosing party cannot file a court document (such as a complaint, petition, order to docket, or notice of hearing) until after you fall 120 days behind. If the foreclosure is nonjudicial, the lender cannot begin the foreclosure by recording or publishing the first notice until after the 120th day of the delinquency. If state foreclosure law doesn't require a document to be recorded, published, or filed with the court, the first notice is the earliest document that establishes, sets, or schedules a date for the foreclosure sale. This is supposed to give you time to work out a way to avoid foreclosure.

Even if you are more than 120 days delinquent, if you submit a complete loss mitigation application (such as an application for a loan modification) before the servicer has made the first notice or filing required to initiate a foreclosure process, it may not start the foreclosure process unless:

- the servicer informs you that you're not eligible for any loss mitigation option (and the time for an appeal is over)
- you reject the workout option that the servicer offers to you, or
- you accept a workout, but fail to comply with the terms of the deal, such as not making payments during a trial modification.

There are two exceptions to this rule: The servicer can proceed with a foreclosure during the 120-day time period if it is joining the foreclosure action of a subordinate lienholder, or if the foreclosure is because you violated a due-on-sale clause. (A due-on-sale clause is a provision in a mortgage or deed of trust that allows the lender to demand immediate payment of the balance of the mortgage if you sell or transfer ownership of the home.)

Servicers must provide homeowners with assistance. Under the rules, mortgage servicers are supposed to work with you if you're having trouble making monthly payments. If you fall behind in payments, the servicer must attempt to contact you to discuss the situation no later than 36 days after the delinquency. No later than 45 days after you miss a payment, the servicer must inform you in writing that mortgage workout options may be available. Simply put, the servicer must send you a "loss mitigation package"—an application that allows you to apply for a mortgage workout option.

Single point of contact. The rules also require the mortgage servicer to assign personnel to help you by the time you fall 45 days delinquent and sometimes sooner. (This is technically called the "continuity of contact" rule, but is often referred to as the "single point of contact" requirement.) Personnel must be accessible to you by phone and able to advise you about the status of your loss mitigation application and applicable timelines. Because of this rule, lenders now have lower loan-to-employee ratios and provide improved service when it comes to loss mitigation. (In the past, servicers were overwhelmed with loss mitigation requests and didn't have enough staff to keep up with all of the requests for help.)

Loss mitigation applications. If you submit a loss mitigation application 45 days or more before a foreclosure sale, the servicer must acknowledge it within five days, excluding weekends and holidays, after receiving the application. The servicer must also tell you whether it needs more information and, if so, what information it needs.

Generally, the servicer is required to evaluate the application for all loss mitigation options within 30 days after receiving the application. Under the 2014 mortgage servicing rules, a servicer need only evaluate you for a loss mitigation option once. New servicing rules (scheduled to start October 2017) require servicers to provide borrowers with foreclosure protections more than once over the life of the loan. For instance, under the new rules, borrowers who catch up on payments after submitting a complete loss mitigation application are eligible for re-evaluation. This benefit should prove useful if, after a modification, you fall behind again due to a hardship, such as a job loss or the death of your spouse.

Restrictions on foreclosure when you request help. If you submit a complete loss mitigation application more than 37 days before a foreclosure sale, the servicer may not move for a foreclosure judgment or order of sale, or conduct a foreclosure sale, until it evaluates the application and:

- informs you that you are not eligible for any loss mitigation option and the time to appeal is over if you're eligible to appeal (the servicer must give you the reasons if it denies you a trial or permanent loan modification option)
- you reject all loss mitigation offers, or
- you fail to comply with the terms of a loss mitigation option such as a trial modification.

You can appeal a loan modification denial so long as the complete loss mitigation application was received 90 or more days prior to a scheduled foreclosure sale.

If you submit your application 37 days or fewer before a foreclosure sale, the servicer must review the application in accordance with any requirements established by the owner or assignee of your mortgage loan.

Your timeframe to accept or reject an offer. If you submit a complete loss mitigation application 90 days or more before a foreclosure sale, the servicer must give you at least 14 days to accept or reject an offer of a loss mitigation option. If a complete loss mitigation application is received less than 90 days before a foreclosure sale, but more than 37 days before a foreclosure sale, the servicer must give you at least seven days to accept or reject a loss mitigation offer.

New rules. The Consumer Financial Protection Bureau recently finalized new rules and made changes to rules already in effect (most go into effect in late 2017).

- Servicers must communicate with, and provide protections to, family members who inherit a home upon the death of the borrower. These people—called "successors in interest"—must receive the same protections under mortgage servicing rules as the original borrower.
- Servicers must give additional information to borrowers who are in bankruptcy, including providing periodic statements and an early intervention notice letting the borrower know about loss mitigation options.
- Servicers must notify the borrower when a loss mitigation application is complete.

More information about the rules and proposed rules can be found at www.consumerfinance.gov. (Run a search for "mortgage servicing rules" and follow the links.)

Also, California, Colorado, Nevada, and Minnesota have passed laws that restrict dual tracking and provide other protections to homeowners facing foreclosure. If you live in any of these states and are facing foreclosure, it is recommended that you speak to an attorney to find out how these laws may be able to help you.

Despite the new laws designed to induce servicers and lenders to work with homeowners to avoid a foreclosure, homeowners (and consumer advocates) have found that servicers often don't comply and continue to conduct foreclosure sales before properly reviewing modification requests. You should be aware of when a foreclosure sale might happen and know the date before which you should take other steps to prevent the foreclosure sale—such as filing for bankruptcy or suing to stop the foreclosure in nonjudicial foreclosure states.

The lessons are obvious: Get started as soon as you can, and be assertive if you don't get a timely response.

If a foreclosure sale looms in the near future—two weeks should have the alarm bells ringing—consult a lawyer immediately. You may want to file bankruptcy to halt the sale. Bankruptcy is the only sure way to stop an imminent sale. (See Chs. 5 and 6 for more on bankruptcy.)

Why Lenders Sometimes Delay Foreclosing

Just because a lender can foreclose doesn't mean it will foreclose. Lenders delay foreclosing for a number of reasons.

Delay is frequently due to abrupt policy changes on the part of the major banks, whether they are servicers, investors, or lenders. Whenever word leaks out about an irregular practice engaged in by one major lender, both that lender and other major lenders will announce a moratorium on foreclosures until they investigate the matter further.

Take, for example, the "robo-signing" scandal in 2010, which was uncovered in a deposition in a Chapter 13 bankruptcy. In the deposition, a bank official admitted to signing thousands of documents every week, falsely stating under oath that he had personal knowledge of the information in those documents. It turned out that this practice, known as robo-signing, was used by a broad spectrum of mortgage servicers and entities seeking foreclosures in judicial foreclosure states. Once word of the robo-signing scandal spread, virtually all the major servicers and lenders announced temporary holds on foreclosures, at least in judicial foreclosure states where signed affidavits typically are required. This delay lasted for several months.

Delay is also frequently caused by changes in federal or state law or federal regulations that require banks to take additional steps prior to initiating foreclosure. For example, when the Consumer Financial Protection Bureau issued the mortgage servicing rules effective as of January 10, 2014, foreclosures stalled. Foreclosure delays generally tend to occur whenever new regulations go into effect since lenders and servicers often back off from foreclosing until they are confident they have appropriate procedures in place to be in compliance with the latest requirements.

CAUTION
Avoid foreclosure rescue scams. Companies that offer to rescue you from foreclosure on the eve of a foreclosure sale are all too often con artists. (See "Don't Get Scammed by a Foreclosure 'Rescue' Company" in Ch. 1.)

Using a HUD-Approved Housing Counselor

As a general rule, the sooner you hook up with a HUD-approved housing counselor, the better. These counselors work for free (they are paid through government grants and in some cases grants from major mortgage lenders who really do want to avoid foreclosures if at all possible) and are well trained in the various foreclosure-prevention programs and techniques of negotiation. You can have no better advocate if you are trying to avoid a foreclosure or negotiate a mortgage modification.

Finding a HUD-Approved Counselor

The federal Department of Housing and Urban Development (HUD) has a list of approved counselors. You can find a counselor at www.hud.gov/offices/hsg/sfh/hcc/hcs.cfm or by calling 800-569-4287.

You can also find a counselor by visiting The Homeownership Preservation Foundation at www.995hope.org or by calling 888-995-HOPE. Counselors can also be accessed through the Making Home Affordable website at www.makinghomeaffordable.gov.

For general information about HUD-approved housing counselors, including their training, their funding, and why they want to help you stay in your home, visit www.hud.gov/offices/hsg/sfh/hcc/hcc_home.cfm.

TIP

Know your options if you don't use a HUD counselor. If you decide to handle your own negotiations, first get a good understanding of the different types of loss mitigation options available, such as loan modifications, repayment plans, forbearance agreements, short sales, and deeds in lieu of foreclosure. (Loan modifications, repayment plans, and forbearance agreements are discussed later in this chapter, while short sales and deeds in lieu of foreclosure are covered in Ch. 8.)

Once you call your servicer or contact a HUD-approved housing counselor, your servicer will send you a "workout package" of forms, along with some information about your options. After you fill out and return the forms, you and your servicer can start talking about possible arrangements.

The servicer will have some discretion to make deals, but will have to contact the lender for anything out of the ordinary. For example, say you are three months behind on your mortgage because you were laid off, but you are now back at work and can make up the missed payments over six months in addition to meeting your current obligation. Most mortgage servicers have authority to sign off on this kind of short-term arrangement. But if you need two years to make up the missed payments, the servicer might have to get permission to make a deal.

If your servicer is not responsive to your attempts to work things out, contact your lender directly. If you don't know who your lender is—which is quite common due to the rapid changes in the marketplace—you can find out from your servicer. The servicer is required by law to give you that information—and you can sue if it doesn't.

Can a HUD-Approved Housing Counselor Always Help You?

Housing counselors can do a lot, but they are limited by mortgage servicer and lender policies regarding what are termed loss mitigation guidelines. This means you might not qualify for a mortgage workout no matter what you or the counselor does. The days of actually negotiating a loan modification are long gone. Now, the loss mitigation process is ruled strictly by the numbers and whether or not you meet certain eligibility criteria.

Still, even if you think you won't qualify for a modification, it certainly doesn't hurt to talk to a counselor and submit a loss mitigation request to the servicer—either before the foreclosure officially starts or even if the foreclosure has already started. Under federal and some state laws, the servicer can't start or continue with a foreclosure while your application is pending and you might get a more affordable mortgage payment for the future. Or you may be eligible for another workout option that you hadn't previously considered.

What Happens When You Contact a HUD-Approved Counselor

When you call a HUD-approved counselor, you will be scheduled for an interview (by phone or in person) that will probably take between 60 and 90 minutes. The counselor will want to get a handle on your income, your debts, your property, your mortgage, the value of your home, and what kind of arrangement you think you can live with. You likely will need to do some homework before your appointment.

The counselor will discuss your situation with you and help you figure out what options are best, as well as give a recommendation on proposed next steps. He or she will also explain what documents you will need to provide to your mortgage company and may be able to contact the mortgage servicer for you.

If Your Case Is Easy to Resolve

You have missed only two or three payments because of a temporary economic setback through no fault of your own, and you can show that you'll be able to make your payments in the future.

The counselor will call a dedicated loss mitigation hotline made available by your mortgage servicer and get an okay to a workout on the spot. Typically, you'll get an agreement that lets you make up the missed payments over a period of between three months and a year, depending on your situation. Or the agreement may add the missed payments to the end of your mortgage.

Information to Gather Before You Call

- Information about your first mortgage loan (have your monthly mortgage statement handy)
- Recent bank statements
- Recent pay stubs (and other income documentation)
- Utility bill showing name and address
- Benefit statements from Social Security, disability, unemployment, retirement, or public assistance
- Your last two tax returns
- If you're self-employed, an up-to-date profit and loss statement
- Monthly household expenses
- Information about any second mortgage or home equity line of credit on the home
- Account balances and monthly payments due on all of your credit cards, student loans, car loans, and so on, and
- Information about your savings and other assets.

It's hard to generalize about how long it takes to get an agreement in your hand if your case looks like an easy one to the counselor. It all depends on the volume of cases being worked on by your counselor and lender, and the priority assigned to your case. These types of cases are usually resolved pretty quickly, though it could take a few weeks.

If You Need Serious Help to Keep the House

You have missed four or five payments and are on the verge of foreclosure. If you're going to be able to make future payments, you need some type of modification of your mortgage principal or interest payment, and you need a way to deal with the missed payments.

You will work with the counselor to prepare and submit a loss mitigation application to the servicer. If the application is approved, the lender will make the changes in your mortgage that will make it possible to stay in your house.

During the mortgage crisis, servicers were unable to keep up with workout requests and those who needed a modification to avoid a foreclosure were often disappointed when their request was denied or the house was sold while the application sat in limbo. Now, mainly due to changes in the law, servicers generally try to work with those who are facing financial difficulties to keep them in their home if at all possible. They have increased their personnel and streamlined the process to stay current in responding to loan modification applications.

Servicers Must Appoint Personnel to Help You

Federal mortgage rules require servicers to provide "continuity of contact" to homeowners seeking foreclosure alternatives. Under this rule, the servicer must assign a single person or a team of personnel (often called a single point of contact) to respond to a delinquent borrower's inquiries and assist the borrower with available loss mitigation options. The contact must occur no later than the 45th day of the borrower's delinquency. (The continuity of contact rule doesn't apply to open-end lines of credit, reverse mortgages, qualified lenders under the Farm Credit System, any loan that is secured by a property that isn't your principal residence, and small servicers and certain government agencies.) Additionally, the California and Nevada Homeowner Bill of Rights require servicers to provide borrowers with a single point of contact during the loss mitigation process.

If the Only Way to Avoid Foreclosure Is to Sell or File for Bankruptcy

If the foreclosure has already started, you are unlikely to have enough income to stay current on your payments (even if they are reduced, and even if you could reduce your overall debt load by filing for Chapter 7 bankruptcy).

Your counselor will probably tell you that a satisfactory workout isn't going to happen. The counselor will likely suggest unloading your house in a short sale (which usually means selling it for less than you owe on it) or offering a deed in lieu of foreclosure to the lender (giving the house to the lender in exchange for a promise not to sue you for what you still owe on the mortgage).

Some counselors might suggest that you consult a lawyer about the possibility of filing for bankruptcy. Many, however, avoid the "B" word if at all possible, because the lenders (or in many cases, their funders) don't like it. Keep in mind that foreclosures are not always a bad thing, and bankruptcy is sometimes the most appropriate response. For example, a short sale might be marginally better for your credit record in the future, but you most likely would have to leave your house much sooner than you would if you let the foreclosure continue. That means you would give up the opportunity to save money by staying in your house for months—perhaps many months—without making payments. Finally, in a short sale you may be liable for the deficiency or, if your lender forgives you for the deficiency, the income tax on that forgiven debt, whereas bankruptcy would help you avoid these liabilities. Keep in mind that a counselor who attempts to sell you on a short sale or talk you out of bankruptcy may be passing on the lenders' and servicers' views, which may not best serve your economic interests.

If you still want to keep your home even if your counselor tells you a workout is not in the cards, it's time to think about bankruptcy. Filing for Chapter 13 bankruptcy might allow you to keep your house. (See Ch. 5.) At this stage, filing for Chapter 7 bankruptcy won't keep you in your house in the long run, but it can help you stay there payment-free for an extra couple of months. (See Ch. 6.)

The Making Home Affordable Program

In 2009, the federal government initiated a series of programs that were intended to help homeowners avoid foreclosure. The first two programs were called the Home Affordable Refinance Program (HARP) and the Home Affordable Modification Program (HAMP). A number of additional and supplementary programs were subsequently promulgated by the Treasury Department. The majority of programs under the Making Home Affordable program ended December 31, 2016, and most MHA programs (including HAMP) are no longer available. As of this writing, the Home Affordable Refinance Program (HARP) remains available. To find out the application deadline for remaining MHA programs, visit the Making Home Affordable website at www. makinghomeaffordable.gov.

Refinancing Your Mortgage

Before the housing crash, many homeowners periodically refinanced their mortgages. The two primary reasons were to either reduce the mortgage payment or extract equity from the house. Borrowers assumed that housing values would continue to go up and that debt accumulated through refinancing (and through additional mortgages, such as home equity lines of credit, or HELOCs) would ultimately be absorbed by the increase. When the great housing crash grew into full bloom near the end of 2008, virtually all refinancing activity ground to a halt. Homeowners unable to refinance were left holding the bag. When the government stepped in to address the burgeoning foreclosure crisis, it naturally turned to refinancing as one of the primary remedies.

The government came up with the Home Affordable Refinance Program (HARP) to help those homeowners who were unable get traditional refinancing because the value of their home had declined. While nearly all of the Making Home Affordable programs ended on December 31, 2016, the end-date for HARP is September 30, 2017. The expiration date has been extended before and may be extended again. To find out whether HARP is still in effect at the time you are reading this book, visit www.harp.gov.

The Federal Housing Finance Agency (FHFA) has announced that Fannie Mae and Freddie Mac will implement a new refinance program for borrowers with high loan-to-value (LTV) ratios, which will replace HARP when it expires. Also, the economic recovery continues, and property values are rising. Homeowners who are no longer underwater could be eligible to complete a traditional refinance.

CAUTION

Check the MHA website. Below is a brief overview of HARP on the chance that it will still be available if and when you need it. Check www.harp.gov and the Making Home Affordable website for the latest news about HARP and associated programs (www.makinghomeaffordable.gov).

The Home Affordable Refinance Program (HARP)

HARP was intended to stimulate a return to refinancing as a means for borrowers to reduce mortgage payments and to move into stable mortgages, such as 15- or 30-year fixed mortgages. The program was originally designed to help millions of underwater or almost-underwater homeowners refinance, but had very limited success when first introduced. Consequently, in the fall of 2011, President Obama announced an overhaul to the HARP program, which changed it in several ways. The most significant change was the removal of the limit on the amount that homeowners could be underwater. (The original version of HARP only permitted refinances for mortgages that were up to 125% of the current value of a home.) Now, to be eligible for HARP, you must meet all of the following requirements:

- Your loan is owned by Fannie Mae or Freddie Mac. (If you're not sure whether Fannie Mae or Freddie Mac owns your mortgage, use the look-up tools at www.fanniemae.com/loanlookup and www.freddiemac.com/mymortgage.)
- Your loan originated on or before May 31, 2009.
- Your home is your primary residence, a 1-unit second home, or a 1- to 4-unit investment property.
- Your current loan-to-value ratio is greater than 80%.
- You are current on your mortgage payments.
- You have not had a late payment in the past six months and no more than one late payment within the last year.

As of late 2016, there have been more than 3.4 million refinances through HARP since the inception of the program. To find an interactive map showing the general number of HARP-eligible homeowners by metropolitan area, county, or zip code, go to www.harp.gov and click on "Are You Eligible?" and then "View Eligibility Map." (You can also find a lot of good information about HARP on this website.) To find out if you are personally eligible for HARP, call your mortgage servicer.

Basic Workout Options

If you aren't eligible to refinance your mortgage, you still may be able to work something out with your servicer.

Repayment Plan: Keeping Current and Catching Up

With a repayment plan, you arrange to make up missed payments over time and stay current on your ongoing payments. This approach is usually the most feasible and easiest to negotiate with your servicer. For it to work, your income will have to be able to cover both current and makeup payments.

For example, say you are four months behind on your payments of $2,000 a month, for a total of $8,000. Paying an extra $800 a month over the next 11 months would bring you current. Why 11 months, when you could pay back the $8,000 in ten? The eleventh month would account for 10% interest you'd likely be charged on the arrears. The actual numbers might be a little different, but you get the idea.

If you could pay only $2,400 a month (the $2,000 payment plus $400 to make up the arrears), your plan would be for 20 months, plus additional time to pay the interest.

The longer it will take you to catch up, the likelier it is that your servicer will have to get permission from the lender. If the lender will have to sign off on your proposed plan, and you are running up against your foreclosure sale date, you should definitely ask—in writing—for an extension that the servicer thinks will be sufficient to either work out an arrangement or give you time to fight the foreclosure. Some servicers will tell you right up front whether a proposed plan will work or is off the table. Other servicers will string you along. You'll just have to make sure that you aren't forgoing other possible solutions (such as bankruptcy, a court action challenging the foreclosure, a statutory reinstatement, or redemption of the mortgage), just because the servicer tells you the solution is "in the pipeline."

Don't Forget: Statutory Reinstatement or Redemption

Many states give you, by law, the right to reinstate your mortgage (make it current) or redeem the loan (pay off the entire loan). (See Ch. 1.) Your state's page in the appendix lists the time limits for the exercise of these procedures if they're available in your state. Typically, you must exercise them before the foreclosure sale date, although some states give you a period of time after the sale date to redeem the mortgage and reclaim the home by paying it off in full (plus interest and costs).

   If you think either of these options might work for you, pay attention to the deadlines. If your funds are not delivered on time, the foreclosure sale will proceed or you may miss your opportunity to redeem. This means you could lose your home if there is a delay in courier service or a bank processing error. If you can, hand deliver your funds in person to the proper contact or arrange a wire transfer well before the deadline. Or, if you mail in your funds, send the check via an overnight courier so that it can be tracked.

Forbearance: Getting a Break From Payments

Under a forbearance agreement, the servicer (or lender) agrees to reduce or suspend your mortgage payments for a period of time. In exchange, you promise to start making your full payment at the end of the forbearance period, plus an extra amount to pay down the missed payments. Forbearance is most common when someone is laid off or called to active military duty for a relatively short period of time and cannot make any payments now but will likely be able to catch up soon.

   In forbearance, unlike a repayment plan, the lender agrees in advance for you to miss or reduce payments for a period of time. But both

forbearance and repayment plans require extra payments down the line
to bring the loan current. Forbearance for three to six months is typical;
forbearance for longer periods is less so.

Modification: Lowering Your Payments

Unlike repayment plans and forbearance, mortgage modifications are
designed to lower your monthly payments over the long term. Almost
all lenders offer "proprietary" (in-house) modifications to borrowers
who are struggling to make their monthly mortgage payments and who
meet eligibility criteria for assistance. According to the December 2016
housing scorecard produced by the U.S. Department of Housing and
Urban Development and the U.S. Department of Treasury, lenders
offered 4.9 million proprietary loan modifications between April 2009
and October 2016.

Many homeowners can't come close to making their current payments
now or in the future. There are many reasons, including:

- Their income streams were disrupted by layoff or injury and new
  jobs at the same pay are just not available.
- They were in over their heads from the beginning, because of
  predatory loan practices or their own misstatements about their
  income and debt loads.
- Their interest-only loans caused principals to reach preset caps,
  which in turn dramatically pushed their monthly payments
  upwards to unaffordable levels.
- Their interest rates reset higher (currently not as big a problem as
  was originally feared, due to continued low short-term interest
  rates engineered by the Federal Reserve).
- Something happened in their lives that required them to reprioritize
  their budgets—for instance, a medical emergency or a child in
  trouble.

If you can't afford your mortgage payment now or won't be able
to in the near future, mortgage modification is the best approach to
remaining in your house.

Tips for Completing Your Modification Application

Here are some suggestions for completing your application:

- Fill out all of the paperwork (don't forget to sign the application) and attach any and all documentation that the servicer requests. For example, if the servicer requests copies of your two most recent pay stubs, this means you must actually send your latest pay stubs. Do not send two random pay stubs that you just happened to have handy.
- When sending items such as copies of your bank statements, be sure to send copies of all statement pages—even if they're blank.
- Send all of the forms and supporting documentation at the same time. This way it is less likely that any of the items will get misplaced.
- If you mail the application to the servicer, send it by some method that you can track (FedEx, UPS, etc.).
- Write your name and complete loan number at the top of each page.
- Don't pay for modification assistance. Loan modification companies may charge $1,000 or more for services that you can get for free from a HUD-approved housing counselor. Because some states prohibit people from taking money up front to rescue homeowners from foreclosures, some modification companies use lawyers—who can accept up-front payments in most states (but with restrictions in some states, such as California)—to pitch their services. Lawyers can be helpful in certain situations—for instance, to challenge a foreclosure in court or to file bankruptcy—but they have no magic keys to the kingdom of mortgage modifications. You and your wallet will typically be better off with a free HUD-approved housing counselor.

Here are some of the ways your servicer might modify a mortgage to reduce your payments and perhaps to reduce the outstanding balance of your loan to the value of your home:

- Reduce your mortgage's interest rate to the current market rate, if it's lower than what you're supposed to be paying now.
- Convert from a variable-rate to a fixed-rate mortgage, which could bring the payment down if the interest on the variable-rate

mortgage has already reset, and will prevent a jump in payments if the reset looms in the near future.

- Extend the loan's repayment period—for instance, from 30 years to 40. This will bring down the monthly payment but delay for many years the time when you can begin to build equity.
- Reamortize the loan. This involves adding the amount of the missed payments to the principal balance and issuing a new loan at a new interest rate for a new period of time. Reamortization can result in an increased payment (for example, if the interest rate stays the same or increases) or a reduced one (for example, if the interest rate is reduced and the loan period is increased).

Before signing off on new mortgage terms, ask yourself whether you would be better off keeping your house or giving it up. If you can get a lower payment, you might be more inclined to keep it. But the decision may depend on the size of the reduction and the amount of your negative equity. It might make more sense to use the foreclosure process as a way to put away some money. If you decide to let the foreclosure go through, the modification process is likely to lengthen the time you can stay in the home because mortgage lenders must suspend foreclosure proceedings during the processing period.

The Impact of a Loan Modification on Your Credit

The impact of a loan modification on your credit depends on how the lender reports the modification. According to FICO (the largest and most ubiquitous credit scoring company), if your lender reports the modification as "paid as agreed," the modification will not affect your FICO score. Unfortunately, the lender is likely to report the modification as "paying under a partial payment agreement" or something else indicating you're not paying as agreed. This will negatively impact your credit score—although certainly not as badly as a short sale, deed in lieu of foreclosure, or foreclosure. Once you start making timely payments under the modification, your score should improve. And keep in mind that as the negative information ages, its impact on your credit score will fade.

Workouts for Government-Backed Mortgages

Special workout options are available to you if your mortgage is:

- owned or guaranteed by the Federal National Mortgage Association (Fannie Mae) or the Federal Home Loan Mortgage Association (Freddie Mac)
- insured by the Federal Housing Administration (FHA), which operates under regulations and guidelines issued by the federal Department of Housing and Urban Development (HUD)
- guaranteed by the Veterans Administration (VA), or
- financed by a direct loan from the Rural Housing Service (RHS).

You should know if one of these agencies has purchased, insured, or guaranteed your mortgage, because you will have been informed in writing. But if you don't remember and don't want to turn your house upside down looking for the paperwork, ask your housing counselor, mortgage servicer, or lender.

If you are working with a HUD-approved housing counselor. You have all the usual workout options plus some additional ones, giving you a much better chance of working something out that the lender will approve of. You can get help and information about these different options from the counselor.

If you are working directly with your mortgage servicer. Your mortgage servicer should give you information about the special options available for your particular type of mortgage, and even distribute any explanatory materials produced by the governmental entity for its customers.

Fannie Mae offers the Flex Modification program to borrowers who are having trouble making their mortgage payments. Fannie Mae's program combines aspects of HAMP, as well as the Fannie Standard and Streamlined Modification, which it replaces on October 1, 2017. Eligible borrowers can expect to receive a 20% payment reduction through a mortgage modification. To qualify, your mortgage loan must meet the following criteria:

- The loan must be a conventional first-lien mortgage loan.
- A loan secured by a principal residence must be 60 days delinquent or, if less, the default must be imminent.

- A loan secured by a second home or an investment property must be at least 60 days delinquent.
- The property can be vacant or condemned.
- The mortgage loan must have originated at least 12 months before the modification evaluation date.

You can't participate in the Flex Modification program if:

- You had a previous liquidation workout option, such as a short sale or deed in lieu of foreclosure.
- You are making payments on a forbearance plan, repayment plan, or Trial Period Plan (unless Fannie Mae otherwise agrees).
- You have another offer for a loan modification or workout option.
- You received three or more previous loan modifications.
- You failed a Fannie Mae Flex Modification Trial Period Plan within 12 months of being evaluated for eligibility.
- You were 60 days or more delinquent within the first 12 months of receiving a Fannie Mae Flex Modification (and weren't reinstated).

Fannie Mae. If you encounter problems with your mortgage servicer when trying to arrange a workout on a mortgage owned or guaranteed by Fannie Mae, call 800-2Fannie (800-232-6643) or the appropriate regional office, listed below.

Freddie Mac. Freddie Mac also offers the Flex Modification program, which should reduce a borrower's payment by 20%. To qualify, you must submit an application and meet the following requirements:

- You must have suffered an eligible hardship.
- You must have a verifiable income. (This doesn't apply if you're 90 days delinquent or 60 days delinquent on a step-rate mortgage within the 12 months following an interest rate adjustment. You also don't have to submit an application and the servicer doesn't have to confirm your hardship.)
- The mortgage must have originated at least 12 months before the evaluation date.
- The mortgage must be a conventional first-lien mortgage currently owned or guaranteed in whole or in part by Freddie Mac.

Fannie Mae Regional Offices		
Midwestern	Illinois, Indiana, Iowa, Michigan, Minnesota, Nebraska, North Dakota, Ohio, South Dakota, Wisconsin	312-368-6200
Northeastern	Connecticut, Delaware, Maine, Massachusetts, New Hampshire, New Jersey, New York, Pennsylvania, Puerto Rico, Rhode Island, Vermont	215-575-1400
Southeastern	Alabama, District of Columbia, Florida, Georgia, Kentucky, Maryland, Mississippi, North Carolina, South Carolina, Tennessee, Virginia, West Virginia	404-398-6000
Southwestern	Arizona, Arkansas, Colorado, Kansas, Louisiana, Missouri, New Mexico, Oklahoma, Texas, Utah	972-773-HOME (4663)
Western	Alaska, California, Guam, Hawaii, Idaho, Montana, Nevada, Oregon, Washington, Wyoming	626-396-5100

If you run into problems with your mortgage servicer, call 800-FREDDIE and ask to speak to someone about loss mitigation. This department will assess your situation and either explain the Freddie Mac servicer rules or help you arrange a workout.

FHA-insured loans. If you have an FHA-insured loan, your lender must send you a copy of HUD Publication HUD-2008-5-FHA, Save Your Home: Tips to Avoid Foreclosure, no earlier than the 32nd day of delinquency, but no later than the 60th day. The document will outline all of your FHA loan workout options. An FHA-insured loan entitles you to a special loss mitigation (mortgage workout) process that requires the servicer to solicit you proactively for loss mitigation. In addition to sending you the brochure, the servicer must complete a "waterfall" to determine if you qualify for a loss mitigation option.

The lender must first evaluate you for a forbearance plan that allows you to suspend or reduce payments for a period, or a repayment plan to bring the loan current. An extended plan might be provided if you're unemployed and actively seeking a job. If you don't qualify for these options, then you must be evaluated for a loan modification that would possibly add overdue payments to your loan balance, reduce the interest rate, or extend the number of years you have to pay off the loan. Another option, a Partial Claim, gives the borrower a second interest-free loan to bring the delinquent loan current. The loan isn't paid off until you pay your first mortgage or sell your house. Those who won't be able to keep up with the mortgage payments even if given a workout plan might be able to complete a short sale or deed in lieu of foreclosure.

If you have an FHA-insured loan, call your servicer to get details about loss mitigation options or the waterfall process. Or, you can call HUD's National Servicing Center at 877-622-8525.

VA-insured loans. Borrowers with VA-insured loans should contact their mortgage servicer (the party primarily responsible for helping you avoid foreclosure). If the servicer isn't helpful, a loan technician in one of the various VA Regional Loan Centers can intervene to ensure the servicer explored all options to avoid foreclosure. To learn more, call 877-827-3702 or go to www.benefits.va.gov and click on "Home Loans" and then "Mortgage Servicing Assistance." This website also has a link that will take you to the contact information for the Regional Loan Centers.

Rural Housing Service (RHS) loans. If your loan is guaranteed by the RHS, you can call the Centralized Servicing Center (CSC) toll-free phone number at 800-414-1226 or go to http://rdhomeloans.usda.gov/fcls.html to learn about workout options.

Foreclosure Avoidance Mediation Programs

Many states have mediation programs to assist borrowers in finding ways to avoid foreclosure. Some states, such as Oregon and Connecticut, have instituted statewide foreclosure avoidance mediation programs, while in other states there are certain counties or municipalities that have implemented such programs. The programs vary, but most force the lender to at least discuss non-foreclosure options with you before it can complete the foreclosure. If you participate, you may have a better chance of achieving some type of workout. Or, by participating you may be able to delay the foreclosure.

Mediation, sometimes called a conciliation conference, consists of a meeting between you, your lender, and an impartial third party (the mediator). At the meeting, the parties discuss the borrower's financial situation and try to work out a way to keep the home or give up the property without going through a foreclosure. Generally, the foreclosure is postponed while the mediation talks are ongoing and, by working together, the parties are sometimes able to reach an agreement to avoid foreclosure by way of a:

- loan modification
- repayment agreement
- forbearance agreement
- short sale, or
- deed in lieu of foreclosure.

Visit the "Foreclosure" area on www.nolo.com, for articles on state foreclosure mediation programs. Or check *Foreclosures and Mortgage Servicing*, by John Rao, et al. (National Consumer Law Center), for more information on state foreclosure avoidance mediation programs.

Hardest Hit Fund Programs

In February 2010, the U.S. Department of the Treasury created the Hardest Hit Fund to provide targeted aid to homeowners in those states most affected by the housing market crash. As part of this program, billions in aid money was allocated to the 18 states, plus the District of Columbia, that experienced the most extreme home price declines, as well as high unemployment rates.

Hardest Hit Fund states are Alabama, Arizona, California, Florida, Georgia, Illinois, Indiana, Kentucky, Michigan, Mississippi, Nevada, New Jersey, North Carolina, Ohio, Oregon, Rhode Island, South Carolina, Tennessee, and Washington D.C. These states (and D.C.) each developed their own programs, which are administered by that state's housing finance agency, to distribute the funds and assist distressed homeowners in avoiding foreclosure. The states have until the end of 2020 to make use of the funds allocated under the Hardest Hit Fund.

The assistance programs vary from state to state, but may include:

- mortgage payment assistance for unemployed or underemployed homeowners
- principal reductions to help homeowners obtain more affordable mortgages
- bringing a delinquent mortgage current with a one-time payment
- eliminating homeowners' second lien loans, and
- helping struggling homeowners transition into more affordable residences after moving out of their homes.

To qualify for assistance, you'll have to submit an application and meet certain criteria. Eligibility requirements vary from state to state; however, they usually include the following:

- You must be a resident of the state in which you apply for assistance.
- You must occupy the property.
- Your total annual income must be less than the amount designated by the state program.
- You must have limited financial resources.
- You must have suffered a hardship, such as unemployment, underemployment, divorce, the death of a spouse, or medical hardship.
- The unpaid principal balance on your mortgage cannot exceed a particular amount.

In many state programs, the homeowner will receive a 0% interest loan (paid directly to the servicer) that is forgiven over a specified period (generally 20% over five years). If you stop occupying the property as your principal residence before the end of the forgiveness period, you'll have to repay the remaining balance.

 CAUTION
Beware of scammer copycat websites posing as Hardest Hit Fund application sites. The Hardest Hit Fund programs never charge a fee for their services. You don't need to pay to apply for assistance.

For general information about the Hardest Hit Fund, visit the U.S. Department of Treasury website at www.treasury.gov (search for "Hardest Hit Fund"). The Making Home Affordable website (www.makinghomeaffordable.gov) also contains information about Hardest Hit Fund programs. For additional state information, check the state program's website.

Alabama

Under Alabama's "Hardest Hit Alabama" program, eligible homeowners can apply for the following types of assistance:

- **Mortgage payment assistance, including money to bring the loan current.** Unemployed and underemployed homeowners who are receiving unemployment compensation benefits, and homeowners who have experienced a substantial reduction in household income, might qualify for this type of help.
- **Loan modification assistance.** Funds are available to reduce an outstanding principal balance, pay delinquent escrow or past-due payments, or restructure the loan.
- **Short sale help.** If you choose a short sale, the assistance will cover the remaining principal balance and closing costs.

You don't need to be behind on your mortgage payments to qualify. Generally, your household income limit can't be more than $77,700 (the limit for lien extinguishment with a short sale is $55,500). Your mortgage balance cannot be more than $258,690. The property must be a single-family primary residence or manufactured home attached to real property. To qualify, you must have suffered a hardship such as unemployment, underemployment, divorce, the death of a spouse, medical hardship, or disability. The maximum program amount is $30,000, or $60,000 if you combine programs. For more details, go to www.hardesthitalabama.com or call 877-497-8182.

Arizona

The Save Our Home AZ program provides money to eligible homeowners for:

- mortgage principal reductions
- mortgage payments for the unemployed and underemployed

- a second mortgage payoff, and
- short sale relocation assistance.

Other requirements include a mortgage balance of $500,000 or less and an owner-occupied property located in Arizona. To find out if you qualify, go to www.saveourhomeaz.gov/self-assessment or call 877-448-1211.

California

California's Keep Your Home California has several options available for residents, including:

- **Unemployment Mortgage Assistance Program.** Payment of up to 18 months of mortgage payments ($3,000 per month maximum) for homeowners collecting unemployment benefits.
- **Mortgage Reinstatement Assistance Program.** Provides up to $54,000 to help homeowners bring delinquent payments current and reinstate their loans.
- **Principal Reduction Program.** Provides funds to underwater home-owners suffering from a financial hardship or an unaffordable mortgage payment. This program pays down up to $100,000 of the principal balance of the mortgage loan with the average amount received being $73,500.
- **Transition Assistance Program.** Provides up to $5,000 to complete a short sale or deed in lieu of foreclosure and relocate to new housing (for instance, to cover rent, moving expenses, a security deposit, or transition assistance counseling services).
- **Reverse Mortgage Assistance Pilot Program.** Provides up to $25,000 to eligible senior homeowners for past due and upcoming property expenses (up to 12 months) for things such as property taxes, homeowners' insurance, and HOA dues or assessments.

The outstanding property mortgage cannot exceed $729,750, and the programs serve low- and moderate-income homeowners primarily. However, the income limits are relatively high in some counties (for instance, $104,650 in Orange County). To learn more, go to http:// keepyourhomecalifornia.org or call 888-954-KEEP (5337).

Florida

Florida has two programs for unemployed homeowners: the Unemployment Mortgage Assistance Program (UMAP) and the Mortgage Loan Reinstatement Payment (MLRP) Program.

UMAP provides money for up to 12 months of monthly mortgage payments and mortgage-related expenses (property taxes, homeowners' insurance, and mortgage insurance) to a maximum of $24,000. To qualify, you must be underemployed, unemployed, or have had at least a 10% reduction in income due to a qualifying financial hardship. Qualifying homeowners can also get up to $18,000 towards past-due amounts to reinstate the first mortgage.

Under MLRP, homeowners who are behind on mortgage payments and who have gone through (and recovered from) a qualifying financial hardship can get funds to put towards a past-due amount, up to $25,000. Also, Florida offers a principal reduction program that provides up to $50,000 to reduce the principal balance of the first mortgage to no less than 100% loan-to-value.

To learn more, go to www.flhardesthithelp.org or call 877-863-5244. For more information about a principal reduction, go to www.principal reductionflhhf.org.

Georgia

HomeSafe Georgia offers the following three forms of assistance to eligible homeowners:

- **Help with mortgage payments.** Homeowners who have suffered unemployment or underemployment in the last 36 months can receive up to 24 months of monthly payment assistance while searching for a new job or while completing training. Those who are behind in payments can get up to 12 of the 24 months to get current on the loan. Some program applicants are required to pay part of the monthly mortgage amount.
- **Reinstatement help.** Homeowners who are behind on mortgage payments and have suffered a military, medical, or death-related hardship in the last 36 months may qualify for up to 12 months

of mortgage assistance (plus money to cover fees) to reinstate the loan. The money is paid in a lump sum to the lender to bring the mortgage up to date. The delinquency must be related to the hardship, and the homeowner must have enough income to continue to make the payments after the loan is reinstated.

- **Mortgage payment reduction.** Homeowners who have experienced a significant permanent reduction in income in the last 36 months due to disability, the death of a spouse or the homeowner, or exhaustion of unemployment benefits (followed immediately by drawing Social Security retirement benefits) may qualify for up to $45,000. The money is paid directly to the lender to reduce the principal balance and enable a recast or modification. As a result, the homeowner gets a more affordable payment.

To find out more, go to www.homesafegeorgia.com or call 877-519-4443.

Illinois

Eligible Illinois homeowners who have suffered at least a 15% loss of income due to a qualifying hardship event (such as unemployment, underemployment, disability, death, or divorce) can receive up to $35,000 in the form of:

- a one-time payment covering a mortgage arrearage, including fees and penalties, or
- 100% mortgage payment assistance for up to 12 months (including a loan reinstatement, if applicable).

Illinois' I-Refi program helps homeowners with an upside-down mortgage due to declining property values (even if the owner is current on payments). Underwater homeowners may qualify for up to $50,000 to reduce the balance and refinance the loan based on the current market value of their home.

The official website of the Illinois Hardest Hit Fund program is www.illinoishardesthit.org. You can also call 855-873-7405 to get more information.

Indiana

Indiana's "Get Hope" program provides up to $30,000 in mortgage modification assistance to eligible borrowers. The program will cover the monthly mortgage payment, including principal, interest, property taxes, and homeowners' insurance for up to two years, or the homeowner can use the funds to reinstate a delinquent mortgage or reduce a monthly payment.

The program also provides transition assistance when completing a short sale or deed in lieu of foreclosure as long as the home remains in a marketable condition. You may qualify for $2,500 for moving and relocation expenses. Lenders can receive up to $5,000 to extinguish and release subordinate liens as part of a short sale or deed in lieu of foreclosure agreement.

To receive assistance, you must have experienced a qualifying involuntary financial hardship. Free foreclosure prevention counseling is available to all Indiana homeowners.

You'll find more information at www.877gethope.org, or you can call 877-GET-HOPE (877-438-4673).

Kentucky

The Kentucky Unemployment Bridge Program assists eligible homeowners with mortgage payments. To qualify, the homeowner must show:

- an income loss due to unemployment
- a reduction in income due to substantial underemployment, or
- a qualifying disability within the last three years.

The program will pay a monthly mortgage payment for up to 12 months, or $15,000 total. You can use a portion of the money to reinstate (bring current) a delinquent mortgage. Free transitional counseling is available for those pursuing a short sale, deed in lieu of foreclosure, or foreclosure.

For details, go to protectmykyhome.org or call 866-830-7868.

Michigan

The Step Forward Michigan Program provides up to $30,000 to eligible homeowners to help with overdue mortgage payments, property taxes, and condominium association fees. To qualify, you must have an eligible hardship (such as job loss, a medical event, a reduction of your gross income, death, divorce, or a one-time critical housing repair) that caused you to fall behind, and you must have enough income to make future payments.

You can learn about eligibility requirements at www.StepForward Michigan.org or by calling 866-946-7432.

Nevada

Nevada's programs to help struggling homeowners include:

- **Principal reduction program.** Qualifying homeowners can receive up to $100,000 for a first mortgage principal balance reduction along with another modification program.
- **Mortgage assistance for the unemployed or underemployed.** If you've suffered an income loss, you could qualify for up to $54,000 in assistance for up to 18 months.
- **Reinstatement assistance.** If you are behind in mortgage payments, you may be able to get up to $54,000 to cure first mortgage loan arrearages.

Learn more at www.nevadahardesthitfund.nv.gov or by calling 888-320-6526.

New Jersey

If you've suffered a qualifying involuntary financial hardship (such as job loss, underemployment, a medical problem, divorce, disability, or death) that caused or will cause you to fall behind on your mortgage payments, you might qualify for one or both of New Jersey's programs.

- **New Jersey HomeSaver.** Eligible homeowners can receive up to a $50,000 mortgage balance reduction and get a more affordable monthly payment through modification options.
- **New Jersey HomeKeeper.** As much as $48,000 is available for past-due amounts or monthly mortgage payments (including principal, interest, taxes and insurance) for up to 12 months.

You can only receive assistance from one program at a time. The overall benefit cap per household is $98,000.

Find out more at www.njhousing.gov/foreclosure or by calling 855-647-7700 or 609-278-7660.

North Carolina

The NC Foreclosure Prevention Fund offers eligible homeowners the following options:

- **Mortgage payment program.** Homeowners who are struggling due to job loss or temporary unemployment, reduced income, or temporary financial hardship (such as divorce, illness, the death of a spouse, or a natural disaster) may qualify for up to $36,000 to make mortgage payments for as many as 36 months. One-time assistance while you search for a job, or long-term assistance while you attend an approved job retraining program, is also available.
- **Loan modification (recast).** An individual who has suffered an eligible hardship and cannot afford a mortgage payment due to a decrease in income (after reemployment or the establishment of a fixed income) might qualify for a principal balance reduction and loan modification.
- **Second Mortgage Refinance Program.** Homeowners can lower their monthly payments by refinancing a second mortgage. The benefits include a zero-interest, deferred loan up to $50,000. If you participated in the mortgage payment program and are employed, you might qualify for a second mortgage refinance if you can show you have a financial need.

Go to www.ncforeclosureprevention.gov or call 888-623-8631 for more information.

Ohio

Under the Save the Dream Ohio program, residents who received unemployment assistance on or after January 1, 2014, might be eligible for up to $35,000 to bring a delinquent first mortgage current or to pay your mortgage payments for up to nine months (or a combination of both).

Visit https://savethedreamohio.gov or call 888-404-4674 to get more information about eligibility requirements and to learn how to apply for assistance.

Oregon

Oregon offers refinancing, reinstatement, mortgage payment, property tax, and reverse mortgage assistance. Its Home Rescue Program provides eligible homeowners with up to one year's worth of mortgage payments ($20,000 maximum) and, if needed, up to $15,000 in funds to reinstate a delinquent loan.

Learn more about Home Rescue and other Oregon programs by visiting www.oregonhomeownerhelp.org or by calling 503-986-2025.

Rhode Island

Under Rhode Island's Hardest Hit Fund program, eligible homeowners might qualify for funds to:
- pay a mortgage payment
- pay a mortgage arrearage due to a financial hardship
- pay unpaid property taxes
- obtain a loan modification, or
- relocate after leaving a home.

Among other requirements, the homeowner must demonstrate a financial hardship, such as unemployment or underemployment, the death or disability of a main wage-earner in the household, or unforeseen medical expenses.

To find out if you're eligible for assistance, go to www.hardesthitri.org. You can also get information at www.hhfri.org. For information about protecting yourself from foreclosure or coping with the loss of your home, call the Rhode Island Housing Help Center at 401-457-1130.

South Carolina

South Carolina's SC Help program offers up to $36,000 to eligible homeowners who are having difficulty making mortgage payments due to a hardship such as unemployment, underemployment, loss or drastic reduction of self-employment income, catastrophic health-related expenses, divorce, or the death of a spouse. SC Help funds can be used for:
- monthly mortgage payments
- reinstatement assistance

- $5,000 in moving expenses after a short sale or deed in lieu of foreclosure, or
- loan modification assistance.

Go to www.schelp.gov or call 855-435-7472 to get additional information.

Tennessee

Tennessee offers the Principal Reduction Recast Program with Lien Extinguishment (PRRPLE). To qualify, you must be facing a financial hardship that, through no fault of your own, has resulted in income loss. The program lowers an eligible borrower's monthly mortgage payments by providing:

- a principal balance reduction of the first mortgage loan, combined with a loan modification, or
- a principal reduction that extinguishes the mortgage lien.

Go to www.keepmytnhome.org to learn more. The website also has information about how to get free and confidential foreclosure prevention counseling.

Washington D.C.

Washington D.C.'s HomeSaver program provides the following assistance to eligible homeowners:

- A one-time payment of up to six months' worth of payments. To qualify, you must be receiving unemployment benefits when you apply or have experienced an involuntary reduction of income of at least 25%.
- Up to 24 months' worth of mortgage payments ($38,400 maximum). To qualify, you must be receiving unemployment benefits at the time you apply or have experienced an involuntary reduction of income of at least 25%.
- A one-time payment of up to $38,400 to get caught up on delinquent mortgage payments if you're employed but have received unemployment benefits within the last six months.

- Assistance of up to $38,400 if you are at risk of foreclosure or a tax sale due to overdue property taxes.

To learn more about eligibility criteria, go to www.homesaverdc.org or call 202-777-1690.

> **CAUTION**
>
> **Keep in mind that Hardest Hit Fund programs change frequently and determining whether you're eligible for a particular program can be a complicated process.** Check your state's website for updates and details about the application process. Additionally, you should be aware that not all lenders participate in every program.

Special Protections for Service Members on Active Duty

If you're on active military duty, and you took out a mortgage before you went on active duty, you are entitled to a raft of protections against foreclosure. The federal law that provides these benefits is called the Servicemembers Civil Relief Act (SCRA).

Judicial Foreclosure Is Required

Probably the most important protection for families in nonjudicial foreclosure states (see Ch. 2) is that the SCRA requires a court order before your house can be sold in foreclosure. If the lender forecloses without a court order while you are on active duty or within one year thereafter, the sale is invalid (unless you sign a waiver). (This protection period will be reduced to the time of active duty service plus 90 days beginning January 1, 2018, unless action is taken by Congress.) Even threats to foreclose without going to court are likely illegal under the Fair Debt Collection Practices Act (FDCPA), a state debt collection statute, or an Unfair and Deceptive Acts or Practices (UDAP) statute.

Also, courts tend to interpret the SCRA liberally in favor of military service members. Because judicial foreclosures are much more expensive and typically take much longer than nonjudicial foreclosures, you may have a better chance of working something out with the lender.

You can delay (the legal term is "stay") a foreclosure procedure for a period of time, not less than 90 days, so long as you meet certain criteria and if you request it from the court in writing. A HUD-approved foreclosure counselor (or military legal services if you are deployed out of the country) can help you with a letter to the court.

A Court Can Adjust Your Mortgage

During a foreclosure, the court may provide "equitable" relief as appropriate if your ability to pay or meet the other mortgage obligations is materially affected by your military service. This means that, so long as you took out the mortgage before going on active duty, the court may reform the mortgage by, for example:

- reducing the mortgage payments, or
- suspending payments altogether during the time you're on active duty.

The court may make an adjustment on its own or in response to your request.

In addition, even if a foreclosure has not yet started, you can make an application to a court for relief such as a payment reduction or an expanded repayment period if you're behind. Again, you must have taken out the mortgage before going on active duty, and you must apply for the relief during your military service or within 180 days thereafter. You'll eventually have to repay all of the principal and interest payments that you skipped.

Default Judgments Can Be Reopened

If the lender starts a foreclosure lawsuit and you don't respond to it, the court will order a default judgment against you. But you can reopen the judgment if it is entered while you're on active duty or within 60 days after your active duty ends. You must take action to reopen the judgment within 90 days after your release from active duty. To get the judgment reopened, you'll have to show that that:

- your military service materially affected your ability in making a defense to the action, and
- you have a meritorious or legal defense to the foreclosure or some part of it.

Interest Rates Must Be Reduced

The interest rate on a mortgage incurred before you entered active duty must be reduced to 6% while you're on active duty and one year thereafter. (The interest rate is also limited to 6% for all other types of obligations, such as car loans and credit cards, while you are on active duty.) Past payments of interest over 6% while you were on active duty must be forgiven (refunded), and the mortgage payment must be reduced to reflect the lower interest rate while it is in force.

To get the interest rate reduction, you must notify the creditor in writing of your duty status and include a copy of the military orders requiring active duty status. You must send this notice no later than 180 days after your active duty status ends. It can be retroactive to the day your active duty started. Keep in mind that you might not get the reduction if a court determines that you can afford the higher rate.

> **EXAMPLE:** Susan is a National Guard member. She and her husband sign a mortgage to buy a house at a subprime interest rate of 9%. Their payments are $1,900 a month. Six months later, Susan is called to active duty and deployed overseas. Her husband continues paying the mortgage at the required rate while Susan serves in Iraq for 15 months. When she returns home and is released from active duty, she learns from a military counselor that she was entitled to have the mortgage payments reduced while she was on active duty.
>
> She promptly sends a notice to the lender of her entitlement to the 6% interest rate, with a copy of her deployment orders, and demands that retroactive adjustments be made. She receives a check for $6,000. That's 15 months times $400, the amount her payment would have been lowered had the interest rate reduction been made when she went on active duty.

Lenders cannot report negative information to a credit reporting agency just because you asked for or received benefits under the SCRA. Nor can a creditor deny you credit, revoke existing credit, or change the terms on an existing account because you asserted your rights under the SCRA.

Cash for Illegal Foreclosures

As part of a national mortgage settlement, the U.S. Department of Justice announced in early 2015 that some service members (around 950) and their coborrowers would receive compensation from five of the nation's largest mortgage servicers (JPMorgan Chase, Wells Fargo, Citi, GMAC/Ally, and Bank of America) for nonjudicial foreclosures that took place between January 1, 2006 and April 4, 2012 and that violated the SCRA. (As noted earlier, the SCRA prohibits nonjudicial foreclosures against service members who are on or recently left active duty, and took out their mortgages before their service began.)

Service members (or their dependents) who think that their SCRA rights have been violated should contact an Armed Forces Legal Assistance office. To find an office near you, go to http://legalassistance.law.af.mil.

More State Protections

In addition to the federal law, many states have their own statutes that provide additional protections for service members. Your state's page in the appendix lists the citations for your state's law.

How Chapter 13 Bankruptcy Can Delay or Stop Foreclosure

Chapter 13 bankruptcy can help you save your house in a number of different ways. How? It gives you time to make up your missed payments, can make your mortgage more affordable in the long term by reducing your overall debt load, and may allow you to eliminate a second mortgage. It also gives you a friendly forum for challenging the legality of your mortgage and any pending foreclosure. And even if you decide to give up your house, Chapter 13 can help you substantially delay your move-out date.

You get these crucial benefits by proposing to the court a feasible Chapter 13 debt repayment plan. In most cases, a plan will pass muster if it shows enough probable income to meet your regular and necessary living expenses (including your mortgage and payments toward any arrearage that has occurred) and to pay off certain debts, such as back taxes and child support. If you have any money left over, it would go to repaying your unsecured debt such as credit card bills and court judgments. Chapter 13 plan requirements are explained in more detail below.

It won't be easy to stick to a repayment plan for three to five years, but if you can, you'll be well rewarded. All of your remaining unsecured debt will be wiped out—and you won't lose your house.

The benefits of Chapter 13 bankruptcy start the minute you file. That's because filing for bankruptcy immediately stops a foreclosure in its tracks. As soon as you file, the federal bankruptcy court automatically issues what's known as an automatic stay. This is a court order that bars all of your creditors, including mortgage lenders, from making any attempt to collect a debt you owe unless they get court permission. And once the bankruptcy judge approves your repayment plan, you will be safe from foreclosure over the entire plan period, as long as you keep making the required plan payments and your loan payments.

RESOURCE

More information on Chapter 13 bankruptcy. This chapter gives only an overview, to help you determine whether or not Chapter 13 bankruptcy might help you save your house—or at least keep you living in it longer. To learn more about this powerful remedy, see:

- the bankruptcy and foreclosure areas of www.nolo.com
- *The New Bankruptcy: Will It Work for You?* (Nolo), which explains your bankruptcy options, and
- *Chapter 13 Bankruptcy: Keep Your Property & Repay Debts Over Time* (Nolo), a guide to Chapter 13 bankruptcy.

Using Chapter 13 to Keep Your House

In a typical Chapter 13 case, the court will protect your property from foreclosure provided you resume paying your normal monthly mortgage payments and pay back your mortgage arrears within your plan period, which will be between three and five years. In this way, the Chapter 13 bankruptcy allows you to gradually bring your loan current, in small affordable steps. This is what makes your Chapter 13 plan such an important tool for saving your home—when the court approves your plan, the lender is ordered to go along with it.

If you stick to your Chapter 13 repayment plan, you can:

- spread out missed mortgage payments (your mortgage arrears) over the life of the repayment plan, three to five years (this essentially forces your lender to accept a mortgage reinstatement plan)
- pay a fraction (or sometimes, nothing) of most unsecured debts during the plan period and eliminate any remaining balance when you complete your plan, freeing up money for you to pay toward your mortgage

- ask the court to reduce ("cram down") certain secured debts to the value of the collateral (for example, you might be able to reduce your $20,000 car note to the actual value of the car, say $12,000, thereby reducing your monthly payments)
- contest the legality of your mortgage or a proposed foreclosure, if appropriate
- contest any claims for costs and fees that are added to the missed payments you'll repay as part of your plan (these costs are commonly made erroneously)
- get rid of (strip off) liens on your home created by second and third mortgages, as long as they are wholly unsecured by your home (that is, if your home were sold the proceeds would be insufficient to pay back any portion of the lien)
- remove a judgment lien if it would otherwise mean you'd lose part of your exemption on the property
- postpone the collection of delinquent student loans, and
- resume your regular monthly mortgage payments.

TIP

You can get a loan modification during your Chapter 13 case. If you file for Chapter 13 bankruptcy, you can still apply for a loan modification. Many homeowners have gotten loan modifications from their lenders during their Chapter 13 bankruptcy cases.

Repay Your Mortgage Arrears Over Time

If the only reason you are filing Chapter 13 is to get time to get your mortgage current, and you could get a similar deal from the servicer, you'll be better off not filing for bankruptcy, at least as far as your credit score is concerned. On the other hand, if your mortgage servicer refuses to work with you, then Chapter 13 may be your best option for saving your home.

EXAMPLE: Freddie owes $3,600 in missed mortgage payments. He receives a notice of default that gives him a month to pay up or lose his house. His mortgage servicer refuses to work with him because of a previous notice of default—the lender doesn't think he's a good credit risk.

Freddie had fallen behind on his mortgage because he was laid off, but now he's working again. If he files for Chapter 13 bankruptcy and is able to reduce payments on unsecured debt (like credit cards), he'll be able to afford a repayment plan, under which he will resume normal payments on his mortgage and also make up the arrears over three years. He proposes to pay down the arrears at the rate of $110 a month: $100 for the debt plus $10 a month for the trustee's fee.

You will be able to keep your house through Chapter 13 only if your plan will enable you to stay current on your mortgage as well as pay off an arrearage over the life of your plan. And you must propose a plan showing not only that you can make plan payments but also that you can keep current on all your other reasonable and necessary monthly expenses, such as utilities, transportation, car note, insurance, and the like. Further—and this is a deal breaker for some would-be Chapter 13 filers—you must pay some types of debts in full during the course of the plan. For example, if you owe recent back taxes, the court won't approve your repayment plan unless it shows that you can pay off the taxes in full while your plan is in effect.

Also, you must be able to pay your unsecured creditors at least as much as they would have received in a Chapter 7 bankruptcy from a partial liquidation of your property. As a result, if you have a significant amount of equity (or other property that isn't protected by bankruptcy), the required monthly payment might be too high for you to afford. (See the discussion of Chapter 7 bankruptcy in Ch. 6.)

Finally, your plan must provide for a payment to the trustee of roughly 10% of the amount of all payments you make to creditors through the repayment plan. (This fee covers the operating costs of the Chapter 13 bankruptcy program.)

Make Your Mortgage More Affordable by Eliminating Other Debts

Americans are up to their eyeballs in debt. In fact, it's not uncommon for people of moderate means to have credit card debt exceeding $50,000. If you are looking to save your house, and Chapter 13 bankruptcy might get the job done, chances are great that you'll also greatly reduce, if not eliminate, your debt load. Chapter 13 gives you three to five years not only to work out your mortgage problems but also to deal with your unsecured debt (debt not secured by collateral) once and for all.

To eliminate credit card and other unsecured debt in Chapter 13 bankruptcy, you must be willing to commit all of your disposable income to repaying all or part of your debt (taking into account that you must also pay down other debts such as mortgage arrears or recent back taxes) over a three- to five-year period. Any unsecured debt that remains at the end of your plan is discharged (canceled), unless it is one of the types of debt that survives bankruptcy, such as child support or student loans.

Ask the Court to Reduce ("Cram Down") Certain Secured Debts

Chapter 13 bankruptcy judges can reduce (cram down) certain secured debts to the market value of the collateral that secures the debt. They can also reduce interest rates to the going rate in bankruptcy cases (roughly 1.5 points above the prime rate). If you can get the judge to reduce your payments on a secured debt, you will have more money to pay toward your mortgage—and a better shot at proposing a Chapter 13 plan that the court will confirm.

> **EXAMPLE:** Allison bought a new car for $24,000, taking a seven-year note for $38,000 (including the principal and interest), with monthly payments of $475. Three years later, when Allison files for Chapter 13 bankruptcy, she still owes $24,000, even though the car's market value has fallen to $14,000.

As part of her Chapter 13 plan, Allison asks that the note be crammed down to $14,000 and that the interest rate on her loan be reduced to 4%, the approximate going rate in bankruptcy cases. The court approves this cramdown, and Allison's monthly car payment is cut roughly in half.

A cramdown is usually available only for:
- cars bought at least 30 months before you file for bankruptcy
- other personal property items (furniture, jewelry, computers) bought at least one year before filing
- rental or vacation homes (but not your primary residence), and
- loans on mobile homes that your state classifies as personal property (not real estate).

The catch is that you must repay the cramdown amount in your plan. As a result, most people don't use it to reduce a balance owed on real estate.

Contest the Foreclosure

You may be able to fight a foreclosure in your state's courts whether or not you file for bankruptcy. But if you file for Chapter 13 bankruptcy, you can ask the bankruptcy court to decide whether the facts upon which a proposed foreclosure is based are erroneous.

For example, suppose you contest the foreclosure on the ground that your mortgage servicer failed to properly credit your payments. A bankruptcy court decision in your favor on this point would eliminate the basis for the foreclosure should you later drop your Chapter 13 case or convert it to a Chapter 7 bankruptcy. Unlike some state courts, the bankruptcy court is a comparatively friendly forum for homeowners challenging foreclosures. (See Ch. 7 for more on the grounds for contesting a foreclosure.)

CAUTION

Don't file for bankruptcy unless you can do so in good faith.
Because Chapter 13 provides such an excellent opportunity for hanging up a foreclosure action, it has become a favorite means to that end. Some people file, keep the case alive as long as possible, file again as soon as it's dismissed, and so on. This can land you in big trouble down the line.

Merely filing a case puts the automatic stay into effect, without any review of your filing history by the judge, so it takes a while for the court to spot you as a bad-faith filer. But when it finally does, it can ban you from further filings—and refer you to the U.S. Attorney for a perjury prosecution if you made any significant misstatements in your paperwork.

Turn a Second or Third Mortgage Into an Unsecured Debt

If you're like many homeowners, your home is encumbered with a first mortgage, a second mortgage (often used for the down payment in an 80-20 financing arrangement), and even a third mortgage (maybe in the form of a home equity line of credit). Most likely, the holder of the first mortgage is pushing the foreclosure. But if you have fallen behind on your first mortgage, you are probably behind on your second and third mortgages as well. Would it help you keep your house if you no longer had to pay the second or third mortgage? You know the answer: Reducing your overall mortgage debt load could only help you meet your first mortgage obligation.

One of the great features of Chapter 13 bankruptcy is that in many (but not all) bankruptcy courts you can get rid of (strip off) all mortgages that aren't secured by your home's value. Let's say that you have a first mortgage of $300,000, a second mortgage of $75,000, and $50,000 out on a home equity line of credit. Presumably, the value of your home when you took on these debts was at least equal to the total value of the mortgages, or $425,000. But if the house is now worth less than $300,000, as a practical matter the house no longer secures the second and third mortgages. That is, if the house were sold, there would be nothing left for the second or third mortgage holders.

If your second and third mortgages were considered secured debts, your Chapter 13 plan would have to provide for you to keep current on them. However, when they are stripped off, they are reclassified as unsecured debts. This means you have to repay only a portion of them—just like your other unsecured debts. And as explained earlier, the amount of your disposable income, not the amount of the debt, determines how much of the unsecured debt you must repay.

> **EXAMPLE:** Sean files for Chapter 13 bankruptcy and proposes a three-year plan to make up his missed mortgage payments. He also owes $60,000 in credit card debt and has disposable income of $300 a month. His house's value is $250,000. He owes $275,000 on his first mortgage, $30,000 on the second, and $15,000 on a home equity loan.
>
> Because his house's value has fallen below what he owes on the first mortgage, there is no equity left to secure the second mortgage or home equity loan. So his Chapter 13 plan would classify these two formerly secured debts as unsecured. When they're added to the $60,000 in credit card debt, he's got a grand total of $105,000 unsecured debt. Because all he has is $300 per month in disposable income, his plan would repay a little more than 10% of his unsecured debt—including a little over 10% of his formerly secured second and third mortgage debt.

This also means that under your Chapter 13 plan you won't have to make up payments missed on your second or third mortgages. And because you're no longer making current payments on the second or third mortgage, the total amount you pay each month will be reduced by a considerable amount. Finally, because the lien has been completely removed from your property, if later on your home value increases so that you have more equity, the former second mortgage holder would still be out of luck. Because the lien is gone, the former lender doesn't have any right to the equity in your property. (Compare this scenario to what happens in Chapter 7 bankruptcy when you have unsecured mortgages. See, in Ch.6, "Eliminating Payments on a Second or Third Mortgage.")

⚠ CAUTION

Find out whether your court will let you get rid of liens. Although eliminating a lien when there is no equity to secure it is logical and permitted by many courts, some courts refuse to allow it. They reason that stripping a lien from a house is tantamount to modifying a residential mortgage, something that is not allowed by the bankruptcy laws. At some point, this issue is likely to be resolved by higher federal appellate courts. For now, if this is a major reason you are considering Chapter 13 bankruptcy, you need to know how your court would address it. Contact a local experienced bankruptcy attorney to get that information.

An Overview of the Chapter 13 Bankruptcy Process

When you file for Chapter 13 bankruptcy, your court papers must disclose what you own (real estate and personal property), your debts, and your financial transactions going back several years. You also will have to show that you've filed income tax returns for the previous four years.

But before you can even file for bankruptcy, you must complete some basic credit counseling. And you'll have to get some personal financial management counseling after you file but before you get your Chapter 13 discharge.

Coming Up With a Repayment Plan

The heart of a Chapter 13 bankruptcy is your repayment plan. It shows how much income you have to repay your debts, how long the plan will last, and what debts (and what proportion of them) you propose to repay.

There is no set percentage of your debt that you must repay. It all depends on how much disposable income you have available for this purpose. (Disposable income is the amount that remains after subtracting allowable expenses.) Keep in mind that courts will consider income you receive from roommates, domestic partners, and other members of your household if they are chipping in to help you save your home.

A Chapter 13 repayment plan lasts several years: three if your income is below the median income for your state and five if it is over. (See Ch. 6 for how to determine whether your household income is above or below your state's median.)

Your plan must show that your income (plus proceeds from any property you plan to sell) will let you do all of the following:

- stay current on all your contractual obligations, such as a mortgage and car note (unless you plan to voluntarily give the house or car back to the lender)
- pay off any arrears you owe on these contractual obligations
- meet your normal monthly expenses
- pay off certain priority debts, such as back taxes and child support or alimony, in full over the life of your plan (if the delinquent family support was assigned to a third party for collection, you don't have to pay it in full during the plan; the remaining balance won't be discharged though)
- devote all of your disposable income to repayment of a percentage of your unsecured debt, such as credit card and personal loan debt
- pay your unsecured creditors at least as much as they would have gotten had you filed for Chapter 7 bankruptcy—that is, the value of your assets that would be sold in a Chapter 7 bankruptcy to pay your creditors (see Ch. 6), and
- pay the bankruptcy trustee (the official who collects the money you pay under your plan and distributes it to your creditors) a fee of about 10% of all payments you make under the plan (this amount can be large or small, depending on whether you pay your current mortgage payments directly to your lender or through the trustee).

Not everyone can propose a plan that the court will approve. For example, a plan must provide for paying most types of priority debts in full. So if you owe $50,000 in back taxes, and your disposable income would pay only $25,000 of the taxes over the life of your plan, the judge will refuse to confirm the plan. (Many of these roadblocks to plan confirmation, however, can be overcome. Be sure to talk to a bankruptcy attorney before you scrap your plan to file for Chapter 13.)

RESOURCE

More information on repayment plans. See www.nolo.com for more on the requirements for Chapter 13 bankruptcy plans.

The Creditors' Meeting

About a month after you file for Chapter 13 bankruptcy, you are required to attend a creditors' meeting, conducted by the trustee assigned to your case by the court. At this meeting the trustee will go over your proposed plan and explain how the trustee thinks it should be changed.

TIP

Know when your first Chapter 13 payment will be due. It's common to think that you won't need to make a payment until after the court approves your plan, but that's not how it works. Not only will you be required to make your first payment soon after filing your case, but, if you fall behind, your matter will likely get dismissed. To avoid this pitfall, find out your payment due date before you file and, of course, budget accordingly.

The Confirmation Hearing

About a month after the creditors' meeting, your case will be set for a confirmation hearing in the bankruptcy court. At the confirmation hearing, the bankruptcy judge will decide whether or not to approve your proposed plan. Before the hearing, the trustee and your creditors will have an opportunity to file an objection to your repayment plan with the court. If the objection raises a valid point, you might want to continue the hearing date, correct the problem, and file an amended plan. If you don't agree with the objection, you can file a response stating your reasons. Ultimately, the court will review all of the submitted documents, listen to any argument presented at the hearing, and then do one of the following: confirm (approve) your plan; give you a chance to fix an issue; order your case to be dismissed; or allow you convert your case to Chapter 7 bankruptcy.

The Typical Chapter 13 Timeline	
Day 1	Papers filed to start the bankruptcy
Day 14	Repayment plan must be filed
Day 31	First plan payment must be made (check with your court)
Day 46	Creditors' meeting held
Day 76	Confirmation hearing held
Day 106	Second confirmation hearing held, if necessary

Completing the Plan

It's tough to complete a Chapter 13 repayment plan. That's because a person who files for Chapter 13 bankruptcy is in a fragile economic condition to begin with. All it takes is a layoff, medical emergency, divorce, or simply fatigue at living within a strict budget for so long to cause someone to fall behind on plan payments. In fact, only about one-half of all Chapter 13 bankruptcies are successfully completed.

If your income does drop significantly during the course of your Chapter 13 bankruptcy, you may be able to modify your plan or get a hardship discharge. More likely, however, you will be given the choice of converting your case to a Chapter 7 bankruptcy or having it dismissed entirely. Most people faced with this choice opt to convert to Chapter 7 bankruptcy and discharge what's left of their debts. But you might choose dismissal instead if you have nonexempt property you would be forced to part with in a Chapter 7 bankruptcy (for example, your family grand piano, which the trustee could sell for $5,000).

Just because you might not complete your Chapter 13 bankruptcy doesn't mean you shouldn't start it. If and when you do default, you may be in a better situation to keep your house or at least sell it for a profit.

If you do complete your plan and meet the other Chapter 13 require-ments (such as giving the trustee an annual financial report and keeping current on your taxes and any child support obligations), you will receive a bankruptcy discharge. It usually cancels whatever nonpriority unsecured debt (but not student loans) that has not been paid off in your plan.

There are a few exceptions to a Chapter 13 discharge, the most common of which are:

- debts you didn't list in your bankruptcy papers
- civil judgments arising from willful or malicious acts
- debts for death or personal injuries arising from drunk driving
- back child support or alimony not paid off as part of your plan
- taxes first due less than three years prior to your bankruptcy filing date, for which a return was filed less than two years before your bankruptcy filing date, and which were assessed within 240 days of your bankruptcy filing date (other conditions might apply)
- debts arising from your fraudulent acts (if proven by the creditor in bankruptcy court), and
- court-imposed fines and restitution.

Relief Under Chapter 13 After a Chapter 7 Discharge

The bankruptcy code prohibits you from receiving a Chapter 13 discharge if your case is filed within four years of the filing of a prior Chapter 7 case (in which a discharge was granted). However, according to most courts that have ruled on this issue, you are entitled to file a Chapter 13 bankruptcy at any time after a Chapter 7 even if you won't qualify for a discharge of your debt.

Why would you want to file a Chapter 13 bankruptcy if you can't discharge debt under it? Simply, many Chapter 7 debtors are left with liens and debts that survive the Chapter 7 bankruptcy, and Chapter 13 provides a structured way to deal with them. Because, by definition, your Chapter 7 bankruptcy has discharged all (or most) of your debt, you don't really need the Chapter 13 discharge. For instance, a number of homeowners who file Chapter 7 are left with second mortgage liens on their home—because liens aren't discharged in Chapter 7 bankruptcy. Chapter 13 would provide a way to pay off such a lien over the life of the plan, or in some instances get rid of it altogether. However, some courts will not allow lien stripping in a Chapter 13 bankruptcy if you are not eligible for a discharge. Check with a local bankruptcy attorney to determine the rule in your jurisdiction.

Another reason: Suppose you come out of Chapter 7 owing a lot of back child support (which is not discharged in Chapter 7). You can file a Chapter 13 and propose a repayment plan that would be considerably more affordable than what you are being offered by the child support enforcement agency. Again, you wouldn't be discharging the child support but rather obtaining protection from the court against unreasonable repayment demands, garnishments, and the like.

Why You Need a Lawyer in a Chapter 13 Case

- Chapter 13 bankruptcy can require negotiating with creditors and the bankruptcy trustee to reach agreement on an acceptable repayment plan.
- Chapter 13 bankruptcy requires at least one appearance in court before the bankruptcy judge (the confirmation hearing) and often several more.
- Chapter 13 cases can have many variables, such as valuation of property, reducing liens to the value of the collateral, creating a plan that doesn't discriminate among debtors, and often, requests for plan modifications or hardship discharges.
- An experienced lawyer can help you understand the specifics of your case, including the types of debts you have and the amount or percentage you must repay.
- Local rules, court procedures, and how judges interpret the law vary by jurisdiction and court. A knowledgeable local bankruptcy attorney will know what's standard in your area.

Will You Need a Lawyer?

It's hard to handle your own Chapter 13 bankruptcy; you most likely will need an attorney to represent you, especially if you are trying to save your house. This is because an involuntary dismissal (a greater possibility if you are representing yourself) would greatly set back your plans to keep your house. However, you do have the right to represent yourself, and you may have to if you flat out can't afford to pay the attorneys' fees. (See Ch. 10 for information on finding, choosing, and working with a lawyer and other helpful resources.)

An Attorney May Be More Affordable Than You Think

If you currently are not paying anything on your mortgage but could afford to pay at least some of it, it might only take you a couple of months to save enough money to pay a lawyer to represent you in Chapter 13 bankruptcy.

RELATED TOPIC

How to find a good attorney. Ch. 10 provides tips on how to choose a lawyer.

How Chapter 7 Bankruptcy Can Delay or Stop Foreclosure

Chapter 7 bankruptcy will delay a foreclosure rather than block it permanently. You're more likely to be able to keep your house if you file for Chapter 13 bankruptcy (see Ch. 5). But even if you think you'll need to give up your house sooner or later, Chapter 7 bankruptcy can still be very valuable when you're facing foreclosure.

Filing for Chapter 7 bankruptcy offers different benefits, depending on your situation.

If you want to keep your house and are current on your house payment, you can get other debt canceled, freeing up money that may make it easier to pay your mortgage.

It's important to understand that a Chapter 7 bankruptcy will not wipe out (discharge) a second or third mortgage. If you keep your house, you'll remain responsible for all of the debt associated with the home, even if its value is less than what you owe on the first mortgage.

If you decide to give up your house, you may be able to:
- delay foreclosure proceedings for two to four months, and
- get all or most of your debts permanently canceled so that you can have a fresh start after foreclosure.

Bankruptcy is a wonderful way to deal with various debts. Simply put, with a few exceptions, qualifying debts all go away. Credit card debts, medical bills, and most money judgments arising from lawsuits over breach of contract or negligence are all dischargable. So if you are up to your neck in these types of bills, bankruptcy is something to seriously consider. Whether you want to free up income to pay your mortgage (by eliminating payments on dischargeable debts), or whether you are headed toward a foreclosure and want to get a fresh start, Chapter 7 bankruptcy might be the right chapter for you.

Of course, Chapter 7 bankruptcy is not for everyone. You have to qualify to file and there are the obvious psychological barriers. And if you have good credit, it will take a hit with bankruptcy. Of course, most people filing for bankruptcy already have bad credit, in which case filing for bankruptcy won't make a huge difference, credit wise. In fact, with a little work, there's a good chance that your score will recover fairly quickly.

CAUTION
If you're interested in modifying your mortgage, see a HUD-approved counselor or bankruptcy lawyer before you file for bankruptcy. If you are seeking a modification of your mortgage principal or payments, or are attempting to refinance your current mortgage either in or out of the government programs described in Ch. 4, talk to a HUD-approved housing counselor before filing bankruptcy. A lawyer can also advise you about the modification process in bankruptcy.

How Chapter 7 Bankruptcy Helps You

Whether or not you plan to give up your house, you can buy some time just by filing for bankruptcy. As soon as you do, foreclosure proceedings must stop—at least for a while. When you file for bankruptcy, the federal bankruptcy court automatically issues a court order called a stay. It bars creditors, including mortgage lenders, from taking any measures to collect a debt you owe unless the creditor seeks permission from the bankruptcy court to proceed, and the court grants permission after notice and a hearing.

The automatic stay immediately stops foreclosures as well as other creditor actions. If, for example, your home is due to be sold at auction on December 5 at 10 a.m., and you file for bankruptcy at 9:59 a.m. that day and notify the lender of the filing, the sale is "stayed" and has no effect even if it goes ahead after you file. But if you file at 10:01 a.m., just one minute after the sale, the sale would go through.

In most cases, it takes only about four months for a Chapter 7 bankruptcy case to go through court. After the court grants a Chapter 7 discharge, the party seeking to foreclose on your home is free to take the next step under your state's foreclosure laws.

Keep in mind that there is no guarantee the foreclosure will remain stayed during the entire bankruptcy. A foreclosing lender can file a motion asking the court to lift the automatic stay so that it can move forward with the foreclosure (more below). A good rule of thumb is to seek help from a knowledgeable attorney whenever significant assets are at risk.

What Happens to Your Property in Chapter 7 Bankruptcy?

Chapter 7 bankruptcy is what most people think about when they think about bankruptcy. It's called "liquidation" bankruptcy because it cancels your debts, but you might have to let the bankruptcy court liquidate (sell) some of your property for the benefit of your creditors.

When you file Chapter 7, most types of property you own automatically become part of your "bankruptcy estate," under the control of the bankruptcy court. The bankruptcy trustee may have authority to sell some of the property in the bankruptcy estate to pay your creditors. But every state lets you claim some or all of your bankruptcy estate as exempt, meaning you get to keep it.

As a general rule, exemption laws let you keep necessities, such as furniture, clothing, personal effects, tools of the trade, cars, books, TVs, and home computers. Most states also allow you to keep at least some equity in the house where you're living when you file for bankruptcy; this is known as a homestead exemption. When home equity is low, very few people lose property to the bankruptcy trustee.

RESOURCE

Check the exemptions in your state. What property you may exempt, and to what value, varies by state. You can find the exemptions in your state on Nolo.com. In the "Bankruptcy" section choose "Bankruptcy Information for Your State."

Whether you can keep a certain piece of property also depends on how much equity you have in it. Exemptions protect equity in property. If you have no equity, you can keep the property without using an exemption. For example, if your car is worth $20,000 but the remaining car loan balance is $20,000, you have no equity and wouldn't need to use an exemption in order to keep it. (You'd still have to pay back the loan, however.)

You may have to give up other (nonexempt) property to be sold to help pay off your debts. Many people don't have any nonexempt property. But if you own luxury items outright, such as a boat, an RV, a valuable coin collection, corporate securities, an ownership interest in a business, or an expensive car in which you have considerable equity, they might be sold by the bankruptcy trustee to repay some of your debts.

What Happens to Your Debts in Chapter 7 Bankruptcy?

Once the bankruptcy trustee has paid creditors whatever money is available, your remaining qualifying debt is canceled (discharged). There are certain kinds of debts, though, which can't be discharged in bankruptcy. These include:

- student loans (with rare exceptions)
- most back taxes
- back child support and alimony
- criminal fines and penalties (state or federal)
- liabilities arising from willful and malicious actions such as assault or theft
- liabilities for personal injury or death arising from drunk driving
- debts arising from acts the creditor proves were fraudulent (for instance, misstatements on a loan application)
- traffic tickets, and
- HOA (homeowners' association) fees that accrue after you file for bankruptcy.

Using Chapter 7 Bankruptcy to Keep Your House

You can use Chapter 7 bankruptcy to save your house if both of the following are true:

- You are current on your mortgage payments when you file (or you can get current in a hurry), and
- Your equity in the house (if any) is adequately protected by the exemption laws available to you in your state.

If you are not (and can't get) current on your payments, Chapter 7 bankruptcy will be only a temporary remedy unless you are able to modify your loan (which isn't guaranteed). The lender will be able to proceed with a foreclosure within two or three months. You should instead explore Chapter 13 bankruptcy, which provides a way for you to keep your house by spreading out your missed payments over several years. (See Ch. 5.)

Staying Current on Your Payments

Suppose you are current on your payments but expect to fall behind in the very near future for one reason or another. This might be the case if your mortgage interest rate is due to reset higher, you've reached the principal cap on an interest-only loan, or you have just lost some work hours or been laid off.

In these and similar situations, filing for Chapter 7 bankruptcy may be a big help. Except for a few categories of debt, such as those mentioned above, you can eliminate virtually all your unsecured debt in about three months (and you can even stop paying them before you file). That's right, all your credit card debt, personal loans, medical debts, money judgments and car repossession deficiencies go away. Once your unsecured debt load is eliminated or greatly reduced, you will have a much better chance of being able to pay your mortgage.

Protecting Your Equity

In every Chapter 7 case, the bankruptcy trustee is primarily interested in finding property belonging to the debtor that can be sold for the benefit of the creditors. Unless selling the property would produce money for the creditors, the trustee isn't interested in it. The measure of value in property that might benefit creditors is the equity. The primary purpose of exemptions is to protect equity by requiring the trustee to pay you the amount of the exemption if the property is sold. Selling property that's entirely covered by an exemption would benefit you, not your creditors, so the trustee won't sell it—and you'll get to keep it (subject to any outstanding loans against it).

> ⚠️ **CAUTION**
>
> **Once you file, you may not be able to change your mind.** If you file for Chapter 7 and then discover that you won't be able to keep your house because it has too much equity, you probably won't be allowed to back out and dismiss your bankruptcy case. Your right to dismiss is based on the best interests of your creditors, and if the creditors would receive a distribution from the sale of your house, their interests may require the bankruptcy to go forward. If the trustee sells your home, you'll receive the amount you're entitled to exempt, and your creditors will get paid out of the remaining proceeds.

Most states let you keep at least some home equity when you go through Chapter 7 bankruptcy. Protection for home equity varies dramatically from state to state; you get $500,000 in Massachusetts, $136,925 in Ohio, and just $15,000 in Alabama. In some states, two exemption lists, one state and one federal, are available. You can pick the one that's most advantageous to you. (If you haven't resided for at least two years in the state where you file for bankruptcy, however, you must use the exemptions for the state where you resided before the beginning of that two-year period.)

If your equity is under the amount that's protected and you're current on your payment, you should be able to keep your house when you go through Chapter 7 bankruptcy.

> **EXAMPLE:** Stuart and Stephanie have built up $25,000 of equity in their house, and they've managed to stay current on the mortgage payments. But credit card and medical debts (their young son has been ill) have piled up alarmingly, and they're considering bankruptcy.
>
> They live in Maine, which lets them keep $95,000 of equity under the state's homestead exemption. If they filed for bankruptcy, the trustee would not take their house and sell it. That's because after paying off the mortgage, only $25,000 would be left—and that wouldn't be available to creditors because it's within Maine's $95,000 homestead exemption, which means it would have to be paid to Stuart and Stephanie.

If you have a lot of unprotected equity, however, the bankruptcy trustee is going to want to get at it, so that it can go to your creditors.

> **EXAMPLE:** Petra owns a house in South Carolina, which she inherited from her grandfather. The house carries a mortgage of $300,000 but is valued at $500,000, meaning Petra has equity of $200,000. In South Carolina, you may protect only $59,100 worth of equity in your house. Petra is in a jam. She can't borrow against her equity because she can't afford to pay down another loan, but she needs the protection of bankruptcy against several creditors who are threatening to sue her. She's managed to keep current on her mortgage payments, but she won't be able to keep that up if her creditors sue her and garnish her wages.
>
> If Petra filed for Chapter 7 bankruptcy, the bankruptcy trustee would sell her house, pay off the mortgage, give Petra her $59,100 exemption and use the rest to pay Petra's creditors and the bankruptcy trustee. If there were anything left over after that, Petra would get that as well. If this is not the result Petra wants—and it probably isn't—she should not file for Chapter 7 bankruptcy.

RESOURCE

How much home equity can you keep? If you have home equity and you want to find out how much your state protects or what other property is protected under your state's exemption laws, visit Nolo.com and in the "Bankruptcy" section choose "Bankruptcy Information for Your State."

You Cannot Eliminate Payments on a Second or Third Mortgage

When property values fall, second and third mortgages are frequently left unsecured. In other words, the property no longer has sufficient value to guarantee their payment.

After the 2008 economic downturn, many properties were worth less than the amount the homeowner owed. Although this situation has reversed itself in many states, property equity in some areas still hasn't bounced back. (You can get details about the hardest hit states in Ch. 4.)

If your home is worth less than what you owe on your first mortgage, you can wipe out a subsequent mortgage (such as a second or third) in a Chapter 13 bankruptcy. However, this option is not available in a Chapter 7 case. A homeowner who keeps a house in a Chapter 7 bankruptcy will remain responsible for all loans secured by the property, regardless of the value of the property.

> **EXAMPLE:** Paula owes $200,000 on a first mortgage, $100,000 on a second mortgage, and $50,000 on a third mortgage. Her house is worth $275,000, leaving the second mortgage partially unsecured, and the third mortgage wholly unsecured. If she files for Chapter 7 bankruptcy and keeps the home, she'll remain responsible for all three mortgages. If, however, she files for Chapter 13 bankruptcy, she can file a motion asking the court to strip off the wholly unsecured third mortgage. (Partially secured mortgages remain in a Chapter 13 bankruptcy. Only wholly unsecured mortgages will qualify for discharge.)

Using Chapter 7 Bankruptcy to Delay a Foreclosure Sale in Good Faith

The instant you file for bankruptcy, all foreclosure proceedings must cease. This means that if you file for bankruptcy at 11:59 a.m., a foreclosure sale at 12:00 p.m. would be void. Because of this instant relief, many people turn to bankruptcy as a last resort when their efforts to work something out with their lender have failed to materialize. As mentioned, a Chapter 7 bankruptcy filing will give you two or three months of relief before the foreclosure can proceed again, but it's definitely not a permanent fix.

As a general rule, filing for Chapter 7 bankruptcy is a bad idea if you have little or no debt that would be discharged and your only reason for filing is to buy some extra time in your house. You won't be able to get another Chapter 7 discharge for eight years, so why waste it just to get a little extra time? Also, the courts frown on filers using bankruptcy for tactical purposes. However, if you are facing foreclosure, you also probably have some serious debt issues. If your Chapter 7 would eliminate that debt as well as buy you some more time in your home, the equation changes and Chapter 7 bankruptcy becomes a valid option you could file in "good faith."

How Much Time You'll Get

A Chapter 7 bankruptcy takes about three to four months (sometimes longer) from the date of filing to the date of discharge (cancellation) of your debts. Unless the judge gives the lender permission, no foreclosure sale can take place during that time.

The lender can, however, file a formal request (motion) asking the bankruptcy court to lift the automatic stay and let the foreclosure sale proceed. Lenders usually must provide at least 25 days' advance notice of the hearing on their motion unless they get the judge's permission to shorten that time. Generally, the lender must hire a lawyer to file the motion, so it is a relatively expensive procedure. For this reason, some lenders skip the expense, let the bankruptcy proceed and simply reschedule the foreclosure sale once it's complete. This leaves your three-to four-month delay intact.

A lender who thinks it's worthwhile to ask the court to let the foreclosure go ahead usually files a motion 30 to 45 days after you file. A court hearing on the request will be scheduled about 25 to 30 days later. The court will likely grant the motion to lift the stay unless you can show that any of the following apply:

- The proposed foreclosure is illegal in some way.
- The lender hasn't complied with state procedural requirements (see Ch. 7).

- The party bringing the foreclosure hasn't produced the necessary paperwork or evidence to show it has authority to seek the foreclosure.
- There is substantial equity in the property that you cannot protect with an exemption. In this case the trustee would likely sell the property.

If the court lifts the stay, the lender will then be free to resume the foreclosure process. If the court refuses to lift the stay, then the foreclosure will be stalled until you receive your bankruptcy discharge.

After the discharge (or after the court lifts the stay), the lender can proceed with the foreclosure. Unlike Chapter 13 bankruptcy, Chapter 7 doesn't force the lender to let you make up your missed payments over time or preserve your right to keep ownership of your house.

Timing Your Filing

Sometimes you don't have the luxury of deciding when to file for Chapter 7 bankruptcy. If your wages are about to be garnished, you'll most likely file as soon as possible. However, if there's no emergency, it sometimes helps to wait until your filing has the best possible effect on delaying your foreclosure sale. In most cases, this means waiting to file until just before the sale date.

Keeping the Money You Saved Before Filing for Bankruptcy

If you're sure you'll be giving up your house sooner or later, it makes excellent financial sense to keep living in it and give it up later. If you are current on your mortgage when you make this decision, you'll likely be able to save at least three or four months' worth of mortgage payments before foreclosure proceedings even begin. And depending on how long you have before the actual sale, you will probably be able to save at least several more months' worth of mortgage payments. (More on this in Ch. 9.)

If you would like to file for Chapter 7 bankruptcy, you should first figure out whether you'll be able to keep what you've saved before you file, or whether you'll have to give it up to be used by the trustee to pay down your unsecured debt. This issue doesn't arise for any money you save after you file your Chapter 7 bankruptcy; it applies only to what you have in the piggy bank on the day you file.

You can keep your savings through the bankruptcy process if you can claim it as exempt. Every state has its own rules about how much money is exempt from creditors—in other words, how much you are allowed to keep when you go through bankruptcy. And there is a separate set of federal exemption rules; in states that allow it, you may pick whichever system works best for you. However, most states don't allow you to keep much—if any—savings. But that's not always the case.

For example, in California, under the exemption system that just about everybody uses when there is no home equity to protect, you can protect roughly $28,225 worth of any type of property, including cash in a bank account. You can also keep such commonly owned items as household furnishings and personal effects, as well as $8,000 in the tools you need in your profession and $5,350 of vehicle equity. So, if you have $10,000 in the bank, you could keep that $10,000 and still have enough remaining to protect other property.

To find out how much money you are allowed to keep when filing for Chapter 7 bankruptcy, check your state's page in the appendix.

It may be that the exemptions available to you in your state won't let you keep the cash you've saved as well as all your other property. In that case, you'll have to pick and choose what property you keep and what you give up. For example, if you have $50,000 worth of home equity, and your state makes you choose between the home equity and your savings account, you may have to give up the savings account. In the end, the only way to know for sure how much property (and cash in the bank) you can keep in a Chapter 7 bankruptcy is to review the exemptions.

EXAMPLE 1: Jon lives in California. He has no home equity. He has not been paying his $2,500 mortgage for seven months before he files for bankruptcy to stave off a scheduled foreclosure sale. With money earned from his job, he has put $2,000 a month in a bank account, giving him savings of $15,000. In addition to hand-me-down furniture and normal personal effects, Jon's only other property is a classic 1967 Chevrolet Camaro Rally Sport worth $20,000.

In one of the two available exemption systems in California, Jon is entitled to exempt $5,350 worth of motor vehicle equity and $28,225 of any other type of property (the wild card exemption). Jon wants to hold on to his Camaro but will have to use $14,650 of the wild card exemption to supplement the $5,350 motor vehicle exemption to fully exempt it. That leaves him $13,575 from the wild card exemption. Because there is no specific exemption for a bank savings account (as there is for a motor vehicle, for example), Jon will be able to exempt only $13,575 of his savings. He'll have to give up the rest ($1,425) as nonexempt property, to be used by the bankruptcy trustee to pay down his unsecured debt. If he is eligible to make retirement plan contributions, he might be able to exempt his cash by depositing $1,425 into an IRA account.

EXAMPLE 2: Amy lives in Massachusetts in a house she inherited. She has home equity of $200,000, but she doesn't have enough income to borrow against her equity and she has a lot of credit card debts to deal with. Bankruptcy seems like the best way out. Amy checks Nolo.com and learns that the Massachusetts homestead exemption fully protects her equity. Unfortunately, the Massachusetts exemption system provides very little protection for savings, so if Amy has saved money before filing for bankruptcy, she'll have to give it up (unless she can legally deposit it into a retirement account).

If Amy had no home equity she needed to protect, she could use the federal exemptions (an alternative system to the Massachusetts state exemptions) to protect her savings, because they provide $13,100 "wildcard" protection for any type of property (including a bank account) for single filers and $26,200 for joint filers.

The Chapter 7 Bankruptcy Process: An Overview

Chapter 7 bankruptcy is a very straightforward process. It typically consists of six steps:

Step 1: Before filing, complete a mandatory credit-counseling course by phone or online.

Step 2: File the official bankruptcy forms (fillable forms are available online) listing all your property and creditors and providing information about your financial transactions during the previous two years.

Step 3: Mail the bankruptcy trustee, who handles the case for the court, a copy of your most recently filed income tax return, plus any other documents the trustee asks for.

Step 4: About 30 days after you file, attend a creditors' meeting, usually the only personal appearance you'll have to make. The creditors' meeting occurs in a small hearing room and is conducted by the trustee. Creditors seldom appear. At this meeting, you are required to answer (under oath) any questions the trustee has about the information in your papers, or provide other information the trustee thinks is relevant. A typical meeting lasts five minutes or less. You are not required to have a lawyer represent you at this meeting—you will have to answer the trustee's questions directly, whether or not you have a lawyer with you.

Step 5: No later than 60 days after the creditors' meeting, you must attend mandatory budget counseling (by phone or online) and file a simple form telling the court that you have completed it along with a certificate of completion from the counseling agency.

Step 6: Remain in a holding pattern (don't operate a business with inventory or sell or give away any property without the trustee's permission) until the court sends you a written discharge of your debts. That will come about 60 to 75 days after the creditors' meeting. During that period, creditors can, but seldom do, object to your getting rid of a debt. The trustee arranges for you to turn over nonexempt property, if you have any, but most people who file for Chapter 7 bankruptcy don't have any nonexempt assets.

The Chapter 7 Bankruptcy Timeline	
Before you file	Mandatory credit counseling
Filing date	Papers filed to start the bankruptcy
About a month after you file	Creditors' meeting held
Up to 60 days after the creditors' meeting	Mandatory budget counseling
60 days after the creditors' meeting	Court sends written discharge of your debts

Do You Qualify for Chapter 7 Bankruptcy?

When radical changes in the bankruptcy law were implemented in 2005, a new urban legend was born to the effect that almost no one could file for Chapter 7 bankruptcy anymore. Not true. In fact, pretty much anybody who could file before 2005 can file now.

To qualify for Chapter 7 bankruptcy, you must pass either the income test or the means test. Here is how they work.

The Six-Month Gross Income Test

You may qualify for Chapter 7 bankruptcy if your average monthly gross income in the six-month period prior to the month in which you file for bankruptcy is below the annual median household income for your state.

A household is defined by most courts as all members of an economic unit; that is, an arrangement where income and expenses are shared for the benefit of all. For example, domestic partners and their children are one economic unit, as are groups of people living together as "families." Roommates, on the other hand, are typically not considered an economic unit, assuming they handle their income and expenses separately and only share the rent. Similarly, arrangements in which a debtor lives with his or her parents, but the income and expenses are not shared, are not considered economic units. A few courts reject the economic unit definition of "household" and instead look to the tax rules. In these courts, if a member of the household is not a dependent of the bankruptcy debtor for tax purposes, he or she would not be considered part of the household.

To see whether or not you qualify under this income test, add up all your gross income for your household for the six calendar months immediately preceding the current month. Then multiply the total by two.

Figuring Your Gross Income

Total household income for last six calendar months $ _____

                                  ×   _____ 2

Average annual income   = $ _____

Then compare this figure to the median household income for your state. You can find the most current figures (they change at least once a year, sometimes more) on the website of the U.S. Trustee at www.justice.gov/ust (choose "Means Testing Information" and then click on the appropriate date range under "Data Required for Completing the 122A Forms and the 122C Forms").

If you pass the means test, you are halfway there. You also have to provide information about your current income and living expenses (called Schedules I and J). You should be fine if your current living expenses are reasonable, necessary, and use up virtually all of your monthly income. If you have more income per month than you really need for living expenses, the trustee might seek to dismiss your case.

> **EXAMPLE:** Preston and Megan live in Kansas with their two children. In September they examine their gross income from all sources (which includes bonuses, commissions, overtime, and even lottery winnings) for the months March through August. Their total income for that period is $36,600. They multiply that figure by two to arrive at an annual figure of $73,200.
>
> They find that Kansas has a median annual household income of $83,528 for a family of four. Their annual gross household income is less than the Kansas median annual household income, which means they pass the income test and can file for Chapter 7 bankruptcy.

TIP

If you wait, you may qualify later. If your income is higher than the median income for your state based on your gross income for the previous six months, but your income has recently gone down, you might consider waiting for another month or two to file. The delay may render your income for the new six-month period low enough to produce an average below your state's median.

The Means Test

If your household income is above the median for your state and household size, you may still be able to file for Chapter 7 bankruptcy if you pass what's called the means test. You'll have to show that your allowable expenses and certain standard deductions leave you with inadequate funds to repay a substantial portion of your unsecured debts. (An unsecured debt is a debt that isn't attached to particular collateral—for example, credit card debt.)

If you pass, you can file for Chapter 7 bankruptcy. If you don't pass, the court may consider you to have enough money to pay back at least some of your debts through a Chapter 13 bankruptcy. But check with a bankruptcy lawyer first. An experienced bankruptcy lawyer might be able to help you pass the means test.

The Actual Income and Expenses Test

Even if you pass the income or means test, some bankruptcy courts will require you to file for Chapter 13 bankruptcy rather than Chapter 7 bankruptcy if, looking forward, your actual income will exceed your actual expenses by more than about $200 a month. This determination is based on the income and expense schedules that must be filed with every bankruptcy.

Will You Need a Lawyer?

Will you need a lawyer to represent you in Chapter 7 bankruptcy? Opinions on this differ. Surprised? Don't be. Put any two lawyers in a room, and ask them the same question. You will probably get four different answers.

Those who feel you can go it alone point to the fact that for the vast majority of filers, there's no court appearance (although you will have to appear at the meeting of creditors) and no legal advocacy is needed.

If you do decide to represent yourself, be aware that the legal system holds you to the same legal standards as those expected from a licensed attorney. You are responsible for knowing and correctly following the laws and for completing your paperwork properly. When you appear at the meeting of creditors, the trustee will not provide you with legal advice or help. Instead, the trustee will scrutinize your case looking for assets to take and reasons to have it disallowed.

If you file under the wrong chapter or make other mistakes, you will bear the consequences. For some mistakes, you may need to amend your papers and attend one or more extra creditor meetings. But other mistakes can be much more costly. For example, the trustee or your creditors may ask the court to deny your bankruptcy or you might lose assets or other valuable legal rights.

A good lawyer can help you successfully navigate the bankruptcy system. In addition, your attorney can advise you on how to keep your home. If you think you might want to represent yourself, first get a good do-it-yourself book and read it carefully, so you know what you are taking on (Ch.10 has some recommendations). It may also make sense to meet with a bankruptcy attorney (many will provide an initial consultation for free), to see if your case has any tricky issues and to find out how much representation would cost.

Fighting Foreclosure in Court

I f you're in a state that requires foreclosures to go through court (see Ch. 2 and the appendix to find out if you live in a judicial foreclosure state), you'll have the right to present your objections to the foreclosure to a judge for review. If you're in a nonjudicial foreclosure state, you'll have to file an action in court against the foreclosing party (or file bankruptcy) to have a judge review the foreclosure.

In judicial foreclosure states, you may have a decent shot at delaying or stopping a foreclosure, even if you don't file for bankruptcy, in any of the following situations:

- The foreclosing party brought the foreclosure based on false information (for example, your payments were credited to the wrong party and you were never behind, or the lender substantially overstated the amount you had to pay to reinstate your mortgage, depriving you of your reinstatement rights under state law).

- You can prove that the foreclosing party didn't follow state procedural requirements for bringing a foreclosure (for example, by failing to properly serve on you a notice of intent to foreclose required by state law).

- The foreclosing party isn't legally entitled to bring a foreclosure action (for example, state law says that only the actual holder of the promissory note can foreclose on the mortgage and the foreclosing party does not meet that description).

- The person signing the affidavits in support of the foreclosure did not have personal knowledge of the information in the documents (in other words, the person signing the affidavits was a robo-signer).

- The notary public attesting to the validity of a signature in the documents did not follow regulations governing notarization.

- The original lender or mortgage originator engaged in unfair lending practices through fraudulent behavior or by violating a state or federal law with regard to certain mortgage provisions or disclosures to borrowers.

As you'll see, to successfully fight a foreclosure in court you will probably need to hire an attorney to represent you. The foreclosing party will have an attorney, and trying to do battle with an attorney in court when you aren't one yourself can be an exercise in futility. If you absolutely have to represent yourself, though, there are resources that can help you, and they're discussed in Ch. 10.

How Long Can You Delay the Sale of Your House?

As you might expect, contesting a foreclosure in a judicial foreclosure state is very different than doing so in a nonjudicial foreclosure state. (If you don't know which kind you're likely to come up against, see Ch. 2 or your state's page in the appendix.) And the amount of delay you're likely to get depends on the procedure, too.

Judicial Foreclosures

In judicial foreclosures, just filing an answer to the foreclosure petition or complaint might give you several additional months. This is because once you contest the case, you're entitled to your day in court. The lender may file a motion for summary judgment (which is when the court grants judgment in favor of the foreclosing party because there is no dispute as to the important facts of the case) in response to your answer, though you'll typically still get a hearing. (You must respond to the motion for summary judgment or else you'll lose.) If the court decides that you have a legal defense to foreclosure, the court will deny summary judgment to the lender. This means that the case will now go to trial.

It's impossible to generalize how long it will take to get to trial; some states and courts are faster than others. But it's likely to take anywhere from two to six months or longer.

If you don't respond and let the case go by default, you are probably looking at a month or so before the court issues a foreclosure judgment. In most states, the judge then orders a sale to be held. In Connecticut or Vermont, however, the judge can transfer title then and there, without a sale.

Nonjudicial Foreclosures

In nonjudicial foreclosure states, the only way to raise a defense to the foreclosure (other than filing for Chapter 13 bankruptcy) is to file an action in state court seeking a court order (temporary injunction) holding up the sale until you have gotten a chance to argue your case. In most states you must post a bond (a kind of insurance policy) to protect the owner from financial losses during the delay caused by the case. This requirement alone can be expensive and might defeat the purpose of your bringing the case if your primary goal is to buy some extra time to live in your house payment free.

Also, if you must hire a lawyer for this court process, your costs will be considerable—maybe several thousand dollars. Your case may be dismissed just a month or two after you file it, meaning you will have spent a lot of money for very little delay. Of course, if you have a good shot at saving your house, the risk may be worth it.

TIP

Delaying foreclosure with a foreclosure mediation program. If your state or county has an official foreclosure avoidance mediation program, by participating you may be able to delay the foreclosure and force the lender to discuss loss mitigation options with you. You can learn more about these programs in Ch. 4.

When It May Be Worth Fighting

If it's clear that the foreclosing party failed to follow the law and that as a result, you were deprived of an important right, it may be worth it to go to court and contest the foreclosure. After all, if you could get the foreclosure lawsuit dismissed or significantly delayed, you may be able to stay in your house much longer than you would otherwise. And that, of course, could have significant financial and emotional benefits. (See Ch. 9.)

Often, however, you can't really tell whether a foreclosure is illegal unless you have access to internal bank documents. You most likely won't be able to access these documents unless you file a lawsuit and seek production of the documents in what are called "discovery" proceedings, such as depositions, interrogatories, and motions to produce documents.

Other Strategies for Fighting Foreclosure

This section lists the most common circumstances in which you may want to contest a foreclosure in court. But there are others. Over the years, attorneys have come up with a panoply of theories to contest foreclosures, drawing on the common law—law fashioned in cases decided by our courts. None of these theories are widely used; however, it's possible that one might be useful in your case.

For example, you might be able to block foreclosure by arguing that your loan terms are unconscionable—that is, so unfair that they shock the conscience of the judge. In one case, for example, the borrower spoke very little English, was pressured to agree to a loan that he obviously couldn't repay, was not represented by an attorney, and was unaware of the harsh terms attached to the loan (such as an unaffordable balloon payment).

Check *Foreclosures and Mortgage Servicing*, published by the National Consumer Law Center, for more information on these common law defenses.

You're on Active Duty in the Military

If you're on active military duty, you have some special protections under the Servicemembers Civil Relief Act (SCRA). Foreclosure on a mortgage you took out before you were on active duty must be a judicial foreclosure, no matter what the custom is in your state. You can waive this requirement, but the waiver must be in writing and be executed while you are on active duty or afterwards. The right to a judicial foreclosure can't be waived beforehand.

If a foreclosure is begun against you while you're on active duty, you can stay (postpone) the action for a period of not less than 90 days by requesting it from the court in writing. (See Ch. 4 for more detail on these rules.)

The Lender Didn't Follow State Foreclosure Procedures or Mortgage Terms Governing Foreclosures

Because every foreclosure means that someone loses a home, many courts require the foreclosing party to strictly follow state law and respect the terms of the mortgage or deed of trust. If they don't, you can call them on it.

But if the foreclosing party makes a trivial violation of the rules, the judge will probably let it go. Virtually all judges overlook errors that are inconsequential, such as the misspelling of a name. And the law in some states specifically provides that certain procedural errors (often failure to provide required notices, particularly when the borrower has actual notice of sale) will not affect the right of the foreclosing party to obtain the foreclosure.

If the foreclosing party's error doesn't actually cause you any harm, it's probably not worth fighting over. Most courts will overlook a violation that is technical in nature and doesn't deprive you of a fair procedure, on the principle of "no harm, no foul." For example, say the lender failed to record the notice of default in the local land records office (a typical requirement) on time, but you got your required notice on time. The court might well decide that the failure to record didn't harm you and allow the foreclosure to proceed.

Typical Foreclosure Requirements

In most states, the foreclosing party must take one or more of the following steps, depending on the state and the type of foreclosure (judicial or nonjudicial). If the lender missed a step, you may able to contest the foreclosure. Typically, in a nonjudicial foreclosure, the lender must:

- mail you a notice of default, telling you how much time you have to reinstate the mortgage
- record the notice of default in the local land records office
- mail you a notice telling you the date the property will be sold, and
- mail you a notice telling you how long you have to redeem your home (by paying off the debt or by reimbursing the party that bought the home at the foreclosure sale, if there is a redemption period after the sale).

In a judicial foreclosure, the lender typically must:

- mail you a notice telling you that foreclosure proceedings will soon be started in court
- serve you with a copy of the complaint to foreclose, and/or
- publish notice of the intended foreclosure sale in a local newspaper for a particular number of weeks before the sale.

All of these notices have time limits and specific content requirements. For instance, a notice might have to describe the property, the amount due on the mortgage, the amount necessary to reinstate the mortgage including costs and interest, and information on the person you can contact to discuss the notice. (See Ch. 2 and your state's page in the appendix.)

More serious violations will get a more serious response from the court. For example, if the lender failed to send you a notice of default as required by state law, the lender might have to start over, because the lack of adequate notice deprived you of valuable time to resolve the problem. (You might have worked out an alternative arrangement with the lender, gotten refinancing, or taken advantage of state rules permitting reinstatement or redemption of the mortgage.)

Other serious errors include failing to identify the breach in a notice of default, inaccurately stating the total amount due, or not giving an appropriate amount of time to cure the default in a required foreclosure notice.

The Foreclosing Party Can't Prove It Has the Right to Foreclose

A mortgage loan consists of two basic parts: (1) a promissory note setting out the terms of the loan, and (2) a security agreement (a mortgage or deed of trust) making the real estate collateral for the loan and setting out the terms under which a foreclosure may occur in case of a default. When the loan changes hands, the promissory note is indorsed (signed over) to the new owner of the loan. In some cases, the note is indorsed in blank, which makes it a bearer instrument under Article 3 of the Uniform Commercial Code (UCC). This means that any party that possesses the note has the legal authority to enforce it. (In practice, all states have adopted the UCC or some form of it.) Similarly, the mortgage (or deed of trust) is "assigned" to the new owner. Assignments are typically recorded in the land records.

In the early days of the foreclosure crisis, attorneys representing homeowners were sometimes successful in delaying or derailing foreclosures on the grounds that ownership had not been satisfactorily established due to gaps in the chain of indorsements or assignments. (The legal theory involves a concept called "standing"—that is, who has the right to foreclose.) However, now lenders are more careful about addressing any gaps before starting the foreclosure. Also, courts have heard this issue often and have decided against homeowners in many situations, making it harder to prevail on an argument based on standing. Still, your case may be the exception.

The issue of standing is complicated and the law varies among states. In some courts, the foreclosing party must establish that it has the right to enforce the note (that is, it holds the note or is acting as the note holder's authorized representative) in order to foreclose. If your loan has been transferred multiple times or was securitized, proving just who has this right can be difficult. The original promissory note you signed is stored somewhere, but it can be difficult for a foreclosing party to come up with it, or even a copy of it.

What Is MERS?

The mortgage banking industry created the Mortgage Electronic Registration System, Inc. (MERS) in the mid-1990s to simplify the assignment process when one bank sells a mortgage to another. MERS is not a lender, a servicer, or an investor. Rather, it is a large electronic database of mortgages and mortgage transactions. Mortgage documents typically refer to MERS as the "mortgagee of record" and "nominee," or agent for the purpose of making future transfers to other entities.

MERS then acts as a stand-in for the lender in the county land records, tracking and transferring the mortgages that are registered on its system between different owners. According to MERS, it does not have to record these transfers in the county land records because MERS is the mortgagee of record (or the beneficiary on a deed of trust) as the lender's nominee. This makes it easier and cheaper to transfer the loan from one lender to another since they don't have to pay county recording fees for each transaction.

Attorneys for borrowers have challenged foreclosures involving MERS by arguing that it lacks the legal authority to act as a nominee on behalf of the original lender and subsequent owners of the loan. However, these arguments have not been very successful.

Many courts have rejected borrowers' challenges to MERS's role as a nominee, ruling that MERS had authority to act, was a legitimate organization, and that the mortgage the borrowers signed put them on notice of MERS's role in home loan transactions.

There has also been considerable litigation over whether or not MERS has standing to initiate a foreclosure in its name as the plaintiff in a judicial foreclosure or as a beneficiary in nonjudicial foreclosure proceedings. For example, the Maine Supreme Court held in 2010 that since MERS does not own the promissory note, it lacks standing to begin foreclosure proceedings in that state (*Mortgage Electronic Registration Systems, Inc. v Saunders*, 2 A.2d 289 (Maine 2010)). The Supreme Court of Minnesota, on the other hand, decided in the case of *Jackson v. Mortgage Electronic Registration Systems, Inc.*, 770 N.W.2d 487 (Minn. 2009) that MERS does have standing to foreclose.

As a result of this type of litigation, MERS instituted a significant policy change in 2011, prohibiting all members from conducting foreclosures in its name. Consequently, there shouldn't be any more new MERS foreclosures,

> **What Is MERS? (continued)**
>
> even in states that previously allowed them. (MERS now typically assigns the mortgage or deed of trust to the foreclosing party before the foreclosure starts.) In the unlikely event that MERS is the foreclosing party in your foreclosure case, you will want to be familiar with cases involving MERS. (See Ch. 10 for more information on doing your own legal research.)

Even if the original note is available, the indorsements might not be in order. Florida requires that the foreclosure complaint include the factual basis for the plaintiff's authority to enforce the note and give the location of the note. The plaintiff must also file the original note with the court before it enters judgment. (If the note has been lost, there are certain steps the foreclosing party can take in order to foreclose.) California, on the other hand, does not require the foreclosing party to possess the original note before starting a nonjudicial foreclosure. (*Debrunner v. Deutsche Bank National Trust Co.*, 138 Cal.Rptr.3d 830 (Cal. Ct. App. 2012).)

When it comes to assignments of mortgages, many courts follow the general rule that the mortgage follows the note. This means that when the foreclosing party has the right to enforce the note, a recorded assignment of the mortgage might not be needed. For example, Florida courts have determined that standing can be established from the plaintiff's status as the note holder at the time the foreclosure starts, regardless of whether any mortgage assignments are recorded. (*McLean v. JP Morgan Chase Bank N.A.*, 79 So.3d 170, 172 (Fla. Dist. Ct. App. 4th Dist. 2012).)

However, in other states, the law requires a valid assignment of the mortgage (or deed of trust) in order for the foreclosure to be valid. Nonjudicial foreclosure states, in particular, tend to require an assignment as part of the foreclosure process. In Massachusetts, for example, the Supreme Judicial Court rejected the "mortgage follows the note" concept and affirmed a lower court's invalidation of a foreclosure sale where the lender was unable to prove that it had been assigned the mortgage at the time of the foreclosure. (*U.S. Bank, N.A. v. Ibanez*, 458 Mass. 637 (2011).) (In this case, the foreclosing party obtained and recorded an assignment of mortgage after the foreclosure was over.) The court's decision retroactively deemed thousands of Massachusetts foreclosures potentially invalid because, at the time, it was standard practice to proceed with foreclosure even if there wasn't an assignment. In response, Massachusetts passed a law that limits the amount of time that homeowners can challenge a foreclosure sale based on this type of error. In another Massachusetts case, the court held that the foreclosing party must also hold the promissory note (or be acting on behalf of the note holder) in order to foreclose. (*Eaton v. Fannie Mae*, 462 Mass. 569 (2012).)

In addition, courts have had to address the issue of what happens when the foreclosing party did not have authority to start a foreclosure, but later obtained standing after the foreclosure had already begun. For example, the Ohio Supreme Court ruled that a lender must establish standing at the beginning of the suit; acquiring standing after the foreclosure starts is not good enough. (*Federal Home Loan Mortgage Corp. v. Schwartzwald*, 979 N.E.2d 1124 (Ohio 2012).)

Cases about the ownership of mortgages, deeds of trust, and promissory notes and the legality of foreclosure proceedings can be very difficult to argue. You'll most likely need an attorney to help you review your ability to raise a defense based on standing and argue it in court if you decide to go this route. (If you do decide to represent yourself, Nolo has an excellent book on this topic. See *Represent Yourself in Court*, by Paul Bergman and Sara Berman.) Keep in mind you're unlikely to be successful these days if you simply say that you don't know who owns your mortgage loan, you want the foreclosing party to "produce the note," or that you have a MERS loan (see "What Is MERS?" above). You'll need to know the laws in your state and how to properly present the arguments.

The Mortgage Servicer Made a Serious Mistake

Mortgage servicers make mistakes all the time when they're dealing with borrowers. In fact, there have been many state and federal settlements that have revealed just how error-prone mortgage servicers are when handling home loans (for instance, the National Mortgage Settlement, the Ocwen National Servicing Settlement, the National SunTrust Settlement, and the Independent Foreclosure Review). You may be able to fight your foreclosure based on this kind of mistake—for example, because the mortgage servicer imposed excessive fees or told you that you owed more than you really did.

What to Look For

Many errors occur when a lender or mortgage servicer tells you how much you must pay to reinstate or redeem your mortgage. Many states let you reinstate a mortgage within a certain period of time by getting current on your mortgage payments, including costs, attorneys' fees, and interest. And even if a state doesn't specifically provide a period in which you can reinstate the loan, the mortgage documents may themselves allow it. (See Ch. 2 and your state's page in the appendix.)

In either case, when you receive notice of an impending foreclosure and are told how much you would need to pay to reinstate the mortgage, the amounts must be reasonably accurate and must be justified by language in the mortgage documents. For example, your lender can't require you to pay a fee for a monthly reappraisal or inspection of the property if the mortgage documents don't provide for it, if you were current on your payments when the inspection was made, or if the overall number of inspections or the inspection fee itself is obviously unreasonable. You could properly contest the foreclosure on the ground that the notice you received deprived you of the right to reinstate your mortgage because of the excessive fees.

> **EXAMPLE:** Henry receives a statutory notice of default that tells him he'll have to make up five missed payments and pay costs of $2,800. The costs include $800 for a reappraisal of the property and $2,000 for ten drive-by property inspections at $200 a pop. While he could make up the missed payments, he can't afford the costs so he doesn't reinstate the mortgage within the time allowed in the notice. The lender starts a foreclosure lawsuit.

An attorney advises Henry that the reappraisal and inspection fees are a rip-off, so Henry contests the foreclosure on the basis that the notice of default was faulty. The court agrees and delays the foreclosure for a month to give Henry time to reinstate the mortgage without paying the inflated fees. If Henry doesn't reinstate on time, the foreclosure will go forward.

Determining whether or not your mortgage agreement allows a particular cost or procedure requires careful reading of the document. The fact is, mortgages are often almost undecipherable—you need an expert to make sense of them. The one area of contention is the amount the lender charges the homeowner for attorneys' fees paid by the lender for work on notices and foreclosure documents. As a general rule, such charges must be reasonable, though some state laws specifically limit the amount of attorneys' fees that can be charged in a foreclosure.

If the mortgage has been bought by Freddie Mac, Fannie Mae, or the FHA, there are limits on what attorneys can charge for services related to mortgage defaults or foreclosures. Limits also apply to fees charged by mortgage servicers. If the fees exceed these limits, and reinstatement of the mortgage is conditioned on payment of the fees, the result depends on the kind of foreclosure proceeding:

- **In a judicial foreclosure,** the judge could dismiss the foreclosure proceedings and either reinstate the mortgage or require the lender to start over. Or, in some states, the judge could delay the foreclosure, giving you more time to reinstate.
- **In a nonjudicial foreclosure,** a violation of attorneys' fee limits may be the basis for you to ask the court for an order (injunction) halting the foreclosure proceedings.

In addition to errant attorneys' fees, the most common errors that may have been made by your mortgage servicer—and that may lead a court to stop a foreclosure—are:

- misapplying your mortgage payments to the wrong account
- buying insurance on the property and billing you for it even though you already carried (and were current on) the insurance

required by your mortgage agreement (see "Rules on Force-Placed Insurance," below)

- failing to pay your property tax, resulting in your owing fines to the government, even though you were paying into an escrow account and the servicer was responsible for paying the taxes
- charging you late fees and property inspection fees even though you were current on your mortgage payments, and
- engaging in coercive collection practices and falsely claiming that certain amounts are due.

Rules on Force-Placed Insurance

Most mortgages require that the homeowner maintain adequate insurance on the home so that the lender's interest is protected in case of fire or other casualty. This type of insurance also covers the loss of your personal property if stolen, damaged, or destroyed. If you let your homeowners' insurance coverage lapse, the mortgage servicer can purchase insurance coverage at your expense. This is called force-placed or lender-placed insurance. (This type of policy does not cover your personal belongings.) Force-placed insurance policies tend to be costly because there is uncertainty about what might happen to the home if the borrower is not keeping up with his or her bills.

Under mortgage servicing regulations that went into effect January 10, 2014, the servicer must send two notices to you before imposing force-placed insurance. The servicer must send the first notice at least 45 days before purchasing a force-placed insurance policy. The servicer must then send a second notice (a reminder notice) no earlier than 30 days after the first notice and at least 15 days before charging you for force-placed insurance coverage. This notice must include the cost of the force-placed insurance or a reasonable estimate of the cost.

If you obtain hazard insurance on your own and provide proof to the servicer, the servicer must cancel the force-placed insurance within 15 days of receiving evidence of existing insurance, and refund any premiums charged for duplicate coverage.

How to Get Information About Errors

The more information you can wrest from your mortgage servicer, the better. A federal law called the Real Estate Settlement Procedures Act (RESPA) provides a way for you to challenge common types of errors such as improper charges, improper calculation of interest, or the failure to credit payments properly. It also gives you a way to get the information you need to make such a challenge.

Start by sending the servicer what's known under RESPA as a qualified written request. In it, you identify the borrower, the account, and the information you're after. Under amendments to Regulation X (which implements RESPA) that went into effect January 10, 2014, your inquiry may be categorized as a "request for information" or a "notice of error." These new categorizations expand on the previous qualified written request requirements. There are different time frames for the servicer to respond to you depending on the type of request you send.

TIP
Send your request to the correct address. The servicer can require that you send your inquiry to a particular address. Check for the correct address on the servicer's website, your periodic statements or coupon books, or on notices that the servicer sent you regarding early intervention and loss mitigation.

Request for Information

Within five business days of receiving the request for information, the servicer must provide you with written acknowledgement that it received your request. Within 30 business days, the servicer must provide the information you requested or explain why it is not available, plus give you the name and contact information of someone you can follow up with. (The servicer must respond within ten business days if the information you're seeking is the identity, address, or other relevant contact information for the owner or assignee of your mortgage loan.) The 30-day period may be extended for an additional 15 days if, within that 30-day period, the servicer notifies the borrower of the extension and the reasons for delay in responding.

Notice of Error

Your servicer must respond if you send a written request asserting certain types of errors, including that the servicer did not:

- accept your payments
- apply or credit payments properly
- pay taxes or insurance, or
- provide accurate information regarding loss mitigation options and foreclosures.

Other errors that would trigger this process include the servicer's imposition of fees or charges without a reasonable basis, as well as other errors relating to the servicing of your mortgage loan. Errors related to the origination, underwriting, or a subsequent sale or securitization, however, would not trigger the servicer's obligation to respond under RESPA.

Within five business days of receiving your notice of error, the servicer must provide you with written acknowledgement it received your request.

The servicer must correct the error, provide notification of the correction, and give contact information for you to follow up (or let you know that no error occurred along with the reasons for this determination). The time period in which the servicer must do this depends on the type of error you asserted in your notice.

- If you complained that the servicer failed to provide an accurate payoff statement upon your request, it must respond not later than seven business days after it gets your notice.
- If your notice asserts that the servicer improperly started the foreclosure during the 120-day preforeclosure waiting period, moved for a foreclosure judgment or order of sale, or conducted a foreclosure sale in violation of the CFPB rules on loss mitigation procedures (basically, if you've asserted that the servicer dual-tracked), it must respond prior to the date of a foreclosure sale or within 30 business days after it got your notice (whichever is earlier).
- For all other types of errors, it must respond not later than 30 business days after it gets your notice of error.

The 30-day period may be extended for an additional 15 days if, within that 30-day period, the servicer notifies you of the extension and the reasons for the delay in responding. The servicer can't get the extension if the notice of error pertains to a payoff statement request or certain errors pertaining to loss mitigation and foreclosure.

When the Servicer Does Not Have to Comply

If your servicer determines that it does not have to comply with your error resolution or information request for some reason (for example, the notice of error or request for information is essentially the same as one you previously sent or your request is overbroad), it must notify you no later than five business days after making that determination and give you its reason for the determination.

What Happens to Credit Reporting and a Pending Foreclosure During Your Request?

While this process is going on, the servicer cannot report to a credit reporting agency that a payment is overdue if it relates to your notice of error. If you send a request for information, however, it can continue to report overdue payments.

In most situations, if you request information or send a notice of error after a foreclosure has begun, the servicer can continue with foreclosure proceedings. It must stop the foreclosure, however, if your notice of error is based on the 120-day preforeclosure waiting period or dual-tracking restrictions. In those situations, the issue must be resolved before the servicer can continue with the foreclosure, unless the servicer receives the notice of error seven or fewer days before the foreclosure sale. If that's the case, the servicer only has to make a good faith attempt to respond to your notice of error, orally or in writing, and either correct the error or state the reason it determined that no error occurred.

Remedies If the Servicer Doesn't Follow the Rules

If the servicer fails to comply with the act, you can sue for statutory damages of $2,000 (this amount was increased from $1,000 by the Dodd-Frank Act), reimbursement for your attorneys' fees, and compensation for your other losses.

The Independent Foreclosure Review

In response to the foreclosure crisis of the late 2000s when loan servicing errors were common and egregious, the government required certain mortgage servicers to hire independent consultants to review foreclosures that were initiated, pending, or completed during 2009 or 2010. This was called the "Independent Foreclosure Review."

However, the reviews took considerably longer and were much more costly than expected. Eventually most mortgage servicers reached an agreement to end the process. (The settling servicers were Aurora, Bank of America, Citibank, EverBank, GMAC, Goldman Sachs, HSBC, JPMorgan Chase, Morgan Stanley, MetLife Bank, PNC, Sovereign, SunTrust, U.S. Bank, and Wells Fargo and their affiliates.) As part of the settlement, these servicers agreed to pay roughly $3.9 billion in cash compensation to borrowers whose primary residence was in foreclosure at any time between January 1, 2009 and December 31, 2010 with one of the participating servicers. Payments ranged from $300 to $125,000 for eligible borrowers.

As of December 31, 2016, the checks distributed as a result of the settlement have expired. If you didn't cash your check, the funds might have been transferred to your state's unclaimed property division or remitted to the general fund of the U.S. Treasury. Go to independentforeclosurereview. com for more information. If you have additional questions, you can call the Paying Agent at 888-952-9105. If your mortgage loan was with EverBank or EverHome, you should call Epiq Systems at 877-819-9754.

Financial Freedom and OneWest/IndyMac Mortgage Services didn't participate in the settlement but completed the review process and have sent payments to all eligible borrowers. If you have uncashed funds from that review, the money will escheat (revert) to your last known state of residence. For further information about a state payment, you can call OneWest Bank at 800-500-6097.

You can also go to https://independentforeclosurereview.com for more information on the settlement.

RESOURCE

Sample request for information and notice of error. You can find samples of these letters on the CFPB's website at www.consumerfinance.gov. For the request for information letter, search for "How do I request information from my mortgage servicer about my mortgage loan?" and then click on the "sample letter" link. For the sample notice of error letter, search for "How do I dispute an error with my servicer about my mortgage?" and again click on the "sample letter" link.

The Lender Engaged in Unfair Lending Practices

You may be able to fight your foreclosure by proving one or more violations of federal or state laws designed to protect you against illegal lending practices.

Two federal laws protect against unfair lending practices associated with residential mortgages and loans: the Truth in Lending Act (TILA) and the Home Ownership and Equity Protection Act (HOEPA). (Technically, HOEPA is part of TILA.) Both allow you to sue for money damages, including a refund of any financing costs you paid. Both of them also let you cancel your mortgage under some circumstances. Canceling the mortgage would usually work to defeat the foreclosure, if you could arrange for a refinance to return the remaining loan principal to the lender.

As powerful as these statutes may sound, most lenders are aware of them and either comply with their requirements or structure their loans so that they don't apply. Still, your case may be the exception.

The Right to Rescind the Loan

For the purpose of fighting a foreclosure, the most important provision of these laws is that you may, for some types of loans and some types of violations, be able to retroactively cancel or rescind your loan. This is referred to as the right to an extended rescission.

Both laws require a lender to give you a three-day rescission period when you take out the loan. But your right to rescind is extended for three years if it later comes to light that the lender violated an important part of the law. TILA also permits recission by way of recoupment even after the three-year period expires, if state law allows it. (Recoupment is a defense to a collection action, like a foreclosure.) So, if one or both of these laws cover the mortgage being foreclosed on, and you can show a material violation of these laws, you can cancel the loan and by doing that defeat the foreclosure. But those are a couple of big "ifs." Let's take them one at a time.

What Loans Are Covered

Under TILA the right to extended rescission applies only if you did *not* use the mortgage loan to buy or build your primary residence. So a first mortgage, which you used to buy your house, is not covered. But a home equity loan, equity line of credit, or refinancing loan would be covered. (The law is aimed at predatory lenders who use loans to skim the equity from borrowers' homes, particularly those of older, minority, and low-income homeowners.)

But lenders of second or third mortgages rarely foreclose—so the right to rescind is unlikely to help you with foreclosure. It might, however, help you if you refinanced your first mortgage and the holder of the new mortgage is foreclosing.

HOEPA initially applied only to high-cost loans that were closed-end consumer credit (that is, loans repayable under specific terms over a specified term). Beginning on January 10, 2014, pursuant to the Dodd-Frank Act, the coverage of HOEPA expanded. Under rules promulgated by the Consumer Financial Protection Bureau, most types of mortgage loans secured by a consumer's principal dwelling, including purchase-money mortgages, refinances, closed-end home equity loans, and open-end credit plans (home equity lines of credit or HELOCs) are now potentially subject to HOEPA coverage. However, significantly, HOEPA's right to rescind does not apply to mortgages taken out to purchase a home or a refinancing of that mortgage loan by the same creditor if no new money is advanced.

HOEPA imposes additional requirements on high-cost mortgage loans, which means those made at high rates or excessive costs and fees. A mortgage loan is considered high-cost if the borrower's principal dwelling secures the loan and one of the following is true:

- The loan's annual percentage rate (APR) exceeds a certain threshold.
- The amount of points and fees paid in connection with the transaction exceed a certain threshold.
- The prepayment penalties the lender charges under the loan or credit agreement exceed a certain amount (or can be charged after a certain time period).

The APR Test

A loan is considered a high-cost mortgage if its APR on the date the interest rate is set exceeds the Average Prime Offer Rate (an annual percentage rate that is derived from average interest rates, points, and other loan pricing terms) for a comparable transaction on that date by more than:

- 6.5 percentage points for first-mortgage loans, generally
- 8.5 percentage points for first-mortgage loans, if less than $50,000 and secured by personal property (such as an RV, a boat, or a manufactured home that is considered personal property), or
- 8.5 percentage points for subordinate loans (second or third mortgages, HELOCs, etc.).

The Points and Fees Test

A mortgage is also considered to be a high-cost mortgage if its points and fees exceed:

- 5% of the total loan amount (if the loan is equal to or more than $20,579 as of January 1, 2017), or
- 8% of the total loan amount or $1,029 as of January 1, 2017, whichever is less, (if the loan is less than $20,579). (These figures are adjusted annually.)

The Prepayment Penalty Test

A loan is a high-cost mortgage if there is a prepayment penalty:

- more than 36 months after the loan is taken out, or
- in an amount that exceeds 2% of the amount prepaid.

(If the loan is indeed a high-cost mortgage, a prepayment penalty is not allowed.)

What Is a Material Violation of TILA and HOEPA

To be able to rescind your loan, you must also show that the lender materially violated the law—in plain English, that it violated a significant provision of the law.

Material violations of TILA. Lenders violate this law when they don't make the disclosures it requires, for example the notice of your right to cancel, as well as the annual percentage rate, the finance charge, the amount financed, the total payments, the payment schedule, and more. Typically, these terms are found in a document called a truth in lending disclosure statement. The numbers on these disclosure statements must be accurate to within very narrow tolerances. Depending on the type of loan, the disclosed annual percentage rate (APR) must be within one-eighth of one percentage point of the actual APR. The total finance charge cannot be understated by more than $100 in most cases and by not more than $35 if the creditor has started foreclosure proceedings.

Material violations of HOEPA. The violations must be something that deprived you of the benefits of HOEPA. A lender that makes a HOEPA loan must comply with various notice provisions. The lender is also subject to restrictions on fees and practices. For example, late fees are limited to 4% of the past-due payment and balloon payments are generally prohibited except under limited circumstances. Ultimately, a violation of HOEPA's disclosure requirements or the inclusion of a prohibited term triggers an extended right to rescind the loan.

Who Can Be Held Responsible for TILA and HOEPA Violations

TILA and HOEPA apply not only to the original lender or mortgage originator, but also to any person or entity who became an owner through an assignment. In other words, downstream mortgage holders are held accountable for the sins of the original lenders. Downstream mortgage holders can escape liability only if they can demonstrate that a reasonable person exercising ordinary due diligence could not have determined that the loan was covered by HOEPA.

How to Rescind a Loan

To rescind a loan, you must give the creditor (not the mortgage servicer) a written notice of rescission. In 2015, the U.S. Supreme Court ruled that in order to comply with the three-year deadline to rescind, the borrower only needs to send a rescission notice; the borrower does not need to file suit within the three-year period. (See *Jesinoski, et ux. v. Countrywide Home Loans, Inc.*, 135 S.Ct. 790 (2015).)

If the rescission is successful, the lender must return everything you paid except for payments of loan principal, and you must return the portion of the loan principal that has not yet been repaid. In other words, when you rescind a loan, you can get out from under the loan (and the foreclosure), but you can't keep the loan proceeds. You'll need to refinance, sell the home, or find another source of funding to repay the principal.

RESOURCE

More information on TILA and HOEPA. Any attorney you hire to fight your foreclosure should be intimately familiar with TILA and HOEPA and know how those laws may help you in fighting your foreclosure. If you are representing yourself, consider buying a copy of *Foreclosures and Mortgage Servicing*, published by the National Consumer Law Center (www.nclc.org).

You Have a High-Cost Mortgage

A number of states have special protections for people facing foreclosure on high-cost mortgages. (For specifics, see Ch. 2.)

If your state has a high-cost mortgage statute, and the lender has violated any of its provisions, you might be able to raise that violation as a defense in your foreclosure case. If your state has a high-cost mortgage statute, there's a brief summary on your state's page in the appendix, including any provisions that might help you fight your foreclosure.

When You Can Sue for Money

A number of state and federal laws also give you the right to sue violators for compensation for your monetary losses. But the violations don't mean you can stop the foreclosure itself. The reason? Mortgages have become investment vehicles, and for the system to work, investors must be able to rely on the legitimacy of their investments. If all bad behavior by a mortgage broker, servicer, or lender could retroactively be used to devalue an investment, investors would never invest.

For instance, say that a mortgage broker recklessly encouraged you to sign up for a mortgage you couldn't afford, telling you that you could refinance in a year or two and make the mortgage more affordable then.

You might think that a court would make things right by denying the foreclosure and ordering the lender to rewrite your loan to make it affordable. Unfortunately, this sort of relief is usually not available. However, if you can cast doubt on the legality of your mortgage or the foreclosure proceedings, you may have the leverage against your lender you need to get a modification. (See "The Lender Didn't Follow State Foreclosure Procedures or Mortgage Terms Governing Foreclosures" and "The Foreclosing Party Can't Prove It Has the Right to Foreclose," above.)

The legal doctrine of "promissory estoppel" is another tool borrowers sometimes use to seek monetary damages from banks that broke their promises to homeowners. Under promissory estoppel, someone who makes a promise is prevented (estopped) from reneging on that promise if the person to whom the promise was made reasonably relied on the promise by taking some action (or failing to take action) and suffered monetary damages as a result.

In one class action lawsuit, the named plaintiff claimed that her lender promised her a permanent mortgage modification if she completed a trial period during which she made modified payments to the bank. The plaintiff made the payments required during the trial period, but the bank refused to give her the permanent modification as promised. The homeowner complained that she had reasonably relied on the bank's promise, made the payments, and suffered money damages (the amount of the modified payments, which she would not have made without the bank's promise of a permanent modification) when the bank reneged on its promise.

The case was ultimately settled. The bank involved in the suit agreed to provide the borrowers with:

- an opportunity to reapply for a new loan modification
- paid counseling assistance from qualified, independent, non-profit organizations
- foreclosure stays, in most circumstances, to prevent foreclosure while they applied for a modification, and
- waiver of certain fees and costs if the loan was modified.

This does not mean, of course, that your lender will easily settle if you sue it based on a promissory estoppel theory or that the court in your case will allow you to proceed with a claim of promissory estoppel. While foreclosing lenders are increasingly being held accountable for their actions, this type of dispute is very fact sensitive, especially when it comes to whether you reasonably relied on the lender's promise to your detriment. If you think you may have a claim of promissory estoppel against your lender or mortgage servicer, you should speak with an attorney.

How to Fight a Foreclosure

How hard it is to fight a foreclosure depends to a great extent on where you live. If your state requires the foreclosing party to sue you (this is called judicial foreclosure), then it's easier (and less expensive) to jump into the existing lawsuit. If, in your state, foreclosures proceed without court supervision (nonjudicial foreclosure), then you'll have to bring your own lawsuit—a more worky and costly process. (To see which procedure is followed in your state, check the list in Ch. 2 or your state's page in the appendix.)

If You're in a Judicial Foreclosure State

In these states, the foreclosing party must bring a lawsuit to get the foreclosure started. You will be notified of the foreclosure lawsuit when papers called a summons and complaint are delivered to (served on) you. The papers will advise you of the lawsuit and give you a period of time within which you must respond if you choose to contest it.

And, significantly, the foreclosing party will have the burden of proving to the judge that the foreclosure is justified under the terms of the mortgage.

Whether or not you respond is up to you. Either way, the mortgage holder will be required to prove that the foreclosure is legal (although if you don't respond, the chances are excellent that the foreclosure will go through). The proof will typically consist of a thick bundle of documents purportedly containing various papers that you signed when obtaining or refinancing your mortgage. There will also be notices, signed agreements, internal accountings of payments both made and missed, and written statements under oath (called declarations or, if sworn before a notary public, affidavits) from lender and mortgage servicer officials who claim to have knowledge of:

- your missed payments
- the lender's compliance with your state's laws regarding foreclosure procedures, and
- the circumstances through which your lender came to own the mortgage.

As a general rule, if you don't point out errors or omissions in the paperwork, the court will accept the papers as evidence that will support a foreclosure judgment and order for sale.

If you do respond, you will have the opportunity to tell a judge why you think the papers are wrong and that foreclosure is not warranted. To contest the foreclosure, you can file a very simple form, called an "answer" in most places. In it, you state your factual and legal arguments for opposing the foreclosure.

If you have evidence of your own regarding these issues, you also can file your own sworn statements. For example, if the lender claims that you missed five payments, but you can prove (typically with canceled checks) that you missed only one, you would submit a statement under oath to that effect and attach your canceled checks.

After you file your answer with the court, the foreclosing party may file a motion of summary judgment, which you must respond to, and the court will hold a hearing on the matter. The court will grant judgment in favor of the foreclosing party if there is no dispute as to the important facts of the case. However, if the court denies summary judgment, the case will proceed toward a trial.

Before the trial, discovery will take place. This is the process by which you and the foreclosing party ask each other for facts, documents, and other information prior to the trial. In a foreclosure, each side may ask the other to provide certain information (through a demand for production of documents, interrogatories, and depositions) that may help prove or disprove the right to foreclose.

At the trial, the foreclosing party must prove it has the right to foreclose. Then you must prove that the foreclosing party should not be permitted to foreclose. You will both present your cases, sometimes through witnesses who can be questioned by the judge and cross-examined by the other side. For example, if there is a conflict over missed payments, both you and an official from the mortgage servicer would testify, and the judge would decide which of you is most likely telling the truth.

At the end of the trial, the judge will either:
- order the foreclosure to go ahead (and in many states, set the sale date), or
- dismiss the case, sending the lender back to the drawing board.

In Vermont or Connecticut, a judge who approves the foreclosure can order ownership (title) to be transferred then and there.

If You Are in a Nonjudicial Foreclosure State

Because nonjudicial foreclosures proceed outside of court, you'll have to file a lawsuit to get a judge's attention. And you'll have the burden of proof because you want the judge to stop a proceeding—the foreclosure—that is already authorized by the mortgage.

You'll most likely need to hire an attorney to succeed in your lawsuit, although Nolo's *Represent Yourself in Court* will provide helpful guidance if you choose to do this yourself. Unfortunately, litigation in which an attorney's services are used is always expensive when you have the burden of proof. So unless the lawyer thinks you have a very good case, you may not want to bother with a lawsuit. If the only basis for your challenge is that the foreclosing party made a technical procedural violation, you'll probably gain only a few weeks of delay even if you win.

To get your day in court to challenge a nonjudicial foreclosure, you must file an affirmative lawsuit against the lender and the foreclosing agent (typically, the trustee or the mortgage servicer). In the lawsuit, you ask the court to enjoin (stop) the foreclosure proceedings until a judge can hear your reasons as to why the foreclosure shouldn't proceed.

In this kind of lawsuit, you typically ask the court for three things, in this order:
- a temporary restraining order
- a preliminary injunction, and
- a permanent injunction.

Your application for a temporary restraining order (TRO) must convince the judge that you will suffer "irreparable injury" if the judge doesn't stop the foreclosure immediately. Because you will lose your home if the foreclosure is allowed to proceed, most courts accept that a foreclosure causes irreparable injury.

Were the Affidavits in Your Foreclosure Case Robo-Signed?

In a judicial foreclosure, the lender must prove that it owns the mortgage and that the borrower defaulted on that mortgage. Typically, the lender proves these two things by submitting documents and a written statement signed under oath (called an affidavit) by a person who has reviewed the documents and who has some personal basis for believing the facts in those documents to be true. The idea is to prevent foreclosures on homes where the foreclosing bank cannot prove that it owns the mortgage or where the homeowner is not in default to the degree asserted in the foreclosure papers.

In 2010, it came to light that several large banks routinely used affidavits signed by employees who signed thousands of affidavits a month, spending about 30 seconds on each affidavit, and who didn't have a clue regarding the veracity of the affidavit or the documents in question—hence the name "robo-signers."

A foreclosure is invalid if a supporting affidavit is false—and any affidavit completed by a robo-signer is false by definition. Since the issue of robo-signing came to light, however, several things have happened to significantly reduce new instances of robo-signing (although this is not to say that it never occurs).

- Many banks imposed moratoriums on foreclosures while they reviewed hundreds of thousands of cases and then adjusted their procedures to fix the problem.
- Some states passed laws imposing penalties for robo-signing.
- One of the biggest robo-signing offenders, Lender Processing Services, agreed to a $127 million multistate settlement that requires it to review and correct foreclosure documents from 2008 to 2010 and reform its practices.

The good news is that in judicial states, judges now take a much closer look at the affidavits and underlying paperwork and will refuse to sign off on a foreclosure if the documents are suspicious (though the foreclosure will probably continue once the paperwork is in order). In nonjudicial foreclosure states, a homeowner can bring a lawsuit to stop a foreclosure if false affidavits were recorded as part of the foreclosure process.

TROs are typically granted without a formal notice or hearing, which means the foreclosing party may have only a day or two of notice in which to prepare a response. If no response is filed, the judge may well grant the TRO, but require you to post a bond to protect the foreclosing party from economic harm in case you lose the case down the line. A bond can be costly, assuming you can get one at all. You might be able to get the bond requirement waived if your income is low enough.

Getting the Bond Requirement Waived

The court may grant a waiver if any of the following is true:
- The delay required by the lawsuit will not cause unreasonable harm to the lender.
- The validity of your mortgage is in question.
- The lender's interest in pushing ahead with the foreclosure can be protected by some other method, such as by requiring you to make reasonable monthly payments during the course of the lawsuit.

Whether or not you'll be able to get the bond requirement waived depends largely on if the court believes your claims have any merit.

The TRO will typically last until the date set for a hearing on whether the court should issue a preliminary injunction—which would stop the foreclosure pending a full trial on the matter. A hearing on the preliminary injunction is typically held between ten days and two weeks after the TRO is issued.

At the preliminary injunction hearing, the court will review each party's paperwork—essentially the same paperwork submitted in a judicial foreclosure hearing, described earlier. At this hearing, the court must decide whether:
- you are likely to prevail if the case proceeds to trial, and
- the injury that you would suffer from the foreclosure outweighs the injury that the foreclosing party is suffering by not getting paid (called balancing the equities).

If the judge decides these issues in favor of the foreclosing party, the TRO will end, and your motion for a preliminary injunction will be denied. While you are technically allowed to continue with your lawsuit, the foreclosure will likely proceed in the absence of a preliminary injunction. Your only remedy at this point (and it's a considerable long shot) would be to ask a higher court for an order (called a "writ") overruling the lower court's denial of the preliminary injunction.

But if the judge decides these issues in your favor, then the judge will issue a preliminary injunction. The preliminary injunction may order the foreclosing party to take corrective action—for example, by issuing a new pay-off statement and giving you a chance to reinstate the mortgage. Or it may simply keep the TRO in effect.

Because it often takes a year or two to bring a case to trial on a permanent injunction, getting a preliminary injunction is pretty much equivalent to a victory for you. Typically, the foreclosing party will either attempt to reach a settlement with you, drop the current foreclosure and begin from scratch, or meet any conditions laid down by the court and then go back into court to ask that the injunction be lifted.

The burden is on you to prove that the foreclosing party didn't comply with state laws or the terms of the mortgage. You meet this burden with the documents you file—typically, declarations or affidavits from you and various witnesses that establish the facts you believe entitle you to stop the foreclosure. For example, if you contest the accuracy or legality of the fees the foreclosing party required you to pay to reinstate the mortgage, you would attach a sworn statement to your application for a TRO or preliminary injunction, setting out the facts as you know them.

If the foreclosing party produces documents that contradict yours, then you will need to convince the judge at the preliminary injunction stage that you deserve to have the foreclosure put on hold until you can produce your full case at trial. Because most preliminary injunction hearings don't involve live witnesses, your paperwork may have to carry the day.

Due Process Suffers in Nonjudicial Foreclosures

When attempting to foreclose on your house, the lender must comply not just with your state's laws and the terms of your deed of trust. It must also comply with the due process requirements of the United States Constitution.

In the foreclosure context, this means:

- You must receive adequate notice of the proceedings that may cause you to lose your house.
- You must have an opportunity to question the legality of the foreclosure proceedings before a neutral magistrate.

By agreeing to a nonjudicial foreclosure (as a practical matter, you have no choice) when you get a loan, you give up a fundamental due process right: the right to an evaluation of the foreclosure's legality by a neutral magistrate before a foreclosure sale. To challenge a nonjudicial foreclosure in court, you almost certainly will need a lawyer. Because people facing foreclosure are almost always strapped for cash, lawyers are often unaffordable. For that reason, for many people, the ability to file an action in court challenging a foreclosure is only theoretical.

If You Decide to Leave Your House

Once it appears that foreclosure is inevitable, many people pack up their belongings and their families and immediately look for a new place to live. They fear losing reliable shelter and want to find another home as soon as possible where they will feel secure. Staying in a house facing foreclosure can be terrifying if you think you might end up out on the street. And it may be unbearably depressing if you are reminded every day that you won't be living there indefinitely.

While these reactions to foreclosure certainly are understandable, foreclosure can actually be a time of opportunity. You will almost certainly have enough time to find a new place to live. Meanwhile, it may prove to be a big financial advantage to stay put for a while—maybe a long while.

Giving Up the House: Your Options

- **Sell your home.** If you have equity in your home (the house is worth more than you owe), you may be able to sell it quickly by pricing it aggressively, which means low, and then pay off the mortgage. You may even be able to leave with some money in your pocket.
- **Let foreclosure work for you:** Stay in the house as long as possible without making any payments, to save money for a future move.
- **Short sale:** If you're underwater (you owe more than the home is worth), offer the house for sale and persuade the lender to accept the offer and let you off the hook for the mortgage.
- **Deed in lieu of foreclosure:** Persuade the lender to let you sign over the deed in exchange for cancellation of foreclosure.
- **Walk away:** Move out when it suits you and let the foreclosure proceed. Works best when your lender can't sue you for a deficiency. (Though if you do this, you might become the victim of a zombie foreclosure. See Ch. 9 for more on this subject.)
- **Work out a mortgage modification:** Apply for a modification, even if you think your efforts will ultimately prove unfruitful, to avoid being labeled a "strategic defaulter" when you apply for a mortgage in the future and gain some extra time to live in the home.
- **File for Chapter 7 or Chapter 13 bankruptcy:** Eliminate any deficiencies or taxes you owe as a result of the foreclosure or other remedies.

So try to put fear and negativity aside as you assess your options to come up with the best choice for your circumstances. This chapter lays out the basic approaches to giving up your house and the advantages and disadvantages of each.

Let the Foreclosure Proceed

If you don't fight the foreclosure or take any of the other steps discussed in this book, the foreclosure will move forward on a schedule dictated by your lender's workloads and policies, and the laws of your state. Specific information for your state is in the appendix.

The single most important point to understand is that *you don't have to leave your house just because the lender has started foreclosure proceedings.* In most states, you'll probably be able to stay long enough to plan for the future by saving all or some of the money that you're no longer putting toward the mortgage.

> **EXAMPLE:** Joshua and Ellen got in over their heads and now can't afford the $3,000 monthly payment on their mortgage. They decide to let the house go. They already know that federal mortgage servicing regulations require the lender to wait 120 days after they quit making payments before officially starting the foreclosure. They then turn to their state's page in the appendix to see how much more time they have. They learn that:
>
> - They will receive what's called a notice of default in their state. This notice gives them an additional three months to make things right. If they don't (and remember, they plan to let the house go), they will have another 20 days' notice before the house is sold.
> - They can file for Chapter 7 bankruptcy and delay the sale by three additional months. Bankruptcy will also let them leave without owing the lender anything. (They otherwise could face a deficiency judgment in their situation.)
> - After the foreclosure sale, they'll probably be able to stay in the house for a month or two.

Altogether, they will have at least a year of living in the house without making payments, and if they can save at least $2,000 a month, they will have roughly $25,000 in the bank when they set out to seek new shelter. (See Ch. 9 for more details on how this all works.)

Foreclosure Moratoriums

During the mortgage crisis, foreclosure moratoriums (temporary suspensions) were commonplace as lenders and servicers struggled to respond to emerging scandals (such as the robo-signing debacle) and the latest changes in the law (like the federal mortgage servicing rules). Now, however, moratoriums occur much more infrequently. That is not to say they won't occur. Natural disasters, new state laws, and further federal regulations could lead to additional foreclosure moratoriums in the future.

Also, if you're unlucky enough to have your foreclosure fall around the holidays, lenders sometimes impose moratoriums on evictions following foreclosures at Christmastime. In the past, most major lenders also tended to hold off on conducting foreclosure sales during this time, but that's no longer the case.

How much time you'll get to remain in your house and how much money you can save, depend on these factors:

- how soon in the whole process you decide to stop making payments
- if you apply for a loan modification, how long the process takes before your servicer issues a denial and proceeds with foreclosure (probably about 30 days, longer if you're entitled to an appeal period)
- whether judicial or nonjudicial foreclosure is used in your state (judicial foreclosures usually take longer than nonjudicial ones)
- whether any foreclosure moratoriums are in effect (see above)
- how much notice your state's law gives you to leave the house after the foreclosure sale (typically, 15 to 30 days)

- whether part of your strategy involves filing for bankruptcy before the foreclosure sale, which provides an additional two to three months' delay, and
- if you file for bankruptcy, how much money you can keep under your state's exemption laws—it varies from nothing to $50,000.

All of these variables are discussed in detail in Ch. 9, and your state's page in the appendix will give you an estimate of how long you can remain in your home.

Walking Away From Your House

What about just walking away from your house? If you do, sooner or later the lender will foreclose on the property and sell it. You may think this won't concern you; you'll be gone, onto the next phase of your life. In fact, this may or may not be true, depending on your potential tax liability and potential liability for the unpaid part of the mortgage. Some people might be better off, emotionally, by shutting their old house out of their mind and finding new shelter in some faraway location. But for most people, this option makes the least sense.

If you want to use the foreclosure to your best advantage, you should at least consider remaining in the home for as long as possible—payment free—and consider filing for bankruptcy to rid yourself from any liabilities arising from your former home ownership. And if tax liability is an issue, you should do your best to file for bankruptcy before the foreclosure sale or be prepared to prove that you were insolvent at the time of the foreclosure sale.

Be Community Minded

The longer you stay in your home throughout the foreclosure process, the better off your lender, the ultimate purchaser, and your neighborhood will be. You've undoubtedly read articles about neighborhoods full of vacant homes, which are plagued by theft and vandalism. It's become a very serious problem.

If the owners of those homes stayed put and continued to maintain them, everyone's home values would likely be a lot higher. If you are the first one (or even the second or third) on your block to go through foreclosure, you single-handedly can be responsible for propping up the value of surrounding properties. The point is that you are earning your keep by remaining on the property until a new owner is ready to assume occupancy.

Be Wary of Leaving the Home Before the Foreclosure Sale

If you decide to leave your home before the foreclosure sale takes place, you could end up in a zombie foreclosure. With a "zombie foreclosure" (sometimes called "zombie title"), the homeowner moves out after foreclosure has been started, but then the foreclosure is canceled, the sale is never held, or title is never officially transferred to a new owner. As a result, certain debts continue to accrue in the owner's name and will follow him or her like the walking dead.

Zombie foreclosure numbers tend to be high in states where the foreclosure process takes a long time, such as in judicial foreclosure states like Florida, New York, and New Jersey. Homeowners who are eager to move on with their lives sometimes abandon their homes when the foreclosure process drags on. Zombie foreclosures also often occur in low-income areas where the lender is not anxious to assume responsibility for the upkeep of the property and wants to save on taxes, as well as other costs. If squatters occupy the property or it falls into severe disrepair, the bank may simply wash its hands of the property. Or there may be other reasons that the lender simply doesn't follow through with the foreclosure, such as it already has too much inventory or the costs of foreclosing do not justify completing the foreclosure.

Since title is never transferred out of the homeowner's name, he or she remains liable for any property taxes, HOA dues, and maintenance on the property. Debts associated with these responsibilities can go unpaid for years and then come back to haunt homeowners who have no idea that the foreclosure process was never completed. (In some cases, the bank may not be legally required to inform the homeowner that the foreclosure has stopped or it may not be able to locate a homeowner who has moved out.)

For example, if you leave your property and title is never transferred out of your name, the following things, among others, could happen months or even years later:

- The tax collector may come looking to collect back property taxes.
- An HOA may file a lawsuit to recover unpaid assessments.
- You could be threatened with fines for not complying with housing codes and ordinances.
- The local government may send you a bill for yard maintenance, repairs, trash removal, and/or graffiti scrubbing.

Plus, your credit score will be even more damaged due to the unpaid debt.

This provides yet another reason for you to remain in your home for as long as possible. You will be much more likely to avoid becoming the victim of a zombie foreclosure if you stay through the entire foreclosure process and wait for an official notice to vacate before moving out.

If you do choose to move out early, you should confirm that the lender completes the foreclosure sale and transfers title out of your name. To do this, you can review the land records at the county recorder's office (in person or, in some cases, online) to make sure a new deed has been recorded. If the home remains in your name, you should be aware that you're still on the hook for expenses related to the home, such as property taxes and HOA dues.

Sell the House in a Short Sale

In a short sale, you sell your house before it's auctioned off in foreclosure for an amount that falls short of what you owe on it. For a short sale to work, your lenders must agree to receive less than they are entitled to under the terms of the loans you signed. Why would they do that? They aren't in the business of owning homes, and generally do a poor job of it. Also, foreclosures are expensive for lenders, who might not get all they're owed anyway.

Zombie Homes in Wisconsin

The Wisconsin Supreme Court decided in 2015 that lenders couldn't let "zombie" homes linger in the foreclosure process indefinitely. In the case of *Bank of New York Mellon v. Carson*, 2015 Wisc. 15 (Feb. 17, 2015), the bank obtained a foreclosure judgment, but never held a foreclosure sale. The homeowner had moved out of the home around the time the foreclosure started and was subsequently fined for building code violations after the home fell into disrepair. The homeowner then sued the bank to force it to finish the foreclosure by selling her home at a foreclosure sale.

The Court of Appeals ultimately sided with the homeowner and decided that the bank must proceed to a sale if it obtains a judgment of foreclosure on an abandoned (empty) home. (Previously, a bank could let an abandoned home linger indefinitely in the foreclosure process.) The Wisconsin Supreme Court subsequently upheld this decision and ruled that the sale must take place within a reasonable amount of time. For awhile this meant that a lender couldn't simply walk away from a vacant Wisconsin property in foreclosure, leaving the homeowner with the problem of a zombie home. However, the Wisconsin legislature responded in 2016 by passing a law that states a lender foreclosing on an abandoned home must do one of the following things within 12 months after the court enters a foreclosure judgment: hold a foreclosure sale, or release the mortgage lien and vacate (cancel) the judgment of foreclosure. Therefore, instead of finishing the foreclosure, the lender can cancel the proceedings and walk away from the property, leaving you to face the problem of a zombie home.

Advantages of a Short Sale

The main benefit of a short sale is that you may get out from under your mortgage without liability for the amount of the loan that is left unpaid. You also won't have a foreclosure or a bankruptcy on your credit record. The general thinking is that your credit won't suffer as much as it would were you to let the foreclosure proceed or file for bankruptcy to get out from under any liability you might incur in the course of the foreclosure.

Your credit rating will take a hit regardless of which option you choose—short sale, foreclosure, or bankruptcy.

RESOURCE
For more information on how these options will affect your credit, see Ch. 1 or get *Credit Repair* by Robin Leonard, updated by Amy Loftsgordon (Nolo).

Disadvantages of a Short Sale

Short sales have some drawbacks when compared to letting the foreclosure happen or filing for bankruptcy.

No Chance to Stay and Save

If you sell your house, you will be expected to leave as soon as escrow closes. But if you let the foreclosure happen and stay in the house until you are formally told to leave by written notice, you can build a nest egg that you can draw on in the future to obtain good rental housing. (Again, see Ch. 9 for more about this strategy.)

It's very difficult to accomplish a short sale if you don't get started as soon as you learn about the pending foreclosure, especially if you have to negotiate with several mortgage holders. Needless to say, if you don't complete the short sale before the foreclosure sale, you'll have nothing to sell.

Potential Deficiency Judgment

The sale price is "short" of the full amount you owe to the lender; the difference between the total debt owed and the sale price is the deficiency. For example, say your lender approves a short sale in the amount of $200,000, but you owe $250,000. The deficiency is $50,000.

In many states, the lender is prohibited from getting a deficiency judgment following a foreclosure. However, most states don't prohibit the lender from getting a deficiency judgment following a short sale.

(California is one of the few states that does specifically prohibit deficiency judgments following short sales.)

If you want to avoid a deficiency judgment following a short sale, you'll have to make sure that the short sale agreement expressly states that the transaction is in full satisfaction of the debt and that the lender waives its right to the deficiency. Or you might be able to negotiate a reduced deficiency.

Potential Tax Liability

A short sale may generate an unwelcome surprise: taxable income based on the amount the sale proceeds are short of what you owe. While in recent years homeowners have been able to exclude forgiven debt related to a short sale (or a foreclosure or deed in lieu of foreclosure) from their income under the Mortgage Forgiveness Debt Relief Act of 2007, you can only do this if you took out the mortgage to buy, build, or substantially improve your home (or to refinance debt incurred for these purposes). On the other hand, if you borrowed against your principal residence and used the money for any other purpose, such as to buy a second house, pay college tuition for a child, or take a vacation, and you end up not paying it back in full, the amount your lender writes off (typically whatever amount wasn't paid back) is considered forgiven debt. Although the concept is not at all intuitive, the IRS treats forgiven debt as taxable income, subject to regular income tax.

> **EXAMPLE:** Joan owes $150,000 on her first mortgage and $50,000 on the second, which she borrowed to pay for her daughter's first year of tuition at an exclusive Eastern college. Joan loses her job and is facing foreclosure. She arranges to sell the house for $140,000 and gets permission from her first lender to pay off the first mortgage for $135,000 and permission from her second mortgage lender to pay off the second mortgage for $5,000.
>
> The $15,000 the first mortgage holder will write off (forgive) is not considered taxable income because Joan used it to acquire the house. But the amount the second mortgage holder will write off, $45,000, is forgiven debt and considered taxable income to Joan because it wasn't used to buy or improve her principal residence.

If you face this situation and can prove to the IRS you were legally insolvent at the time of the short sale, you won't have to pay the tax (see "Income Tax Liability for Deficiencies," below). Insolvency is when your total debts are more than the value of your total equity in your real estate and personal property. You can also get rid of this kind of tax liability by filing for Chapter 7 or Chapter 13 bankruptcy, if you file before escrow closes. Of course, if you are going to file for bankruptcy anyway, there isn't much point in doing the short sale, because any benefit to your credit rating caused by the short sale will be negated by the bankruptcy.

Will You Be Able to Negotiate a Short Sale?

Historically, short sale deals have often fallen apart because of the amount of time required to obtain approval from the lender. At the start of the housing crisis, so many people were requesting short sales that lenders simply were not able to keep up with the volume. Sellers and buyers often got frustrated and chose to give up on the deals before the sales were approved. Since then, many lenders have increased their personnel and streamlined the process to better keep up with increased requests for short sales, often because the law required them to.

Under federal mortgage servicing regulations, you have 120 days after falling delinquent before the servicer can start the foreclosure. You can apply for a short sale during this time. If you don't submit an application during this time and the foreclosure starts, you can still apply. So long as you submit your loss mitigation application more than 37 days before a scheduled foreclosure sale, the servicer can't move for foreclosure judgment or order of sale, or conduct a foreclosure sale, while it evaluates your application. Generally, the servicer must complete its evaluation within 30 days.

After its evaluation, the servicer may give you the opportunity to enter into a listing or marketing period agreement (assuming you don't already have an offer). During the listing or marketing period, the servicer will not pursue the foreclosure. If you don't obtain an approved short sale transaction by the end of the marketing or listing period, the servicer can proceed with the foreclosure. (An "approved short sale transaction" is a short sale transaction that has been approved by all relevant parties, including the servicer, other lienholders, or insurers, if applicable, and the servicer has received proof of funds or financing.)

California Prohibits Dual Tracking of Short Sales and Foreclosures (Sort of)

Federal mortgage servicing regulations prohibit dual tracking, but only if you submit your loss mitigation application more than 37 days before a scheduled foreclosure sale. If you miss the 37-day deadline and want to complete a short sale in California, state law may provide you with some additional protection.

Under California's Homeowner Bill of Rights, your servicer cannot continue with foreclosure proceedings once there is an approved short sale. However, since the protection doesn't kick in until the short sale is approved in writing by all parties, this means that the servicer can initiate a foreclosure or continue with a foreclosure if you are considering a short sale, are negotiating with a buyer, or even have a short sale offer. It's not until the lender, and all other parties such as junior lienholders, actually sign off on the deal that the dual tracking ban kicks in.

Still, California provides more protection than most other states when it comes to dual tracking if you decide to do a short sale less than 37 days before the foreclosure sale. If you hope to complete a short sale in this time frame, you should contact a local real estate agent that has substantial experience in this area to discuss whether a short sale of your home is a realistic goal, and, if it is, to start the process right away.

There are strict timelines for homeowners with Fannie Mae or Freddie Mac mortgages. (To find out if Fannie Mae or Freddie Mac owns your loan, go to www.knowyouroptions.com/loanlookup or https://ww3.freddiemac.com/loanlookup.) Under Fannie Mae and Freddie Mac guidelines, mortgage services are required to:

- acknowledge receipt of a short sale offer within five business days
- notify you within five business days if there is outstanding documentation needed (provided you don't qualify for a streamlined process that doesn't require further documentation), and
- review and respond to a short sale offer within 30 calendar days from receipt of the offer.

Still, sometimes it is difficult to get a short sale processed in time. Short sale negotiations often occur in rushed settings because many homeowners start thinking about short sales only when they are about to lose their houses to foreclosure. And generally you've got to have a bona fide offer from a buyer before you can find out whether or not the lender will go along with it.

The Terms

Short sales are also difficult to come by if there are investors in the picture who might not approve of getting less return on their investment than they were counting on.

A short sale will benefit you only if the lenders are willing to accept the amount a buyer is willing to pay and let you off the hook for the rest. For example, if you owe $300,000 and you can sell your house for just $200,000, you are unlikely to be successful in negotiating a short sale. There's a chance, though—the lender might decide that even a 33% loss on the short sale is better than what could happen in a foreclosure, where houses can sit vacant for months and depreciate in value before being bought by a new owner.

Clearly, the closer the offer is to the principal balance of the loan, the quicker the lender will sign off on the sale. It would be nice if there were a hard and fast line for how much a lender will forgo. Real estate agents and HUD-approved housing counselors should have a pretty good idea of the kind of deals lenders are accepting in your area.

You'll want to work with a real estate professional anyway when you're trying to get your house sold at a price that will be acceptable to all the mortgage lenders. A real estate agent's negotiating help can be critical, because the lender may agree with the proposed offer, or it may make a counteroffer. This may go back and forth until everyone is satisfied or the deal falls through.

EXAMPLE: Toby and Tyler face foreclosure on their first mortgage and decide that a short sale is their best option. They contact a real estate agent, who tells them that they should list their house for at least 85% of their mortgage debt—or $225,000—for the sale to be acceptable to the lender. The 85% figure is based on the agent's knowledge of the going rate for lender acceptance of short sales.

As the foreclosure sale date grows nearer, and the house goes unsold at the 85% figure, Toby and Tyler finally get an offer that would pay 75% of their mortgage; they accept, contingent on approval by the lender. The agent takes the offer to the lender and quickly receives a rejection. The buyer raises his offer to 80%, and the lender agrees.

When a Short Sale Might Make Sense

- You can sell your house for a price that the lender (or lenders) will likely sign off on.
- You don't plan to file for Chapter 7 or Chapter 13 bankruptcy (because if you're hoping a short sale will preserve your credit record, a bankruptcy would undermine that goal).
- All your lenders are willing to let you off the hook for the deficiency (the amount by which the sales price falls short of what you owe).
- You have time before the scheduled foreclosure sale to find a buyer and to explore other options (such as filing for bankruptcy). This can be a problem in states (such as Georgia and Alabama) that don't give you much notice before the sale. (Keep in mind you get 120 days before the foreclosure starts to explore options to avoid foreclosure.)

Convincing Multiple Lienholders

Multiple lenders (or anyone else who has a legal claim, or lien, on your property) can fatally complicate short sales. If you have only one mortgage, you have only one lender to convince. If you have two or more mortgages (or other types of home loans or liens on your property), you must convince all of the lienholders. So the more lienholders there are in your picture, the harder it will be to obtain a short sale.

This is especially true if the property's value has substantially decreased, and a sale will probably produce little or no money for a second or third mortgage holder (typically, the holder of a tax lien, home equity loan, or line of credit). If these other lenders won't get anything out of the short sale, they won't have any incentive to release their liens (legal claims on the property) so that a new buyer can have clear title. And more important to you, they won't absolve you from liability for what you owe them—which defeats a central purpose of the short sale.

> **EXAMPLE 1:** Carlos has a first mortgage on his property of $240,000, a second mortgage of $30,000, and $15,000 out on a home equity line of credit. He can sell the house for only $230,000. All of that money would typically go toward the first mortgage. The second mortgage and line of credit lenders wouldn't get anything. They would rather let the foreclosure go through and sue Carlos for the deficiency than accept a small percentage of what they are owed and agree to not sue him for the balance. Without their agreement, he won't be able to sell the house with clear title, because the property would still be subject to the liens of the other mortgage holders.

> **EXAMPLE 2:** Johnny owes $225,000 on his first mortgage, $50,000 on his second mortgage, and $25,000 on a home equity loan. He falls behind on his mortgage payments and decides to put the house up for sale. Johnny receives an offer of $260,000. This amount will more than please the first mortgage owner, because its $225,000 loan will be paid off in full. The second mortgage owner won't be so happy because it will get only $35,000 of the $50,000 it's owed. But considering the fact that it wouldn't get anything if the house went into foreclosure ("junior" liens are wiped out in foreclosures brought by senior lienholders) and would have to sue Johnny to collect what's due, it agrees to the sale.

Unfortunately, when the home equity lender hears that it won't get anything, it nixes the sale. And without all lienholders agreeing to the sale, it can't happen. So Johnny goes back and asks the second mortgage holder to take $25,000 (half of what it's owed) and offers $10,000 to the home equity lender. The second mortgage holder is even unhappier now, since its share is being reduced, but it still wants the sale to go through, so it agrees. In the end, Johnny manages to negotiate a deal where everyone gets something but not as much as they would like.

Scam Alert

Some companies operate scams aimed at defrauding homeowners who are trying to put together a short sale. Make sure you are dealing with a reputable real estate company and with the company that is servicing the loan (the company to which you have been sending your payments). You should also be getting guidance from a HUD-approved housing counselor (see Ch. 4).

Here is how a scam might work. A business calling itself a mortgage company offers to buy your home in a short sale and pay off the lender. You sign the deed over to it. It convinces you that it will deal with the bank (for one reason or another) and that you should move out because the lender won't participate in a short sale unless you do. Then, instead of paying the lender, it turns around and sells the house to an unsuspecting buyer (or rents it out), pockets the proceeds, and walks away when the bank moves forward with the foreclosure. You are not only out of your house, but you have paid nothing to the bank and are on the hook for the entire mortgage balance.

For more information on foreclosure rescue scams, see Ch. 1 and check this book's companion page (see "Get Legal Updates and More at Nolo.com" in the introductory chapter, "Your Foreclosure Companion"). Scams are like viruses—new ones pop up every day.

Offer the Lender a Deed in Lieu of Foreclosure

If you want to simply hand over ownership of your house to the lender and get your loan canceled in exchange, you can propose something called a deed in lieu of foreclosure. If your lender agrees, it will accept a deed to your property and in exchange, promise to not initiate foreclosure proceedings or to drop them if they've already begun. You don't have to sell the house; the lender will do that for you.

Will the Lender Accept a Deed in Lieu?

Getting a lender to accept a deed in lieu of foreclosure can be a hard sell. The problem is that the lender wants cash, not real estate.

On the other hand, if the bank thinks it's a better deal to take your offer than to incur the expense of foreclosure, it will be a done deal. As with short sales, it will be helpful for you to work with a HUD-approved housing counselor. (See Ch. 4.)

Before the lender will accept a deed in lieu of foreclosure, it might require you to put your home on the market for a period of time (three months is typical). Banks would rather have you sell the house than have to sell it themselves.

You can't use a deed in lieu of foreclosure if you have multiple mortgages or if you have liens on the property such as those arising from delinquent taxes, work on your home, or money judgments. You must be able to deed clear title to the whole property. In other words, you can't do two deeds in lieu of foreclosure and split the property between the first and second mortgage lenders, or other lienholders.

Even if the lender approves a deed in lieu of foreclosure, ideally you'll want to have an agreement (in writing) that the lender won't go after you for any deficiency before you decide to complete the transaction. While it used to be standard practice for lenders to release borrowers from any further liability on the debt after a deed in lieu of foreclosure, now lenders may try to hold you liable for the deficiency—or at least part of it. (In most cases, the deficiency amount will be the difference between the total indebtedness and the fair market value of the property at the time of the deed in lieu of foreclosure.) If your lender insists that you pay all or part of the deficiency, you can try to negotiate a lower amount or arrange to repay the deficit over time.

Fannie Mae and Freddie Mac Deeds in Lieu of Foreclosure

Fannie Mae and Freddie Mac allow certain delinquent and current borrowers to give up their properties with deeds in lieu of foreclosure (sometimes called "mortgage releases").

To qualify, borrowers with Fannie Mae or Freddie Mac loans who are delinquent for 90 days or more must be experiencing and able to document one of the following hardships:

- unemployment
- a reduction in income due to circumstances outside their control (for example, elimination of overtime, fewer regular working hours, etc.)
- an increase in housing expenses due to circumstances outside their control
- a divorce or legal separation, or a separation of borrowers unrelated by marriage, civil union, or similar domestic partnership
- the death of a borrower or the death of either the primary or secondary wage earner in the household
- long-term or permanent disability, or serious illness of a borrower or coborrower or dependent family member
- a disaster (natural or man-made) adversely impacting the property or borrower's place of employment
- distant employment transfer or relocation
- a business failure, or
- another hardship that is not covered above.

Borrowers who are current on their mortgages or less than 90 days delinquent qualify if the borrower's eligible hardship involves:

- the death of a borrower or primary/secondary wage earner in the household
- long-term or permanent disability (or serious illness of a borrower/coborrower or dependent family member), or

- the fact that the borrower's debt obligations were previously discharged in a Chapter 7 bankruptcy.

For borrowers who are current on their mortgages or less than 31 days delinquent, the following additional requirements must be met:

- the mortgaged property is the borrower's principal residence, and
- the total monthly debt-to-income ratio exceeds 55%. (Some service members with Permanent Change of Station or "PCS" orders are exempt from one or more of these requirements.)

For the most part, if a borrower meets the above requirements, any deficiency will be waived. However, in certain circumstances some borrowers may have to make a cash contribution or sign a promissory note. (Some service members with PCS orders are exempt from this.) Fannie Mae and Freddie Mac offer up to $6,000 to second lien holders to expedite the process and, in some cases, borrowers may receive up to $3,000 in relocation assistance.

With Fannie Mae, you may be able to stay in the home rent-free for three months after the mortgage release is complete if you meet certain criteria (for example, the home is your primary residence). Or you may be able to sign a 12-month lease and pay rent at market rate if you meet certain criteria (such as you have a verifiable income).

Avoiding Deficiency Judgments

The laws of most states allow the lender to come after you for a deficiency— that is, the amount by which the foreclosure sale proceeds fall short of the loan amount. However, a few states protect homeowners from liability for deficiencies from mortgages on residential homes that were used to purchase the homes or in other circumstances. (See the appendix for your state's rule.)

You don't need to worry about a deficiency if either of the following applies:

- Your state's law prohibits deficiency lawsuits.
- The lender agrees, as part of accepting a short sale or deed in lieu of foreclosure, not to come after you for any deficiency.

But if your state does allow deficiency lawsuits, or you have a second or third mortgage, you could be on the hook for a lot of money even after you lose your house. You can wipe out that debt by filing for Chapter 7 bankruptcy. (See Ch. 6.)

Some foreclosure advisers will tell you that deficiency lawsuits are rare and not to worry about them. While this was true in the past, it's not the case anymore. Lenders are more likely to pursue deficiency judgments now than they used to be, particularly if you have assets that could be recovered. In any event, it's hard to know whether your lender will seek a deficiency judgment. Even if you may not end up in a lawsuit, do you want to take the chance? Bankruptcy is your ultimate safety net when it comes to any liability arising from your former home ownership.

Income Tax Liability for Deficiencies

If you default on your mortgage, it's likely that you or the lender will eventually sell the property at a foreclosure sale for less than what you owe on it. And it's possible that you might be asked to pay income tax on the difference if the lender doesn't come after you for this amount. The theory is that you are receiving a gift of this amount, because you don't have to pay it back. (The lender is forgiving the debt.)

The IRS learns of the forgiven deficiency when it receives an IRS Form 1099C from the lender. This is a form on which a creditor reports income derived because the creditor cancelled (forgave) your debt after a foreclosure, short sale, or deed in lieu of foreclosure.

Whether or not you'll owe tax depends on the circumstances. Here are the basic rules.

Loans for your principal residence. If your default is on a mortgage or another debt secured by your house, and you used the money you borrowed to buy or improve your house (or to refinance debt you incurred for these purposes), you won't owe tax. (Before federal tax law changed in 2007, you might have had to pay income tax in this situation.) This tax break, which became law through the Mortgage Forgiveness Debt Relief Act, applies to debt forgiven in calendar years

2007 through 2016, though it's quite possible that Congress will extend it. They have done so four times now. For the latest news, check this book's online companion page. (To learn how to access the companion page, see "Get Legal Updates and More at Nolo.com" in the introductory chapter, "Your Foreclosure Companion.")

Loans for other real estate. If you default on a mortgage that's secured by property that isn't your primary residence, you'll owe tax on any forgiven deficiency. So, for example, if you walk away from a loan on your second house in the country, expect a Form 1099 in the mail. The same is true for loans on nonresidential real estate.

Loans not used for real estate. Similarly, if you take out a home equity loan and take that world trip you've been dreaming of instead of using the money to improve your house, you may end up on the wrong side of a tax bill.

> **EXAMPLE:** Harry owes $200,000 on his second home, which is foreclosed on and sold at auction for $150,000. The lender files an IRS Form 1099, reporting the $50,000 difference as taxable income to Harry.

If you do face income tax liability, you have two possible ways of getting out from under it: the insolvency exclusion and bankruptcy. To use the insolvency exclusion, you'll have to prove to the satisfaction of the IRS that your liabilities exceed the value of your assets. Filing for bankruptcy works because debt wiped out (discharged) in bankruptcy is not considered taxable income. You'll have to show the IRS that you filed for bankruptcy before the event that would cause the lender to file a Form 1099C. Of course, you'll want to file for bankruptcy only if it otherwise makes sense. (Bankruptcy is discussed in Chs. 5 and 6.)

TIP
You can fight back if an unpaid loan amount is treated as taxable income. If you receive a Form 1099 attributing income to you from mortgage debt forgiveness, but you think you shouldn't owe the tax, file IRS Form 982, *Reduction of Tax Attributes Due to Discharge of Indebtedness*, with your regular tax return.

How Long Can You Stay in Your House for Free?

A s we've mentioned throughout this book, foreclosure can actually provide a great opportunity to save some serious money. That's because legal procedures—including foreclosures—typically take many months. While the foreclosure proceeding goes on, and then afterwards (during the redemption period, perhaps, or until you're evicted), you probably won't have to move—or make any payments.

For example, if your mortgage payments are $2,000 a month, and you stay in the house for nine months without making a payment, you could save $18,000. Of course, you might not be able to save the entire amount of your mortgage payment, but even if you saved half, you would still have a considerable amount of money in the bank when the time comes to leave.

As long as you remain, you also save the house from nine months of deterioration (and vandalism) it would suffer by being vacant. This does your community a great favor.

How long can you stay in your house payment-free once you decide to give it up? There is no way to give you a precise timeline for your personal situation. Each phase of the process, from your first missed payment to your last day in the house, involves variables unique to your situation. However, the information on your state's page in the appendix will give you an idea of whether you're likely to have several months, a year or more, or something in between.

This chapter explains the elements of that basic timeline in more detail. Once you have a rough idea of what to expect, we highly recommend that you talk to a HUD-approved housing counselor (see Ch. 4) to get a reality check on how fast events are moving in your community. A second opinion can only help.

TIP

Filing for bankruptcy shortly before the sale date can buy you more time. If you file for Chapter 7 bankruptcy after the foreclosure sale has been scheduled, the sale will be delayed for several months while the bankruptcy is pending. If you file for Chapter 13 bankruptcy, you can probably delay the foreclosure sale for at least five or six months, especially if you hire a lawyer to navigate the tricky Chapter 13 shoals. (To find out more, see Chs. 5 and 6.)

When You Stay, Everybody Wins

You might feel a little guilty about staying in your house after you become unable to keep making payments on it or after it's actually auctioned off in foreclosure. But what you might not realize is that by staying, you're doing your neighbors—and probably even the lender or new owner—a favor.

It's well documented that foreclosures tend to cluster in certain communities. And when there are several empty houses in a neighborhood, it's very obvious. Lawns are overgrown with weeds or brown for lack of water; flyers pile up on porches. Maintenance is neglected. The signs of neglect quickly attract vandals, thieves, and transients. Graffiti appears on fences as copper pipe and appliances disappear from the vacant houses.

Some cities, including Cleveland, Baltimore, and Minneapolis, have actually sued lenders to recoup the costs of dealing with the problems caused by abandoned houses. The cities say they have had to pay more to their fire and police departments and have lost property tax revenue. They have also demolished some houses that were past saving and sued for the costs of demolition. Success has varied in these types of cases.

When you stay in the house until you're legally required to leave, you'll help maintain its value—and that of your neighbors' houses. So let go of the guilt and remind yourself that you're doing a good deed.

When You Miss Your First Payment

If you have decided that you'll ultimately have to give up your house because your mortgage payments are no longer affordable (if they ever were), the first step toward benefiting from your foreclosure is to stop making your mortgage payments. Open up a savings account in which to deposit as much as possible of the extra money you now have.

> **TIP**
> **Don't forget about modifications.** Before bailing out on your home, find out whether you qualify for a mortgage payment reduction through a modification. You don't have to be making payments on your mortgage when you first begin the modification process, and whether or not you ultimately plan to leave, there is no harm in seeing what you can get through modification. Even if the modification fails, simply engaging in the process can buy you some time in payment-free shelter. (See Ch. 4 for more information.)

Under federal regulations, your lender can't start formal foreclosure proceedings until you're more than 120 days delinquent. In all but a couple of states (check your state's page in the appendix to see what kind of notice you'll get), you'll know when the lender takes the first step toward foreclosure because you will get a notice in the mail or be served with a copy of the lawsuit. If you get help from a HUD-approved housing counselor and try to work something out with your lender (even though you privately think you'll be giving up your house), you might gain a number of extra months before the lender gives up on you and starts foreclosure proceedings. (See Ch. 4 for information about HUD-approved housing counselors.)

So, from the time you decide to stop making payments until the time you receive notice that foreclosure proceedings have begun, you can live in your home for at least four months (maybe five or six) payment-free. But that's not all. Keep reading.

Before Foreclosure Starts, You'll Likely Get a Breach Letter

Many mortgages and deeds of trust require the lender or servicer to send you a notice (commonly called a breach letter) that your loan is in default before proceeding with foreclosure. (The mortgage's acceleration clause permits the lender to demand that the entire balance of the loan be repaid in the event of a default.)

Typically, the breach letter will provide the following information:
- the reason for the default (for instance, failing to make a payment)
- the action required to cure the default (such as paying the missed payment)
- the date that you must cure the default (usually at least 30 days from the notice date), and
- the consequences of failing to cure the default.

If you don't cure in a timely manner, foreclosure proceedings can begin. In most instances, you'll get this letter during the 120-day pre-foreclosure period.

After You Receive a Formal Notice of Foreclosure

Before your house can be sold, you must get some sort of formal notice required by your state's foreclosure laws. (See Ch. 2.) The kind of notice you will get depends on where you live.

If you're in a nonjudicial foreclosure state, you may get:
- a notice of default (allowing you time to reinstate your mortgage by making up all the back payments) followed by a notice of sale (if you haven't reinstated your mortgage by the deadline)
- a combined notice of default and sale (stating that the property will be sold on a certain date unless you make up the missed payments)
- only one notice—a notice of sale announcing that the property will be sold on a certain date unless you pay off the mortgage, or
- in a couple of states, notice only by publication and posting.

If you're in a judicial foreclosure state, you might get a prefiling notice telling you that foreclosure proceedings will begin within a particular period. You will definitely get a summons and complaint telling you that foreclosure proceedings have been filed in the appropriate court and that you have a certain amount of time to respond.

In almost all judicial foreclosure states, if the judge orders the foreclosure sale, you'll get a notice telling you when and where the sale will take place. In Connecticut and Vermont, however, the judge can transfer title to the property as part of the judgment of foreclosure.

Will Contesting a Nonjudicial Foreclosure in Court Gain Time?

To oppose a foreclosure in a nonjudicial foreclosure state, you have to file a lawsuit. Normally, you would file a petition with the local court requesting an injunction (court order) to block the foreclosure. This might delay the foreclosure by a week or two, or longer if the court believed your argument has merit. You would have the burden of proving that the lender hadn't followed proper procedures or had made some other mistake, and it would be very difficult for you to get very far in this type of lawsuit unless you hire a lawyer. (See Ch. 7 for information on fighting foreclosure in court.)

Nonjudicial Foreclosure States

How much time you have from the first formal notice that foreclosure proceedings have started to the date your property will be sold varies widely from state to state. You can probably count on at least 30 days' notice before the sale. In most states, you'll get a couple of months. Check your state's page in the appendix to find out the precise amount of notice you are entitled to.

Judicial Foreclosure States

If you are in a state where foreclosures go through court (see your state's page in the appendix), typically you will have 20 to 30 days to respond. If you file a response contesting the foreclosure action, it may take several months or even longer before the judge rules on whether to grant the foreclosure. Even if you don't contest the foreclosure action, the sale usually won't take place until at least a month after the judge issues the foreclosure order.

So you'll likely have a minimum of two months from the first notice to the date the court orders the sale to take place. You'll have at least double that amount of time if you decide to oppose the foreclosure in court.

Gaining Time by Contesting a Judicial Foreclosure

One of the great benefits of living in a judicial foreclosure state is that you automatically have an opportunity to contest the request for foreclosure. In a judicial foreclosure, the lender (the party filing the suit) has the burden of filing all the paperwork required to prove its case. All you must do is file a written response to the foreclosure complaint or petition, respond to any motions the lender files, attend any hearings that are scheduled, and voice your objections. Merely filing a written response may achieve a delay of at least several months. The more foreclosures that are occurring in that particular court, the longer it will take.

If you are able to convincingly allege one or more defects in the foreclosure process, you may be able to use these facts as leverage against the lender to negotiate an acceptable modification. In other words, you don't necessarily have to "win" in the court to get what you want.

If you are contesting the foreclosure to try to stay in your house permanently, you almost certainly will want to hire a lawyer because of what's at stake. But if your only goal is to slow the process down so you can stay in your house a little longer and save some money, you likely can accomplish this mission without a lawyer. (Ch. 7 explains in considerable detail how you can challenge the legitimacy of a foreclosure.)

The Redemption Period

A redemption period is a specific amount of time (ranging from several days to a year) given to foreclosed homeowners during which they can buy back the property. During this period, you can "redeem" the property and reclaim the home, generally by paying the successful bidder the amount of the winning bid plus interest and allowable costs or by paying off the total amount of the mortgage debt. In some states, you can continue to live in the home (payment free) during the redemption period. (See your state's page in the appendix to learn about the redemption period after a foreclosure in your state, if there is one.)

After the Sale

After the foreclosure sale, when a new deed has been recorded with a new owner's name on it, you go from homeowner to tenant. A commonly held belief is that you aren't legally a tenant unless you enter into a formal landlord–tenant relationship and agree to pay rent. In fact, with a couple of exceptions, you are considered a tenant (typically termed a "tenant at will" or "tenant by sufferance"). You are entitled to remain in your home until you are evicted using the same court procedures that apply to other tenants—except that you may not get as much notice that you must leave. (Sometimes, the eviction is part of the foreclosure lawsuit.)

The first step toward eviction the new owner must take is to send you a written notice stating that you must move out. (See your state's page in the appendix for the rules on what kind of notice you are entitled to in your state.) How soon you are likely to get such a notice depends on who owns your house after the foreclosure sale: a new buyer or the lender.

If Someone Buys the House

If, at the foreclosure sale, your house is sold to a new owner, that new owner will likely want possession of the property as soon as possible. You may receive a termination notice days or weeks after the auction or sale, just to get the process moving. Exactly when you can expect this termination notice will depend on the new owner's agenda and the experience the new owner has in removing tenants.

If the new owner wants to occupy the house and has experience in evicting tenants, you can expect the notice to come sooner rather than later. If, on the other hand, the new owner is a business that buys and resells foreclosed homes, there might be a significant delay before you get a termination notice, just for bureaucratic reasons. And if the new owner is a novice in buying foreclosed homes and has no experience in evictions, you can expect a delay while the new owner finds a property management firm or lawyer to do the work.

Cash for Keys: Getting Paid to Move Out Voluntarily

Your termination notice may be accompanied by an offer to pay you a lump sum if you leave the property by a certain time and leave it in good condition. Some former homeowners report offers as high as several thousand dollars, which, from the new owner's perspective, is cheap compared to what it would cost the owner if you dug in your heels and made a formal eviction necessary. Also, experience shows that unhappy former homeowners can do a remarkable amount of damage to a house if they think the new owner is being unreasonable.

Not all buyers of foreclosed properties are enlightened enough to make this sort of offer and may be willing to spend hundreds or even thousands of dollars in lawyer fees to get you out. That said, you should always be willing to propose a move-out bonus if the new owner doesn't. And if the new owner does propose one, you shouldn't be shy about negotiating for a higher amount.

If Your Lender Ends Up With the House

If the property is not sold to a new owner at the foreclosure sale (that is, nobody makes an acceptable bid), your lender will end up with title to the property. If this happens, you may have some additional time to remain in your home payment-free. It depends on the following factors.

Selling foreclosed properties can be difficult, especially when prices are falling and home values are uncertain at best. If your house is in an area where values are relatively stable, and it is in saleable condition, the lender will likely want you out yesterday, because the conventional wisdom in real estate circles is that vacant houses are easier to sell. Paradoxically, if there are a lot of vacant homes in your area, it will be harder to sell your home. If your neighborhood has a glut of homes for sale—whatever the reason—the lender may not be in such a hurry to get you out, because in those circumstances vacant homes rapidly depreciate in value. In fact, you may be able to negotiate a lease that allows you to remain in the house and pay rent. Because the lender would benefit by keeping the property occupied, at least until property values stabilize, you may be able to arrange very favorable terms.

After You Get a Notice to Leave

When you get a notice demanding that you leave the house, it tells you how long you have to vacate the property. In most states, you'll have between five and 30 days. (Check your state's page in the appendix for specifics.) In most states, once the time period runs out, you still can legally remain in the house until a sheriff physically evicts you under authority of a court order. In some cases, to get that court order, the new owner will have to file an eviction lawsuit (commonly called an unlawful detainer or forcible entry and detainer action). This eviction procedure can often take several months, giving you some additional time in your house payment-free. In other cases, the eviction is an extension of the forclosure action and can happen much more quickly.

But forcing the new owner of the home to take you to court has its downside. It's often best to be prepared to move at the end of the period set out in the written notice to leave rather than wait until the new owner goes to court and gets an eviction order. If you are sued, it's a matter of public record and can hurt your ability to rent or lease in the future. You'll already have bad credit as a result of the foreclosure (or bankruptcy, if you go that route), and many landlords subscribe to private databases that screen prospective tenants for being on the wrong end of previous eviction lawsuits. That fact above all others can lead a prospective landlord to reject your application for a lease or rental agreement.

Another reason to avoid an eviction lawsuit is that if the new owner sues you for eviction, you might also end up on the hook for the rental value of the property for the period you remained in the house after the ownership change. This amount would be what the court determines is the fair rental value of the home. For instance, if comparable homes in the area rent for $1,000 a month, the judge might be willing to give the new owner a judgment against you for that amount. This kind of lawsuit would fly only if the new owner made a formal demand for reasonable rent going forward (which is rare), and you refused to pay it.

If you do face such a demand, you may have an argument against it. You could argue that any rent you owed was more than offset by the fact that you maintained the house and that by staying there you prevented it from depreciating in value. This argument would work better if the new owner were your old lender; if a new owner wanted to move in but couldn't because you refused to leave, the house wasn't at risk of being vacant and neglected.

TIP

Consider filing for bankruptcy. When you're pretty sure you're going to have to give up your house, your prime concern becomes living there payment-free for as long as possible. You may be able to extend that time if you file for Chapter 7 or Chapter 13 bankruptcy. Check out Chs. 5 and 6 to find out whether you are eligible, whether you would benefit from filing for reasons other than delaying foreclosure, and other important information.

Eviction Procedures in a Nutshell

Generally, if the eviction wasn't part of the foreclosure action, you'll receive a formal notice (for instance, a "notice to quit") asking you to leave the property before the eviction officially starts. If you don't leave by the deadline set out in the notice, you must be personally served with a summons and eviction complaint (the new owner must go to court to get you out).

- You have the right to contest the eviction complaint before a judge (by filing a formal written response to the eviction complaint).
- After notice and a hearing, the court issues an eviction judgment.
- The court issues an order giving you a few days to move before the sheriff is allowed to remove you. (In some judicial foreclosure states, the court order authorizing the sale also authorizes the sheriff to evict you after the sale, after a required brief notice is served on you. See your state's page in the appendix.)

Resources Beyond the Book

A t some point, as you make your way through the foreclosure process, you're going to want help from a human being. Someone who knows the territory—a lawyer who's familiar with what local judges will approve or a real estate agent who can tell you how quickly your house will likely sell—can be an invaluable guide. This chapter provides a little guidance about who can help you, where to find them, and how to choose someone who will best suit your needs.

But sometimes you need help from other sources, perhaps because you can't afford an expert's fee, you don't like the answer you got, or you would rather get on top of the information yourself. So we'll also steer you to some books and websites that can provide information and guidance.

Finally, this chapter introduces some techniques for finding the foreclosure-related laws listed on your state's page in the appendix. Virtually all of these laws can be accessed online, in a law library, and quite often in a general public library.

HUD-Approved Housing Counselors

We strongly suggest that you find a HUD-approved housing counselor. These counselors can help you assess your mortgage situation and, if possible, work out a solution with your lender that will keep you in your house. Lenders—which can suffer economically from foreclosures and benefit if something can be worked out—are a principal source of funds for these agencies. (See Ch. 4 for an in-depth discussion of finding and working with a HUD-approved housing counselor.) Consider contacting one of the following:

- The federal Department of Housing and Urban Development (HUD) has a list of approved counselors. You can find a HUD-approved counselor at www.hud.gov (search for "Talk to a Housing Counselor") or by calling 800-569-4287.
- The Homeownership Preservation Foundation website, www.995hope.org, offers free online counseling, among other things. Or you can call 888-995-HOPE and talk with someone.

- The National Foundation for Credit Counseling (NFCC) can put you in contact with a certified housing counselor who can offer guidance on avoiding falling behind in your mortgage payments and resolving your mortgage situation. Go to www.nfcc.org/our-services/housing-counseling for more information.

Some homeowners become convinced that they should pay a company to step in to help them. This is almost always a mistake. There is no proof that private companies offering modification or other foreclosure assistance can get the job done any faster than a HUD-approved housing counselor. Worse, there is plenty of evidence that the forms of help these companies offer are scams in which homeowners spend large sums of money in exchange for few or no results.

Real Estate Brokers

Real estate brokers and agents can be indispensable if you are facing foreclosure and want to sell instead. The major difficulty in doing a short sale is that you typically need a solid offer from a potential buyer before your lender will tell you whether or not it will accept the terms. A local broker or agent who is familiar with a particular lender's practices will have a good idea of what kind of terms the lender will accept.

The broker can also negotiate with your lender for the final terms. Pushing a short sale through can require experience with the lender (or lenders) and experience in negotiating real estate deals.

If you don't already have a broker or agent you trust, ask around for reliable names. Most communities have real estate firms with well-respected brand names, and we see no reason not to trust agents working for those companies.

Real estate brokers and agents are subject to regulation by every state. To find out whether your broker or agent is licensed, check the website of your state's real estate regulatory agency.

Mortgage Brokers

If you wish to refinance, a mortgage broker can help you find the best loan (or any loan at all). Like real estate brokers and agents, mortgage brokers are regulated in all states, and licensed in most. You usually can find out whether a particular mortgage broker is licensed by visiting the website for your state's regulatory agency.

Mortgage brokers, as a group, have taken a lot of heat for the mortgage crisis. Honest and ethical brokers are lumped in with the ones who misrepresented to their customers the nature of the loans they were getting and who handed out loans to people who couldn't afford them. Unfortunately, during the housing bubble, unethical mortgage brokers often out-competed those who were ethical, because by all accounts it was comparatively easy for just about anyone to get a mortgage. In fact, the fault is better laid at the doorstep of the banks, which themselves were usually just intermediaries for Fannie Mae, Freddie Mac, and Wall Street investors who bought mortgages on the say-so of rating agencies.

Use mortgage brokers for what they are best at: finding a source of refinancing at the lowest available interest rate. But when it comes to understanding how the mortgage works and whether or not you can afford it, keep the old Latin phrase *caveat emptor* (let the buyer beware) firmly in mind.

Lawyers

We are firm believers in do-it-yourself law, but we also think that the learning curve for some tasks is just too steep for many people to handle—especially given the other problems in their lives. And foreclosure law is complicated. If you realistically think you can keep your house (see Chs. 3 and 4), hire a lawyer if you can possibly afford it. If you are only trying to delay the inevitable, hire a lawyer if you can, but also consider handling the case (or most of it) by yourself.

You almost certainly will need a lawyer if you are determined to keep your house by:

- fighting a foreclosure in court, or
- filing for Chapter 13 bankruptcy and making up missed payments over several years.

You will probably benefit from having a lawyer if you realize that you'll probably lose the house sooner or later, but you want to delay the foreclosure and stay in your house as long as possible by:

- fighting a foreclosure in court, or
- filing for Chapter 13 bankruptcy.

When can you go it alone? Having a competent lawyer to represent you can always be to your benefit, but the amount you'll have to pay for one can often outweigh the benefits. With that in mind, you might sensibly choose to represent yourself if you are filing for Chapter 7 bankruptcy to get rid of your other debts so your mortgage will be more affordable or so that you'll emerge from your foreclosure with a fresh start.

What Type of Lawyer Do You Need?

Most lawyers who represent people in foreclosure actions specialize in foreclosure defense, real estate transactions, consumer protection, or bankruptcy. As the number of foreclosures grew, so did the number of lawyers who have expertise in all three areas.

How do you know what expertise a lawyer has? Your best shot is to pop the question directly. Ask "Do you have the experience necessary to help me with my foreclosure?" or "How many foreclosure cases have you handled, and what were the results?" This approach may seem naïve, but many lawyers appreciate this approach and will give you honest answers.

As a general rule, if you want to keep your house but you have concluded that you don't want to file for bankruptcy, a foreclosure defense lawyer may be the best choice. A foreclosure lawyer will be comfortable fighting the foreclosure in court, if necessary, as well as analyzing the lender's paperwork and negotiating with the lender to keep you in your house. On the other hand, if it looks like you won't be able to work something out with the lender, a bankruptcy lawyer is likely your best choice. Bankruptcy is a highly technical area, and few nonbankruptcy lawyers know the tricks of the trade.

How to Find the Right Lawyer

If you are looking for a lawyer, it's worth it to shop around. Here are some tips.

Start with personal referrals. This is your best approach. If you know someone who was pleased with the services of a foreclosure or bankruptcy lawyer, call that lawyer first.

See whether you can get free or low-cost help. Many law schools sponsor clinics that provide free legal advice to consumers. And many places have senior law projects, with lawyers who will, without charge, help people over 55 with debt and foreclosure issues. To find something near you, do an online search for "senior legal services" in your area. Many parts of the country also have functioning legal aid offices that will help people who qualify—who are poor enough—deal with foreclosures. And if you don't qualify, you may get a quality referral to a lawyer who won't charge you as much as others in the community might.

Be careful with lawyer referral panels. Most county bar associations will give you the names of lawyers who have expertise in fighting foreclosures. But some bar associations may not do much screening of the lawyers they list. Ask about this when you call.

Check out online directories. Both bar associations and commercial websites provide lists of real estate lawyers online, usually with a lot of information about each lawyer. Start with the lawyer directory on the Nolo website (www.nolo.com). It sets the standard for providing information about how the lawyer goes about the practice of law. Use Google to find other lawyers for your state or city.

Look for a bankruptcy expert. To find a good bankruptcy lawyer, consider using the membership directory of the National Association of Consumer Bankruptcy Attorneys, at www.nacba.org. Membership in this organization is a good sign that the bankruptcy lawyer is tuned in to the nuances of bankruptcy, both generally and how it can be used to save your house or keep you in it longer. Also, because foreclosure and bankruptcy are so closely related these days, a bankruptcy lawyer will also likely be knowledgeable about foreclosures.

Choosing a Lawyer

No matter how you find a lawyer, these suggestions will help you make sure you have the best possible working relationship.

Keep in mind that you're hiring the lawyer to perform a service for you. So fight any urge you have to surrender to or be intimidated by the lawyer. You should be the one who decides what you feel comfortable doing about your legal and financial affairs.

Second, make sure you have good chemistry with any lawyer you hire. When making an appointment, ask to talk directly to the lawyer. If you don't get through, this may give you a hint as to how accessible the lawyer is.

If you are able to talk to the lawyer, ask some specific questions. Do you get clear, concise answers? Is the lawyer making an effort to teach you about your overall situation? If not, look for someone else. Also, pay attention to how the lawyer responds to your knowledge. If you've read this book, you're already better informed than the average client. Does the lawyer appreciate your efforts to educate yourself?

Your main goal at the initial conference is to find out what the lawyer recommends in your case and how much it will cost. Go home and think about the lawyer's suggestions. If they don't make sense or you have other reservations, call someone else.

High-Volume Bankruptcy Law Firms

Some lawyers handle a high volume of cases for fees that are significantly less than the average charged by other local bankruptcy lawyers. These firms depend heavily on paralegals to get the work done, and the lawyer appears only briefly at the beginning of the case and at your creditors' meeting (the one personal appearance you will likely make in a Chapter 7 bankruptcy). If you choose a lawyer by price (which is understandable given the standard fees), you will likely be trading hands-on legal representation for a cookie-cutter approach to your case that might not be in your best interest.

When shopping for a lawyer, it's common to hire the first one you talk to, unless the lawyer's fees are way out of your league or you really don't get along with the lawyer. You would be best served by visiting a few people before making your final decision. But how do you bring yourself to say, "Thanks for the information. I'll think about it and give you a call"? We suggest you repeat this to yourself 100 times before you make your first contact. After you walk away the first time, the rest will come naturally.

How Much Will a Lawyer Charge?

With a few happy exceptions, plenty! It's not a stretch to generalize that if you need an attorney to help you with your foreclosure, you will have difficulty raising the money to pay for it.

Chapter 13 Bankruptcies

Chapter 13 attorneys commonly charge $2,500 to $6,000 a case, depending on the attorney and where you live. If your case appears unusually complex from the beginning, the fee you are quoted may run even higher. If the fees are below a certain amount set by each court (called no-look fees), the court won't examine them; above that amount and the attorney will have to convince the court that they are justified.

If you can come up with a portion of these fees up front, the rest of the fee can be paid over time through your Chapter 13 plan. Exactly how much a bankruptcy lawyer will require up front depends on the individual attorney or firm. On average you can expect to pay about half of the total fee before your case is filed.

Chapter 7 Bankruptcies

Attorneys' fees for a routine Chapter 7 bankruptcy case run from $1,500 to $3,500, depending on the lawyer and the locality. Most attorneys require you to pay the full fee before you file the bankruptcy, because bankruptcy legally discharges (cancels) whatever fees are unpaid as of the filing date.

Lawyers can get permission from the court to charge you for work done after you file, but they would rather not be your creditor after they have worked to get you out of debt. So, their up-front charges take into account the work they might have to do after you file.

Filing for Chapter 7 Bankruptcy: How Much Will It Cost?	
Filing fee (unless a waiver is granted)	$335
Mandatory credit counseling (before filing) and budget counseling (after)	$50
If you fill out and file your own bankruptcy papers with the help of *How to File for Chapter 7 Bankruptcy* (Nolo), or	about $35
If you hire a nonlawyer bankruptcy petition preparer to do the paperwork, or	about $150
If you hire a lawyer to represent you	about $1,500 to $3,500
Total	$420 to $3,850

TIP

Filing for Chapter 7 bankruptcy without an attorney. You may be able to file for a simple Chapter 7 bankruptcy on your own, with the aid of a good self-help guide (see "Books" below for recommendations). For a Chapter 13 bankruptcy, however, you'll most likely need a lawyer.

Fighting a Foreclosure in Court

If you want to fight a foreclosure in a judicial foreclosure proceeding or in a separate court action in a nonjudicial foreclosure proceeding, plan on paying an up-front retainer of several thousand dollars.

Other Tasks

One way to get help from a lawyer—and pay less—is to pay only for specific tasks. Some lawyers will agree to perform certain limited tasks for you instead of taking responsibility for the whole matter. This is called offering unbundled services. For example, if you file for bankruptcy without a lawyer's help, and then your lender asks the court to let it proceed with a foreclosure, you might be able to hire a lawyer just to oppose the lender's request.

The fee will vary depending on the complexity of the task and the lawyer's enthusiasm for providing unbundled services. An attorney might charge only a few hundred dollars to help you work out a modification with your lender. And if you want an attorney to represent you in a judicial foreclosure case where you have no serious challenge to the foreclosure but just want to delay the inevitable, the fee will likely be hundreds of dollars instead of thousands.

As a general rule, you should hire an attorney for an unbundled service whenever the amount of the dispute justifies the fee. If a creditor objects to the discharge of a $500 debt, and it will cost you $400 to hire an attorney, you may be better off trying to handle the matter yourself, even though this increases the risk that the creditor will win. But if the dispute is worth $1,000 and the attorney will cost you $400, hiring the attorney makes better sense.

Unfortunately, many attorneys do not like to work on a piecemeal basis. They worry that by doing a little work for you, they might be on the hook if something goes wrong in another part of your case—that is, if they are in for a penny, they are in for a pound. Also, the bar associations of many states discourage lawyers from providing unbundled services. On the other hand, some state bar associations are encouraging attorneys to offer unbundled services simply because so many people can't afford full representation.

You May Be Able to Afford a Lawyer If You're Not Paying Your Mortgage

A lawyer can often be retained for the equivalent of one or two mortgage payments. Because a lawyer may help you gain many extra months of foreclosure delay and living in your home payment free, hiring a lawyer can be very cost effective.

Foreclosure Websites

If you are facing foreclosure, or worry that you might be facing foreclosure soon, you'll find easy-to understand information about foreclosure and your options at these websites:

- **Nolo's Foreclosure Law Section** (www.nolo.com/legal-encyclopedia/foreclosure). Learn everything you need to know about foreclosure, including how it works, how to avoid it, and your options if you are in danger of losing your home.
- **Federal Reserve System** (www.federalreserve.gov/consumerinfo/foreclosure.htm). The Federal Reserve System has established regional Foreclosure Resource Centers throughout the country to address local concerns about the foreclosure crisis. Click your region to get consumer information and foreclosure resources in your area.
- **Federal Trade Commission (FTC)** (www.ftc.gov). The FTC publishes fact sheets and press releases for consumers on foreclosure scams. Search for "mortgage relief scams."
- **Homeownership Preservation Foundation** (www.995hope.org). The Homeownership Preservation Foundation is a nonprofit that offers free foreclosure counseling. The website also provides links to federal and some state government websites offering foreclosure information.
- **MakingHomeAffordable.gov** (www.makinghomeaffordable.gov). This government website provides comprehensive information about interacting with your mortgage company, mortgage assistance options, information you'll need to when applying for

mortgage assistance, and tips to avoid foreclosure. The website also provides information about Hardest Hit Fund programs, and how to find HUD-approved housing counseling agencies.

- **National Consumer Law Center (NCLC)** (www.nclc.org/issues/foreclosures-and-mortgages.html). The consumer section of NCLC's website has helpful information and links on foreclosure, predatory lending, and foreclosure scams.

- **National Foundation for Credit Counseling (NFCC)** (www.nfcc.org). The NFCC website has a national directory of local member agencies—nonprofit credit counseling agencies staffed by NFCC-trained, and certified counselors. NFCC housing counselors can provide assistance with foreclosure and other homeowner issues.

- **U.S. Department of Housing and Urban Development (HUD)** (www.hud.gov). The HUD website has a section on foreclosure that includes tips on avoiding foreclosure, assistance for FHA-insured homeowners, links to government-assisted rental programs, links to local and state resources, and a national directory of HUD-approved housing counselors who provide assistance free of charge.

Books

If you're facing foreclosure, we encourage you to read every book on this topic that you can put your hands on. You probably will not have to pay more than $100 for the lot of them—not a bad deal considering what's at stake.

Every book will have something different to offer. Each author will be giving you the benefit of personal experiences, favorite tips on strategy and tactics, and opinions on the best approach to dealing with foreclosure. While every book is sure to contradict every other one in some particular, that should not worry you. A little confusion can be very helpful if it makes you think. There is no one truth to these matters, and sooner or later you will sort things out.

That said, in addition to the books referenced in previous chapters, we recommend the following books:

- *How to File for Chapter 7 Bankruptcy,* by Stephen Elias and Albin Renauer (Nolo). As the title says, this book explains everything you need to know about filing for Chapter 7 bankruptcy.
- *Chapter 13 Bankruptcy: Keep Your Property & Repay Debts Over Time*, by Stephen Elias and Patricia Dzikowski (Nolo). This is a guide to the whole Chapter 13 process.
- *The New Bankruptcy: Will It Work for You?* by Stephen Elias and Leon Bayer (Nolo). If you're not sure whether or not bankruptcy is the right way to go for you and your family, this book will highlight the pros and cons and help you evaluate your situation.
- *Credit Repair,* by Amy Loftsgordon (Nolo). If your credit is in the tank and you want to take steps to make it better, this is the book for you. It provides all the steps that have traditionally been necessary to raise your credit score.
- *Foreclosures and Mortgage Servicing.* Authored by the staff of the National Consumer Law Center, this is the best book out there for in-depth legal research on the subject of foreclosure. It covers many of the areas we've addressed—and some we have not—in considerably more detail, including:
  - how to negotiate preforeclosure workout agreements, and current workout options with Fannie Mae, Freddie Mac, HUD, VA, and RHS
  - the best discussion anywhere on how to challenge mortgage servicer abuses
  - foreclosure litigation, including power of sale, due on sale, and substantive and procedural defenses
  - raising loan broker and loan originator-related claims against the mortgage holder
  - special rights to stop foreclosure of FHA, VA, and RHS mortgages
  - mobile home foreclosures, and
  - tax liens and tax foreclosures.

It comes with access to a companion website that contains a lot of the forms, foreclosure laws, and other materials you will need if you want to fight a foreclosure or do your own workout with your lender. You can buy a copy for around $130, or perhaps find a copy in your local law or general-purpose library. For more information, visit www.nclc.org.

Looking Up Foreclosure Statutes

Your state's page in the appendix lists references to the laws governing foreclosures in your state. These references are termed citations, and the laws are known as statutes. By using the citation, you can find and read for yourself your state's laws on such matters as:

- how much notice you are entitled to before your home is sold in a foreclosure
- how much notice you are entitled to before you are evicted after a foreclosure sale
- how much time you have to reinstate or redeem your mortgage after a default
- whether your lender can sue you for a deficiency judgment and if so, under what conditions, and
- what special protections you are entitled to if you have a high-cost mortgage (one with a much higher interest rate than normal).

You can easily locate statutes online or in most states at a law library or even at a public library.

There are two fundamental ways to find your state statutes on foreclosure:

- Once you find a collection of the statutes, you can browse through various levels of subject headings (usually organized hierarchically by numbered title, article, chapter, and section).
- You can go to the state law collection at www.justia.com and search for the keywords you're interested in.

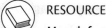 **RESOURCE**

More information on legal research. Legal research is its own subject; if you want to delve into it more deeply, see *Legal Research: How to Find & Understand the Law*, by Stephen Elias and the Editors of Nolo (Nolo). Our goal in this chapter is just to show you how to look up statutes listed on the state pages in the appendix.

Browsing

Here is an example of the steps you could use to find the Vermont foreclosure statutes by browsing. If you go online and follow along, you'll pretty much know how to find the same law for your state.

Start by finding the statute's citation on the Vermont page in the appendix. The citations to Vermont's foreclosure laws are Vermont Stat. Ann., Title 12, Chapter 172, Sections 4931 through 4954.

Step 1: Go to www.justia.com.

Step 2: Scroll down to "Laws: Cases & Codes."

Step 3: Click on "Vermont Law."

Step 4: You'll see seven sets of Vermont Statutes listed. For this example, click the link to 2015 Vermont Statutes—the most recent set at this site. If you find two or more sets of codes for your state, follow the steps in this example for all of them.

Step 5: Find and click on the relevant title. (For this statute, it's "Title 12.") This opens up a list of chapters.

Step 6: Scroll down until you reach the chapter that contains §§ 4931–4954, Vermont's foreclosure statutes. It's "Chapter 172 (Foreclosure of Mortgages)."

Step 7: Click on "Chapter 172."

You're there!

Most other states arrange their statutes in a similar manner: by title, chapter, and section. Use the same method to find the statutes referenced on your state's page.

Some states arrange their statutes in a slightly different manner. For example, if you were looking for Section 2323.07 of the Ohio Revised Code, you would use the first two numbers to find the correct title ("Title 23"). Click on that title, and then Chapter 2323. Next, find the statute numbered "2323.07."

In New York, the citation to the foreclosure laws reads: N.Y. Real Prop. Acts. Law, Sections 1301 to 1391. You would find these statutes by first browsing the list of legal topics until you found "Real Property Actions and Proceedings." Click on that topic and then browse until you find the article (Article 13) that contains "Sections 1301 to 1391 (Action to Foreclose a Mortgage)."

Your state may use a slightly different model from any of these. You may have to use a little ingenuity to get to the right statutes. As a general rule, the number at the left of the citation will be the number you use to start your search, whether it is the title, article, or chapter number. If for some reason the citation number doesn't work, look for a subject heading dealing with foreclosure, real estate, or real property, or if you are in a judicial foreclosure state, civil procedure.

Foreclosure Statutes Can Be Hard to Read

Especially in Eastern states, foreclosure statutes come from English law adopted here in the 18th century. The language is very different from modern English (even modern legal English), and can be hard to understand.

Also, for reasons that escape us, they aren't organized very well. Sometimes one relevant statute will be found in one section of the law while a closely related one will appear elsewhere. For example, some foreclosure laws are found in the code dealing with court procedure, while other laws are found in the part of the code dealing with real estate. So, be prepared to look in several different parts of the code.

Searching Online

To ensure you're looking at the most recent statutes, use Google to find the actual laws online. For instance, by doing an online search for "Vermont's statutes," you'll find in your list of results a link to the "Vermont Statutes Online" on the Vermont State Legislature's website. Clicking on that link will take you to a page listing all of Vermont's foreclosure statutes. Then look for the relevant title, chapter, and sections that you want to review.

Glossary

Acceleration. Requiring a borrower to immediately pay off the balance of a loan. Under a provision commonly found in promissory notes, if the borrower misses some payments, the lender can demand that the total balance of the loan be paid immediately. The loan must be accelerated before the lender can foreclose. In many states, the borrower gets a chance to reinstate the loan (and cancel the acceleration) by paying the arrears, plus costs and interest.

Adjustable-rate mortgage (ARM). A mortgage or deed of trust providing that the interest rate on the underlying promissory note can be adjusted up or down at specified intervals tracking the movement of a federal interest rate or another index.

Administrative expenses. In a Chapter 13 bankruptcy repayment plan, the trustee's fee, the debtor's attorneys' fees, and other costs that a debtor must pay in full. Administrative costs are typically 10% of total payments under the plan.

Amortization. Paying off a loan with regular payments over a set period. Part of each payment is applied to principal and to interest.

Amount financed. The amount of money you are getting in a loan, calculated under rules required by the federal law. This is the amount of money you are borrowing after certain financing costs and fees are deducted. The amount financed is far less than the total amount you pay back, because the total amount of the loan includes the interest on the amount financed.

Annual percentage rate (APR). The interest rate on a loan expressed under rules required by federal law. To determine the true cost of a loan, it is more accurate to look at the APR than the stated interest rate.

Appraisal. An expert's evaluation of what a particular item of property is worth in the marketplace. Colloquially, the term is used to describe any opinion about the value of property. For instance, real estate agents and brokers often informally appraise property, even though they aren't expert appraisers.

Arrears. Overdue payments on a loan. With a mortgage, this may include any missed payments, interest on the missed payments, and the costs incurred by the lender in trying to collect the debt.

Assignee liability. Liability of an assignee (an entity that has been assigned ownership of a mortgage or deed of trust) for unlawful or abusive acts of the original lender or mortgage originator. Assignee liability can be important in lawsuits against a foreclosing party for violations of federal or state laws prohibiting predatory lending practices. In most cases, assignees are off the hook for those practices if they conducted a reasonable investigation into the history of the loan.

Assignment. A document showing that ownership of a mortgage or deed of trust (and the underlying promissory note) has been transferred (assigned) from the original owner to a new owner (assignee). In recent times, mortgages have been the subject of many assignments as they have been "securitized" and sold as investments worldwide. In some cases, the assignments have been made electronically, without anything on paper. When it comes time to enforce the mortgage or deed of trust in a foreclosure, the absence of documentation can sometimes defeat the foreclosure, because there is no documentary proof of current ownership.

Attachment. A legal process that allows a creditor to attach a lien to property that you own because of a contract you signed (a car note, for example), a money judgment you owe, or a special statute that authorizes the lien, as in the case of a tax lien. If the lien is on your house, it can be enforced by foreclosure.

Automatic stay. An injunction automatically issued by the bankruptcy court when someone files for bankruptcy. The automatic stay prohibits most creditor collection activities, such as filing or continuing lawsuits, making written requests for payment, or notifying credit reporting bureaus of an unpaid debt.

Balloon payment. A large lump-sum payment due as the last payment on a loan. For instance, if you borrow $10,000, your note might require you to pay $5,000 of the loan over a three-year period, plus one balloon payment for the rest at the end of that period.

Bankruptcy code. The federal law that governs the operation of the bankruptcy courts and establishes bankruptcy procedures. It's in Title 11 of the United States Code.

Bankruptcy petition preparer. Any nonlawyer who helps someone with bankruptcy. Bankruptcy petition preparers (BPPs) are regulated by the U.S. Trustee. Because they are not lawyers, BPPs can't represent anyone in bankruptcy court or provide legal advice.

Capitalization. Treating items owed on a loan as part of a new principal balance. For example, when missed payments on a mortgage are added to the mortgage principal, to be paid off over time, they are capitalized. If missed payments are capitalized and the loan is reamortized, the lender will recalculate the monthly payment using the existing interest rate and new principal balance.

Chapter 7 bankruptcy. A liquidation bankruptcy, in which the trustee sells the debtor's nonexempt property and distributes the proceeds to the debtor's creditors. At the end of the case, the debtor receives a discharge of all remaining debts, except those that cannot legally be discharged.

Chapter 12 bankruptcy. A type of bankruptcy designed to help small farmers reorganize their debts.

Chapter 13 bankruptcy. A type of consumer bankruptcy designed to help individuals reorganize their debts and pay all or a portion of them over three to five years.

Chapter 13 plan. A document filed in a Chapter 13 bankruptcy that shows how all of the debtor's projected disposable income will be used over a three- to five-year period to pay all mandatory debts—for example, back child support, taxes, and mortgage arrearages—as well as a percentage of unsecured, nonpriority debts, such as medical and credit card bills.

Closed-end loan. Any loan that must be paid off within a certain period of time. Loans that don't have to be paid off within any particular time—for example, credit card debt—are open-ended.

Collateral. Property pledged by a borrower as security for a loan. If a creditor accepts property as collateral for a loan under a security agreement, and the agreement is properly recorded, the creditor has a lien on the collateral and can repossess it if the conditions of the security agreement (typically, making monthly payments on the loan) aren't met.

Complaint. A formal document that initiates a lawsuit.

Confirmation hearing. A court hearing conducted by a bankruptcy judge at which the judge decides whether or not a debtor's proposed Chapter 13 plan is feasible and meets all legal requirements.

Conforming loan. A mortgage loan that is small enough to be bought or guaranteed by Fannie Mae or Freddie Mac. See "Jumbo loan."

Conventional loan. A mortgage loan issued to a borrower with an excellent or very good credit rating. Conventional loans do not include those insured by the federal government or subprime loans.

Cramdown. In a Chapter 13 bankruptcy, the act of reducing a secured debt to the replacement value of the collateral securing the debt.

Credit and debt counseling. Counseling that explores the possibility of repaying debts outside of bankruptcy and covers credit, budgeting, and financial management. Consumers must go through credit counseling with an approved provider before filing for bankruptcy.

Credit bureau. Another name for a consumer reporting or credit reporting agency. These companies sell information about a consumer's credit history to certain categories of people or organizations. Individuals are entitled to one free credit report per year, not including the person's credit score.

Credit report. Also called a consumer report or a credit record, this documents the credit history and current status of a borrower's monthly payment obligations and contains public information such as bankruptcies, court judgments, and tax liens. Chapter 7 bankruptcies remain on a credit report for ten years, Chapter 13 bankruptcies and other negative information for seven years.

Credit score. This is a number that supposedly summarizes your credit history. The score is based on a number of factors, including your debt payment history, how much debt you currently have, how long you've had credit, and how recently your major credit transactions occurred. There are several rating agencies, all of which use their own secret formulas, which means that you never know just how a particular score was arrived at. Lenders use credit scores to decide whether to grant a loan and at what interest rate. FICO scores (the most popular basic credit score) range from 300 to 850; a score in the mid-700s or more generally gets you the best loans at the best rates.

Creditor. A person or an institution to whom money is owed.

Creditors' meeting. A meeting that someone filing for bankruptcy must attend, at which the trustee and creditors may question the debtor about property, court documents, and debts.

Curing a default. See "Reinstating a mortgage."

Current market value. The price that property could be sold for.

Current monthly income. As defined by bankruptcy law, a bankruptcy filer's total gross income (whether taxable or not), averaged over the six-month period immediately preceding the month in which the bankruptcy is filed. The current monthly income is used to determine whether or not the debtor can file for Chapter 7 bankruptcy, among other things.

Debt consolidation. Refinancing debt into a new loan. Homeowners sometimes convert relatively short-term unsecured debt into debt secured by the home—putting the house at greater risk if there is a default in payments on the consolidated debt.

Debtor. Someone who owes money to another person or business. Also, the generic term used to refer to anyone who files for bankruptcy.

Declaration of homestead. See "Homestead declaration."

Deed in lieu of foreclosure. An arrangement under which a homeowner can get out from under a mortgage and prevent a foreclosure, by signing the deed to the home over to the lender in exchange for the lender's agreement not to foreclose. Typically, the lender agrees to not hold the homeowner liable for the remaining amount of the mortgage.

Deed of trust. In about half the states, a loan that is secured by real estate is termed a deed of trust. Deeds of trust are like mortgages. However, unlike mortgages, deeds of trust typically have a power of sale clause that lets the lender have the property sold at a public auction if the homeowner defaults on the payments. Foreclosures under deeds of trust are typically referred to as nonjudicial foreclosures because they take place without court supervision.

Default. Failing to meet the requirements of an agreement. Defaults that lead to foreclosure typically involve the failure to make mortgage payments, but other types of defaults are possible, such as the failure to maintain necessary insurance or to keep the property in proper condition.

Default rate. An interest rate that replaces a contractual interest rate if a borrower defaults on a loan. If the default rate is set out in the mortgage loan agreement, it will typically be considerably higher than the contract rate.

Deficiency. The amount a homeowner owes the lender after a house is sold at a foreclosure or short sale for less than the actual debt. In most states, the lender can recover a deficiency owed by the borrower. However, state laws typically require that the deficiency be measured by the difference between the property's fair market value and the amount of the loan rather than by the sale amount. For example, if a home sells for $300,000 at a foreclosure auction, the fair market value of the home is actually $400,000 and the borrower owes $500,000, the deficiency in most states will be $100,000, not $200,000.

Discharge. A court order, issued at the conclusion of a Chapter 7 or Chapter 13 bankruptcy case, which legally relieves the debtor of personal liability for debts that can be discharged in that type of bankruptcy.

Dischargeable debt. A debt that is wiped out at the conclusion of a bankruptcy case, unless the judge decides that it should not be.

Disposable income. In a Chapter 13 bankruptcy, the difference between a debtor's current monthly income and allowable expenses. This is the amount that the bankruptcy law deems available for a repayment plan.

Equity. The amount of cash you would pocket if you sold your house and paid off all the liens (for example, mortgages, property taxes, money judgments, mechanic's liens, and tax liens). For example, if you owe $300,000 on your house on first and second mortgages, the IRS has a tax lien on the house for $50,000, you sell your home for $390,000, and costs of sale are $20,000, you will pocket $20,000. That's your equity.

Equity stripping. The practice of giving high-cost second mortgages to homeowners, reducing the borrower's equity. Some of these loans violate federal or state truth-in-lending laws, and homeowners may be able to cancel (rescind) the loans later or sue the lender. See "Home Ownership and Equity Protection Act (HOEPA)."

Exempt property. Property described by state and federal laws (exemptions) that a debtor is entitled to keep in a Chapter 7 bankruptcy. Exempt property cannot be taken and sold by the trustee for the benefit of the debtor's unsecured creditors.

Exemptions. State and federal laws specifying the types of property that creditors are not entitled to take to satisfy a debt and the bankruptcy trustee is not entitled to sell for the benefit of the debtor's unsecured creditors.

Fannie Mae (Federal National Mortgage Association). A government-chartered corporation set up to buy mortgages from original lenders and repackage them for private investors. Congress authorized Fannie Mae to stimulate the growth of the housing market by making capital available for new loans. Investors and lenders that deal with Fannie Mae must follow various guidelines regarding mortgage servicing and foreclosure practices.

Federal exemptions. A list of exempt property in the federal Bankruptcy Code. Some states give debtors the option of using the federal rather than the state exemptions.

Federal Home Loan Mortgage Corporation. See "Freddie Mac."

Federal Housing Administration (FHA). A federal agency that insures first mortgage lenders against loss when a loan is made following FHA regulations. The FHA does not lend money; it only insures the loan. The FHA also certifies nonprofit housing counselors.

Federal National Mortgage Association. See "Fannie Mae."

Filing date. The date a bankruptcy petition in a particular case is filed. With few exceptions, debts incurred after the filing date are not discharged.

Forbearance. A lender's willingness to let you skip all or a portion of your monthly payments for a brief period, usually three to six months. You'll have to catch up later, probably with increases in monthly payments. But the lender might be willing to extend the loan so that missed payments can be added to the end of the loan rather than be paid off on top of the regular monthly payment.

Foreclosure. The legal process by which a creditor with a claim (lien) on real estate forces a sale of the property in order to collect on the lien. Foreclosure typically occurs when a homeowner defaults on a mortgage. See "Judicial foreclosure" and "Nonjudicial foreclosure."

Foreclosure "rescue" scams. Scams on people who are facing foreclosure. The scam artist learns about impending foreclosures from public filings, advertisements, and postings and contacts homeowners with promises of help that typically result in the homeowner's losing the house and any remaining equity.

Forgiven debt. Debt that is written off as uncollectable by the creditor. In the foreclosure context, a mortgage owner forgives debt when a foreclosure occurs and the property is sold for less than is owed on the mortgage. Forgiven debt—the amount you don't have to pay back—is taxable as income, and the creditor is required to send you (and the IRS) a Form 1099C stating the amount. Three major exceptions: You won't have to pay tax if you are insolvent when the debt is written off, the debt is discharged in bankruptcy, or you used the money you borrowed to buy or improve the property. (This may change.)

Freddie Mac (Federal Home Loan Mortgage Corporation). Like Fannie Mae, a government-chartered company set up to buy mortgages from original lenders and repackage (securitize) them for private investors.

Ginnie Mae (Government National Mortgage Corporation). A quasi-governmental agency that guarantees pools of FHA- and VA-insured loans that have been packaged into securities for investment purposes.

Good faith. In a Chapter 13 bankruptcy case, when a debtor files with the sincere purpose of paying off debts over the period of time required by law rather than for manipulative purposes—such as to prevent a foreclosure that by all rights should be allowed to proceed.

Government mortgage guarantors. Special government programs that provide mortgage insurance or guarantees to lenders who make purchase-money mortgage loans to certain homebuyers. These programs are offered through the federal government (the Federal Housing Administration, the Rural Housing Service, and the Veterans Administration), or by a state housing finance agency. In addition to being insured, these loans come with rules regarding transactions with homeowners, including a requirement that the lender cooperate with homeowners who are attempting to cure defaults (reinstate mortgages).

Home equity loan. A loan made to a homeowner on the basis of the equity in the house and secured by the house in the same manner as a first mortgage.

Home Ownership and Equity Protection Act (HOEPA). A federal law that provides special protection to homeowners who obtain home mortgage loans at high interest rates or with exceptionally high fees. The protection includes fines and penalties recoverable in a lawsuit against the lender and sometimes a defense to foreclosure in state or federal court.

Homestead. In bankruptcy, a state or federal exemption applicable to property where the debtor lives—usually including boats and mobile homes.

Homestead declaration. A form filed with the county recorder's office to put on record your right to a homestead exemption. Only a few states require recording. In most states, the homestead exemption is automatic—you are not required to record a homestead declaration in order to claim the homestead exemption.

Injunction. A court order prohibiting a person or an entity from taking specified actions—for example, bankruptcy's automatic stay (in reality an automatic injunction), which prevents most creditors from trying to collect their debts.

Interest. The cost of borrowing money over time. Interest on a loan is always described as percentage of the loan payable over a period of time, as in 7% per year. In agreements for the purchase of homes and cars, the interest is computed and amortized over the period of the loan, which makes the amount owed on the secured debt a lot higher than the base loan itself. For instance, if you buy a car for $20,000 and borrow the money over seven years, the amount payable on the note is $20,000 plus the amount of interest that you'll pay over the seven years.

Interest-only loan. A type of mortgage loan, made popular during the 2004–2006 housing boom, where the borrower makes payments only on the loan's interest for a limited period of time. The mortgage payments are much lower than they would be if the payments were applied to the loan as a whole. When the interest-only period ends the borrower must begin making much higher payments to cover both principal and interest. It is the sudden increase in required mortgage payments that pushed many homeowners into foreclosure.

Insolvent. When a person's or business's assets are worth less than their debts.

Joint debtors. Married people who file for bankruptcy together and pay a single filing fee.

Judgment proof. Description of a person whose income and property are such that a creditor can't (or won't) seize them to enforce a money judgment—for example, a dwelling protected by a homestead exemption or a bank account containing only a few dollars.

Judicial foreclosure. A type of foreclosure, used in about half the states, in which the foreclosing party files a lawsuit in the county where the property is located, seeking a judgment that the property can be sold in a foreclosure sale because the homeowner has defaulted on the mortgage. A few states use what are called strict foreclosures, which allow the judge to order title to the property transferred to the foreclosing party without the need for a sale. A few other states have hybrid processes, in which the foreclosure proceeds under a power of sale clause but is subject to some court supervision.

Judicial lien. A lien created by recording a court money judgment against the debtor's property—usually real estate.

Jumbo loan. A loan for an amount that exceeds the conforming loan limit and that usually costs a point or two higher in interest rates as a result. See "Conforming loan."

Lease and buy-back. A scheme in which you deed your home to a third party and then lease it back, paying rent to build up your credit score so you can buy back the loan. Most often it's a scam—the third party pockets your mortgage payments and borrows against the property, and the house ends up in foreclosure.

Lien. A legal claim against property that must be paid before title to the property can be transferred. Liens on real estate can also often be collected through foreclosure, depending on the type of lien. Examples of liens include mortgages, tax liens, and mechanic's liens.

Lien avoidance. A bankruptcy procedure in which certain types of liens can be removed from certain types of property. Liens that are not avoided survive the bankruptcy even though the underlying debt may be canceled—for instance, a lien remains on a car even if the debt evidenced by the car note is discharged in the bankruptcy.

Lifting the stay. When a bankruptcy court allows a creditor to continue with debt collection or other activities that are otherwise banned by the automatic stay. For instance, the court might allow a landlord to proceed with an eviction or a lender to repossess a car because the debtor has defaulted on the note.

Loan term. The loan term is the period during which the loan is due to be repaid in full. Most mortgage loans have 15- or 30-year terms. Many predatory consumer loans (payday loans, car title loans, and refund anticipation loans) have very short terms, which increases the annual percentage rate charged by the lender. Mortgage foreclosure rescue scams also frequently employ short-term loans with outrageous interest payments.

Market value. The highest price one would pay and the lowest price the seller would accept on a property on the open market. Market value is used to determine the amount of equity a homeowner has in the property, which can determine whether it makes sense to fight foreclosure or to file for bankruptcy. Market value also is often crucial in determining whether a mortgage holder can recover a deficiency after a foreclosure sale. For example, assume a property sells for $250,000, the former homeowner owes $350,000, and a court later determines that the property's market value was actually $300,000 (which could have been realized if the minimum bid at the foreclosure auction had been set higher). In that event, if the state's laws use the property's actual market value to limit deficiency awards, the court will issue a deficiency judgment for $50,000.

Materialmen's and mechanic's liens. Liens imposed by statute on real estate when suppliers of materials, labor, and contracting services used to improve the real estate are not properly compensated.

Means test. A formula that uses predefined income and expense categories to determine whether a debtor whose income is more than the state median family income should be allowed to file for Chapter 7 bankruptcy.

Median family income. The figure at which there are as many families with incomes below it as there are above it. The U.S. Census Bureau publishes median family income figures for each state and for different household sizes. In bankruptcy, the median family income is used as a basis for determining whether a debtor must pass the means test to file for Chapter 7 bankruptcy, and whether a debtor filing for Chapter 13 bankruptcy must commit all projected disposable income to a five-year repayment plan.

Meeting of creditors. See "Creditors' meeting."

MERS. MERS stands for "Mortgage Electronic Registration Systems," an entity listed as the mortgagee of record for about half the mortgages in America. MERS operates a database of mortgage transactions conducted by its members, supposedly obviating the need to use county real property recording systems.

Modification. Altering one or more terms of a mortgage, such as reducing the interest rate, reducing the principal due, or increasing the term of the loan to account for missed payments.

Mortgage. A contract in which a loan to buy real estate is secured by the real estate as collateral. If the borrower defaults on loan payments, the lender can foreclose on the property.

Mortgage broker. An individual, usually licensed by the state, who arranges financing for a potential home purchaser by seeking the mortgage products for that particular person.

Mortgage holder. A person or company who currently has the right, under the terms of the mortgage, to enforce it through foreclosure.

Mortgage servicer. A type of business that large mortgage owners hire to administer their mortgage portfolios. The mortgage servicer typically accepts and records mortgage payments, negotiates a workout in case of a default, and even supervises the foreclosure process if attempts at a workout fail. Mortgage owners usually prefer that their homeowners stay current on their loans and stay out of foreclosure, but servicers often have a conflicting economic incentive because when customers default on their mortgages, the servicers get to keep the fees and costs that typically accompany a mortgage default and foreclosure.

Mortgage-backed security. A type of investment backed by mortgage loans that have been packaged into pools or trusts, with payments on the underlying mortgages generating the return for investors. By selling original mortgages to Fannie Mae and Freddie Mac (and other players in the secondary mortgage market, where the packaging occurs) lenders generate more funds for future lending.

Mortgagee. The mortgagee is the lender or other entity that owns the rights and responsibilities granted in a mortgage by the borrower (mortgagor). Typically, the mortgagee is the party who is authorized by state law to bring a foreclosure action.

Mortgagor. Someone who borrows money and signs a mortgage.

Motion to lift stay. A formal request in which a creditor asks the bankruptcy court for permission to continue a court action or collection activities in spite of the automatic stay.

Negative amortization. Negative amortization occurs when payments do not cover the amount of interest due for a loan period. During the housing boom, a popular type of loan that permitted negative amortization was what's called a Payment-Option ARM. This type of adjustable rate mortgage allows the borrower to choose among several payment options each month: a payment of principal and interest, an interest-only payment, or a payment of less than the interest owed that month. If the borrower selects the last option, the amount of unpaid interest is added to the principal, which increases the total amount owed (negative amortization) and results in the borrower paying interest on interest. This drastically increases the total amount owed and the cost of the loan. Typically, if the balance exceeds a certain limit, for example 110% or 125% of the original loan amount, the lender ends the option payments. Negative amortization loans are not readily available anymore.

Negative equity. Negative equity is when a property's market value is less than the total owed on all the liens recorded against it. The popular term for negative equity is "upside down" or "under water." In the bankruptcy context, negative equity can be very helpful in that you can get rid of liens that are no longer secured by equity even though they were secured when you obtained the loans. For example, say you have a first mortgage of $200,000, a second mortgage of $100,000 and a third mortgage of $50,000. Also assume that your home sank from a value of $400,000 to $175,000. In this case you have a negative equity of $175,000 (the difference between your home's value ($175,000) and the amount of the liens created by all three mortgages, or $350,000). Your first mortgage of $200,000 is partially covered by your home's value of $175,000, but you have no equity to secure the second and third mortgages. In this situation, Chapter 13 bankruptcy can remove the second and third mortgage liens from your house's title.

Nonbankruptcy federal exemptions. Federal laws that allow a debtor who has not filed for bankruptcy to keep creditors away from certain property. The debtor can also use these exemptions in bankruptcy if the debtor is using a state exemption system.

Nondischargeable debt. Debt that survives bankruptcy, such as back child support and most student loans.

Nonexempt property. In bankruptcy, property that is unprotected by the exemption system available to the debtor. In a Chapter 7 bankruptcy, the trustee may sell nonexempt property for the benefit of the debtor's unsecured creditors. In a Chapter 13 bankruptcy, debtors must propose a plan that pays their unsecured creditors at least the value of their unsecured property.

Nonjudicial foreclosure. A foreclosure that proceeds outside of court under a power of sale clause included in a deed of trust.

Nonpriority debt. A type of debt that is not entitled to be paid first in Chapter 7 bankruptcy and does not have to be paid in full in a Chapter 13 bankruptcy.

Non-purchase-money security interest. In the foreclosure context, a loan that uses your home as collateral for any purpose other than to buy it—for example, a home equity loan that is used to improve the home or pay for a vacation, college tuition, or medical emergency.

Notice to quit. A formal written notice, given to the occupant of real estate, to leave the premises within a specified period of time or face a judicial proceeding (often called an unlawful detainer, or forcible entry and detainer proceedings) in which a judge can order the sheriff to physically evict the occupant. In some states, a homeowner who continues to occupy the home after a foreclosure must be given a notice to quit before eviction proceedings may go forward. In other cases, the foreclosure order will include a writ of assistance, which is an order of the court directing the sheriff to remove the foreclosed homeowner from the home.

Open-ended loan. A loan without a definite term or end date. Authorized charges on credit cards are open-ended loans. As a general rule, there are no limits on interest rates charged on open-ended loans but some states cap interest rates on closed-end loans.

Origination fee. A fee paid to a lender for processing a loan application. This fee is commonly called points and is charged as a percentage of the loan amount.

Originator. The entity the loan documents identify as the party making the loan, typically a bank or credit union.

Partially secured debt. A debt secured by collateral that is worth less than the debt itself—for instance, when a person owes $15,000 on a car that is worth only $10,000.

Personal financial management counseling. A two-hour class intended to teach good budget management. Every consumer bankruptcy filer must attend such a class in order to get a Chapter 7 or Chapter 13 bankruptcy discharge.

Personal property. All property not classified as real property, including tangible items, such as cars and jewelry, and intangible property, such as stocks and pensions.

Predatory lending. In the foreclosure context, lending money under terms that are likely to cause a default in payments because of the expense of the loan compared to the borrower's income, or due to hidden fees and costs that are not properly disclosed. Certain categories of predatory loans are prohibited by federal and state law, and homeowners can sometimes use a violation of those laws to defend against a foreclosure or sue for fines and penalties.

Prepetition counseling. Mandatory debt and credit counseling that occurs before the bankruptcy petition is filed. Compare personal financial management counseling, which occurs after the petition is filed.

Priority debt. In Chapter 7 bankruptcy, a type of debt that is paid first if the debtor has any assets available to pay creditors. Priority debts include alimony and child support, fees owed to the trustee and attorneys in the case, and wages owed to employees. With one exception (back child support obligations assigned to government entities), priority claims must be paid in full in a Chapter 13 bankruptcy.

Projected disposable income. In bankruptcy, the amount of income a debtor will have left over each month, after deducting allowable expenses, payments on mandatory debts, and administrative expenses from his or her current monthly income. This is the amount the debtor must pay toward unsecured nonpriority debts in a Chapter 13 plan.

Proof of service. A document signed under penalty of perjury by the person serving a document showing how the service was made, who made it, and when.

Property inspection fee. A charge imposed by a mortgage servicer for a cursory inspection (often just a drive-by) to determine the physical condition or occupancy status of mortgaged property. This fee may be unreasonably high and an unreasonable number of inspections may be made, especially if the homeowner has defaulted on mortgage payments. To get current on a mortgage or propose a Chapter 13 repayment plan, the homeowner must pay these fees as well as the missed payments.

Real Estate Settlement Procedures Act (RESPA). A federal law designed to protect consumers from unnecessarily high settlement charges and certain abusive practices in the residential real estate market. RESPA provides a way for a borrower to challenge a stated loan balance provided by the servicer and to get information about how the loan has been processed. It also requires that certain disclosures be made to borrowers.

Real property. Real estate (land and buildings on the land, usually including mobile homes attached to a foundation).

Reamortization. Recalculating loan payments on different terms. For example, if you have paid for ten years on a 15-year loan, your lender might extend the loan for another ten years at a lower interest rate, lowering your monthly payments. Similarly, lenders sometimes add missed payments to the principal loan (that is, capitalize the missed payments). This reamortization may cause the monthly payments to increase because of the increase in the principal and the interest on it.

Redemption right. In foreclosure, the former homeowner's right to buy back the house after a foreclosure sale by reimbursing the new owner the amount of the purchase price or paying off the full value of the mortgage. In some states, even after a foreclosure sale, the new owner can't take possession until the redemption period has passed. For example, if the state's law gives the former owner up to six months to redeem the mortgage after the sale and the right to live in the home during this time, the new owner can't take possession until that time has passed and no redemption has been made.

Refinance. Using a new loan to pay off the current loan to get a better interest rate and perhaps pull some of your equity out of the house. Refinancing is hard to get if you are more than three payments behind or have troubled credit. But a homeowner who is facing a mortgage interest reset, is still current on the mortgage, and has some equity in the property from a down payment or many years of mortgage payments might be able to refinance at a more affordable fixed rate.

Reinstating a mortgage. Getting current on your mortgage by making up missed payments, paying the lender interest on the missed payments, and reimbursing the lender for various costs and fees incurred during the time you were in default. This is sometimes referred to as curing the default.

Repayment plan. A mortgage workout option to catch up on the overdue amount. The typical repayment plan provides for amortizing missed payments (and associated interest, costs, and fees) over a period of time by increasing the monthly mortgage payment to include the extra payments. Also refers to the plan proposed by a debtor in a Chapter 13 bankruptcy.

Rescission. The act of canceling a loan agreement and asking a court to restore borrower and lender to the positions they were in before it was signed. In some cases, federal and state laws allow a borrower to rescind a mortgage loan transaction within three business days after signing the papers. This period can sometimes be extended for years if the lender violated certain federal laws. The right of rescission may sometimes be used as a defense to a foreclosure.

Reverse mortgage. A type of loan designed for people who are 62 or older and have considerable equity in their homes. The reverse mortgage lender provides the borrower with a lump sum, line of credit, or a set monthly payment (or a combination of a line of credit and monthly payments) based on the amount of the equity in the home. Once a triggering event occurs, such as the borrowers' death, the lender will typically foreclose, sell the house, and recoup what it is owed on the loan. Reverse mortgages are heavily regulated.

Second mortgage or deed of trust. A mortgage on property that is already mortgaged or subject to a deed of trust. It comes after a prior mortgage in priority of payment.

Secondary market. The process by which original mortgage lenders sell their loans to buyers (often Fannie Mae and Freddie Mac), who, in turn, package the loans into securities with different risk ratings and resell them to individual and corporate investors with the help of Wall Street brokerages and bond-rating firms.

Secured creditor. The owner of a secured claim.

Secured debt. A debt secured by collateral.

Secured interest. A claim to property used as collateral. For instance, a lender on a car note retains legal title to the car until the loan is paid off.

Secured property. Property that is collateral for a secured debt.

Securitization. The process of converting a mortgage lender's ownership interest in an original mortgage into an investment vehicle that can be handily sold on Wall Street as another type of security.

Serial bankruptcy filing. The practice of filing and dismissing one bankruptcy after another to obtain the protection of the automatic stay, even though the bankruptcies themselves offer no debt relief—for instance, when a debtor files successive Chapter 13 cases to prevent foreclosure even though there are no debts to repay. Courts will ban the debtor from further filings.

Short sale. A sale of a house in which the sale price is less than the mortgage secured by the house. The homeowner must get the lender's approval for a short sale.

State exemptions. State laws that specify the types of property creditors are not entitled to take to satisfy a debt, and the bankruptcy trustee is not entitled to take and sell for the benefit of the debtor's unsecured creditors.

Statutory lien. A lien imposed on property by law, such as tax liens and mechanic's liens, as opposed to voluntary liens (such as mortgages) and liens arising from court judgments (judicial liens).

Stay. See "Automatic stay."

Strict foreclosure. A type of judicial foreclosure used in a few states in which the court not only orders that the foreclosure take place, but also transfers title to the foreclosing party without requiring the property to be put up for sale at an auction.

Strip down of lien. In a Chapter 13 bankruptcy, when the amount of a lien on collateral is reduced to the collateral's replacement value. See "Cramdown."

Subprime mortgage loan. A loan that carries a higher interest rate than a comparable loan, generally because of the borrower's low credit rating or other factors, such as the property's location.

Summons and complaint. Legal documents that are served on a homeowner to initiate a lawsuit—for example, a judicial foreclosure or an eviction. The summons tells the homeowner how and when to respond to the lawsuit. The complaint sets out the reasons why the court should, for example, issue a foreclosure judgment or evict a former owner after the sale.

Tax lien. A statutory lien imposed on property to secure payment of back taxes—typically income and property taxes.

Trustee. An official appointed by the bankruptcy court to carry out the administrative tasks associated with a bankruptcy and to collect and sell nonexempt property for the benefit of the debtor's unsecured creditors. The third party who typically administers a nonjudicial foreclosure is also called a "trustee." A deed of trust gives the trustee the authority to foreclose and sell the home to pay off the loan balance at the request of the lender if the borrower defaults. State law can limit who may act as a foreclosure trustee. In theory, the trustee is a neutral third party, but the trustee is usually chosen by and affiliated with the lender.

Truth in Lending Act (TILA). A federal law that requires most lenders to give borrowers standard disclosures of the cost and payment terms of the loan. The Home Ownership and Equity Protection Act (HOEPA) is part of the Truth in Lending Act. If the lender violates TILA or HOEPA, the homeowner may be able to stop foreclosure by rescinding the loan, depending on its type and whether it qualifies for protection under these federal laws.

Undersecured debt. A debt secured by collateral that is worth less than the debt.

State Information

The information here summarizes some of the important features of each state's law on foreclosures. When you use it, please keep in mind the following point.

This is only a summary of your state's laws and does not tell the entire story. It is intended for owners of single-family residences and doesn't address special laws for agricultural land or the rights of tenants in foreclosed homes owned by their landlords.

RESOURCE

More state-specific foreclosure information. The Foreclosure Center on Nolo.com has lots of state-specific foreclosure articles, and we are adding to the collection every day. You can find detailed articles on state foreclosure procedures, state foreclosure prevention mediation programs, state protections for homeowners in foreclosure, and other developments in state law.

This discusses only the most common method of foreclosure in your state. For example, it provides information about nonjudicial foreclosures for the states where they are the most common procedure, even though judicial foreclosures are allowed in those nonjudicial states in some circumstances.

Laws change. Foreclosure laws and procedures are complex and subject to change by legislatures and to interpretation by courts. For these reasons, you should use the information in this book as a starting point for additional research using the resources described in Ch. 10. Citations to each state's statutes are included so you can look up the laws themselves.

You can cross-check the information in this appendix with the summaries of state law in *Foreclosures and Mortgage Servicing* by the National Consumer Law Center (see Ch. 10). Also check for updates on this book's "Online Companion Page" using the link in the introductory chapter, "Your Foreclosure Companion."

For bills pending in your state's legislature or recently signed into law by your state's governor, visit www.ncsl.org and search for "Mortgages & Loans." Remember, a bill does not become law until it is signed by your state's governor. Most proposed laws will never make it to your governor's pen.

Finally, you can also read posts on Nolo's "Bankruptcy, Debt and Foreclosure" blog at http://blog.nolo.com/bankruptcy, which discusses important changes in foreclosure and bankruptcy law that may affect you.

Alabama

Foreclosure laws change! Check for updates at www.nolo.com/legal-updates.

Topic	State Rule
Most common type of foreclosure process	Nonjudicial under a power of sale in a mortgage
Notice of the foreclosure	Foreclosing party must publish notice in a newspaper once a week for three consecutive weeks; no requirement that the homeowner be served by mail. However, mortgages in Alabama often contractually require the foreclosing party to notify the borrower (usually by mail) before foreclosure proceedings are started.
Reinstatement of loan before sale	Not available (except as permitted by the terms of the mortgage)
Redemption after sale	Available for one year after foreclosure sale (180 days if the loan originated on January 1, 2016, or after) if the property is surrendered to the buyer within ten days after a written demand is made.
Special protections for foreclosures involving high-cost mortgages	None
Special state protections for service members	If a service member dies while deployed overseas, the lender must wait at least 180 days before starting a foreclosure against the surviving spouse or the service member's estate provided that the surviving spouse or the estate notifies the lender and asks for a delay (and the mortgage was taken out after August 1, 2009). Ala. Code §§ 35-10-70, 35-10-71
Deficiency judgments	May be obtained by filing a lawsuit.
Cash exempted in bankruptcy	Using the wildcard exemption, $7,500 for one person, $15,000 for a married couple (will not protect wages, salaries, or other compensation).
Notice to leave after house is sold	Entitled to a written ten-day notice to leave before eviction proceedings may be brought.
Foreclosure statutes	Ala. Code §§ 35-10-1 to 35-10-30, 6-5-247 to 6-5-257

Alaska

Foreclosure laws change! Check for updates at www.nolo.com/legal-updates.

Topic	State Rule
Most common type of foreclosure process	Nonjudicial under a power of sale in a deed of trust
Notice of the foreclosure	Notice of default must be recorded not less than 30 days after default and not less than 90 days before sale. The notice of default must be sent by certified mail to the borrower within 10 days of recording or personally delivered to the borrower within 20 days after recording. Before the sale, the foreclosing party must publicly post and publish a notice of sale (in a newspaper and on the Internet).
Reinstatement of loan before sale	Available any time before sale, but lender can refuse to reinstate if it filed two or more prior notices of default and the borrower cured the defaults
Redemption after sale	Not available after a nonjudicial foreclosure, unless the deed of trust specifically provides a right of redemption
Special protections for foreclosures involving high-cost mortgages	None
Special state protections for service members	Servicemembers Civil Relief Act protections extended to members of the Alaska National Guard and Alaska Naval Militia while on active duty for the state by order of the governor. Alaska Stat. § 26.05.135
Deficiency judgments	Not allowed after a nonjudicial foreclosure
Cash exempted in bankruptcy	$1,890 for one person, $3,780 for a married couple. Under federal bankruptcy exemptions, $13,100 for one person, $26,200 for a married couple.
Notice to leave after house is sold	New owner must give former owner a notice to quit (leave) before filing a civil lawsuit to gain possession.
Foreclosure statutes	Alaska Stat. §§ 34.20.070 et seq.

Arizona

Foreclosure laws change! Check for updates at www.nolo.com/legal-updates.

Topic	State Rule
Most common types of foreclosure process	Nonjudicial under power of sale in deed of trust
Notice of the foreclosure	Foreclosing party must record a notice of sale at least 90 days before the sale date and must mail it by certified mail to borrower within five business days after recording. The notice of sale must also be published in a newspaper for four consecutive weeks and posted on the property at least 20 days before sale, as well as posted in the courthouse building.
Reinstatement of loan before sale	Available until 5:00 p.m. on the day before date of sale (other than a Saturday or legal holiday).
Redemption after sale	Not available after a nonjudicial foreclosure
Special protections for foreclosures involving high-cost mortgages	None
Special state protections for service members	Federal protections under the Servicemembers Civil Relief Act extended to National Guard ordered to active duty by governor in certain circumstances. Ariz. Rev. Stat. Ann. § 26-168
Deficiency judgments	Not allowed after a nonjudicial foreclosure if the property is 2½ acres or less and is a single- or two-family residence. For most other properties, allowed if lawsuit is filed within 90 days of foreclosure sale.
Cash exempted in bankruptcy	$300 for one person, $600 for a married couple.
Notice to leave after house is sold	New owner may begin an eviction action following he foreclosure sale after making a demand for possession.
Foreclosure statutes	Ariz. Rev. Stat. §§ 33-721 to 33-730 (judicial), 33-801 to 33-821 (nonjudicial), 12-1281 to 12-1283, 12-1566

Arkansas

Foreclosure laws change! Check for updates at www.nolo.com/legal-updates.

Topic	State Rule
Most common type of foreclosure process	Nonjudicial under power of sale in a mortgage
Notice of the foreclosure	Foreclosing party must mail a notice to the borrower that includes information about loan modification assistance, among other things, at least ten days before starting a foreclosure. Foreclosing party must record a notice of default and intent to sell, and then mail a copy by certified and first-class mail within 30 days after recording the notice. Notice must also be published in a newspaper for four consecutive weeks prior to sale, posted at the courthouse, and published by a third-party on the Internet.
Reinstatement of loan before sale	Allowed prior to sale
Redemption after sale	Not available after a nonjudicial foreclosure
Special protections for foreclosures involving high-cost mortgages	An intentional violation of the Arkansas Home Loan Protection Act renders the loan agreement void. The lender then has no right to collect, receive, or retain any principal, interest, or other charges at all with respect to the loan, and the borrower may recover any payments made under the agreement. Ark. Code Ann. §§ 23-53-106
Special state protections for service members	Lender may not foreclose on a military service member for nonpayment or any breach occurring during military service without a court order if certain conditions are met. Applies to National Guard members called into active service by the governor for more than 180 days. Ark. Code Ann. § 12-62-716
Deficiency judgments	Allowed for difference between the: indebtedness minus the fair market value of the property or the indebtedness minus the foreclosure sales price (whichever is less). Lawsuit must be filed within 12 months of sale.
Cash exempted in bankruptcy	$200 for one person, $500 for head of household, $1,000 for married couple wherein one is the head of household. Under federal bankruptcy exemptions, $13,100 for one person, $26,200 for a married couple.
Notice to leave after house is sold	The new owner can initiate an eviction action following the sale.
Foreclosure statutes	Ark. Code Ann. §§ 18-50-101 to 18-50-116

California

Foreclosure laws change! Check for updates at www.nolo.com/legal-updates.

Topic	State Rule
Most common type of foreclosure process	Nonjudicial under power of sale in deed of trust
Notice of the foreclosure	Foreclosing party must personally contact (or meet the requirements for attempting to contact) borrowers to explore options for avoiding foreclosure 30 days before recording the notice of default. The foreclosing party then records a three-month notice of default in the county recorder's office and mails a copy to the borrowers within ten business days following recordation. After three months expires (or up to five days prior), the foreclosing property records a notice of sale and mails a copy to the borrowers at least 20 days before the sale date. The sale date cannot be earlier than three months and 20 days after the recording date of the notice of default. The notice of sale is also posted on the property, in a public place, and published in a newspaper.
Reinstatement of loan before sale	Allowed up to five business days before the sale date
Redemption after sale	Not available after a nonjudicial foreclosure
Special protections for foreclosures involving high-cost mortgages	Cal. Fin. Code § 4973 makes a number of abusive loan practices unlawful. Section 4978 provides remedies that include authority for a judge to reform the loan to comply with the law. These provisions don't apply to mortgages held by the secondary market (Fannie Mae, Freddie Mac) or to assignees that have no reason to know of the loan origination violations. Cal. Fin. Code § 4979.8
Special state protections for service members	Protections similar to those under the federal Servicemembers Civil Relief Act extended to members of the National Guard called or ordered into active state service by the governor or into active federal service by the President of the United States. Also applies to reservists who have been called to full-time active duty. Cal. Mil. & Vet. Code §§ 400 to 409.13
Deficiency judgments	Not allowed after a nonjudicial foreclosure
Cash exempted in bankruptcy	Up to $28,225 under California 703 exemption system.
Notice to leave after the house is sold	New owner must give former homeowner three-day notice to quit (leave) and file an unlawful detainer lawsuit to evict.
Foreclosure statutes	Cal. Civ. Code §§ 2923.5, 2924 to 2924l; Cal Code of Civ. Proc. §§ 580a through 580d

Colorado

Foreclosure laws change! Check for updates at www.nolo.com/legal-updates.

Topic	State Rule
Most common type of foreclosure process	Nonjudicial under power of sale in deed of trust. The foreclosing party must file proof of debt ownership and the default with a public trustee, who oversees the process. The mortgage holder must separately obtain a court order in a Rule 120 proceeding authorizing the sale and give the public trustee a copy of the order before the sale date.
Notice of the foreclosure	Thirty days before recording the Notice of Election and Demand, and at least 30 days after the first default in payments, borrower must be served with information about state hotline and how to contact the foreclosing party's loss-mitigation department. After the Notice of Election and Demand has been recorded (110 to 125 calendar days before the sale date), public trustee must mail a Combined Notice of the Sale, Right to Cure, and Right to Redeem to the borrower within 20 calendar days after the recording date. Notice of the Rule 120 hearing must be mailed to the borrower and posted on the property not less than 14 days prior to the hearing date.
Reinstatement of loan before sale	Available until noon the day before the sale provided the borrower files a notice of intent to cure with the public trustee no later than 15 calendar days before the sale date.
Redemption after sale	Available to some lienholders but not to borrower
Special protections for foreclosures involving high-cost mortgages	None
Special state protections for service members	Colorado law provides certain protections against foreclosure for National Guard members when called to state military service or called to state defense force active duty for over 30 days. Colo. Rev. Stat. § 28-3-1406
Deficiency judgments	Allowed, but the borrower can raise a defense against the action for a deficiency judgment if the foreclosing party did not bid the fair market value of the property, minus unpaid property taxes and certain other expenses.
Cash exempted in bankruptcy	None
Notice to leave after house is sold	The new owner must make a demand for possession. If the former owner does not vacate, then the new owner files the lawsuit to evict.
Foreclosure statutes	Colo. Rev. Stat. §§ 38-38-100.3 to 38-38-114

Connecticut

Foreclosure laws change! Check for updates at www.nolo.com/legal-updates.

Topic	State Rule
Most common type of foreclosure process	Judicial ("foreclosure by sale") or; strict foreclosure in which court transfers title directly to foreclosing party without ordering a sale
Notice of the foreclosure	After the foreclosing party files the foreclosure lawsuit, borrower has 15 days after the return date to file an answer. The foreclosing party must give notice to the borrowers about the foreclosure mediation program along with the complaint and summons.
Reinstatement of loan before sale	Not available (except as permitted by the terms of the mortgage)
Redemption after sale	Up until court confirms sale or until the "Law Day" in a strict foreclosure.
Special protections for foreclosures involving high-cost mortgages	None relevant to foreclosure. But certain homeowners who are underemployed or unemployed can ask the court for protection from foreclosure and modification of mortgage terms to give relief from paying of arrearages.
Special state protections for service members	None
Deficiency judgments	May be obtained in foreclosure by sale, and within 30 days after the redemption period expires (the Law Day) in a strict foreclosure.
Cash exempted in bankruptcy	Using the wildcard exemption, $1,000 for one person, $2,000 for a married couple.
	Under federal bankruptcy exemptions, $13,100 for one person, $26,200 for a married couple.
Notice to leave after house is sold	Former owner will be required to move out after the sale under an order of ejectment issued by the court. Check with the marshal to see how much time you have to move out.
Foreclosure statutes	Conn. Gen. Stat. §§ 49-1 to 49-31v; Connecticut Superior Court Rules 23-16 through 23-19

Delaware

Foreclosure laws change! Check for updates at www.nolo.com/legal-updates.

Topic	State Rule
Most common type of foreclosure process	Judicial
Notice of the foreclosure	If the home is an owner-occupied residential property that is one to four units, the foreclosing party must mail the borrower a 45-day notice of intent to foreclose before starting the foreclosure lawsuit. Borrower has 20 days to respond to lawsuit. Foreclosing party must include a mediation notice with complaint. After court grants a judgment of foreclosure, borrower gets a ten-day notice of sale. Notice of sale must also be posted publicly and published in a newspaper two weeks prior to sale.
Reinstatement of loan before sale	Not available (except as permitted by the terms of the mortgage)
Redemption after sale	Available until court confirms sale
Special protections for foreclosures involving high-cost mortgages	None
Special state protections for service members	None
Deficiency judgments	May be obtained by filing a separate lawsuit after a court has issued a foreclosure judgment.
Cash exempted in bankruptcy	$500 if head of family
Notice to leave after house is sold	Eviction of former homeowner may be continued as part of the foreclosure action.
Foreclosure statute	Del. Code Ann. tit. 10, Chapter 49, §§ 5061 through 5067

District of Columbia

Foreclosure laws change! Check for updates at www.nolo.com/legal-updates.

Topic	State Rule
Most common type of foreclosure process	Nonjudicial under power of sale in deed of trust; however, due to issues with the District of Columbia's mediation program, more foreclosures are judicial.
Notice of the foreclosure	Foreclosing party must mail a notice of default along with a mediation notice giving 30 days to elect mediation. If the borrower does not elect mediation (or participates in mediation but does not work out an agreement with the foreclosing party), the foreclosure may proceed. The foreclosing party then sends a notice of the intention to foreclose (including sale information) 30 days before the sale to borrower and sends a copy of the notice to the mayor. The 30-day period begins when the mayor receives notice.
Reinstatement of loan before sale	Allowed up to five business days before the sale, once in two consecutive years
Redemption after sale	Not available
Special protections for foreclosures involving high-cost mortgages	None
Special state protections for service members	None
Deficiency judgments	May be obtained by filing a lawsuit
Cash exempted in bankruptcy	Using the wildcard exemption, up to $8,925 for one person, $17,850 for a married couple. Under federal bankruptcy exemptions, $13,100 for one person, $26,200 for a married couple.
Notice to leave after house is sold	New owner may file a lawsuit to evict former homeowners from the property after giving notice to quit. A summons must be served seven days before trial regarding possession.
Foreclosure statute	D.C. Code Ann. §§ 42-815 through 42-816

Florida

Foreclosure laws change! Check for updates at www.nolo.com/legal-updates.

Topic	State Rule
Most common type of foreclosure process	Judicial
Notice of the foreclosure	Borrower gets 20 days to respond to complaint. Foreclosing party must publish notice of sale in a newspaper for two consecutive weeks at least five days before sale. The judge has the discretion to refer foreclosure for mediation as permitted by law.
Reinstatement of loan before sale	Not available (except as permitted by the terms of the mortgage)
Redemption after sale	Available until the court clerk files a certificate of sale or as specified in the judgment, whichever is later
Special protections for foreclosures involving high-cost mortgages	None
Special state protections for service members	If a military service member took out the mortgage before going on active duty (state or federal), lender cannot foreclose during the time of service or within 30 days thereafter unless a court issues an order ahead of time allowing it. Fla. Stat. Ann. §§ 250.5201 to 250.5205
Deficiency judgments	Allowed as part of the foreclosure action if borrower is personally served. The deficiency judgment is within the sound discretion of the court; however, in the case of an owner-occupied residential property, the amount may not exceed the difference between the judgment amount and the fair market value of the property on the date of sale. Foreclosing party may also file a separate lawsuit for a deficiency. Foreclosing party has one year to request the deficiency judgment.
Cash exempted in bankruptcy	$5,000 for one person, $10,000 for a married couple.
Notice to leave after house is sold	The eviction process is part of the foreclosure action and the right to possession is included in the judgment. It is not usually necessary to file an independent action for possession. The foreclosing party files a motion for a writ of possession. When the motion is granted, the clerk of court issues the writ of possession and the sheriff posts the writ to the property. (The writ gives 24 hours to move out.) If the occupant does not vacate, the sheriff executes the order.
Foreclosure statutes	Fla. Stat. Ann. §§ 702.01 through 702.11, 45.031 and 45.0315

Georgia

Foreclosure laws change! Check for updates at www.nolo.com/legal-updates.

Topic	State Rule
Most common type of foreclosure process	Nonjudicial under power of sale in a Security Deed (deed of trust)
Notice of the foreclosure	Foreclosing party must mail notice to borrower 30 days before sale. Additional notice by publication in a newspaper of general circulation is required.
Reinstatement of loan before sale	High-cost home loans may be reinstated until title is transferred. For other types of loans, the security deed may provide the right to reinstate.
Redemption after sale	Not available
Special protections for foreclosures involving high-cost mortgages	Additional notices required for high-cost loans. Georgia Fair Lending Act, Ga. Code Ann. §§ 7-6A-1 to 7-6A-13
Special state protections for service members	None
Deficiency judgments	If the foreclosure was nonjudicial, no deficiency judgment until a court confirms that the property was sold at its fair market value. (Foreclosing party must file a report of sale with the court within 30 days of the foreclosure sale.)
Cash exempted in bankruptcy	Using the wildcard exemption, up to $11,200 for one person, $22,400 for a married couple.
Notice to leave after house is sold	The purchaser must first make a demand for possession, and then can begin eviction proceedings.
Foreclosure statutes	Ga. Code Ann. §§ 44-14-160 to 44-14-191

Hawaii

Foreclosure laws change! Check for updates at www.nolo.com/legal-updates.

Topic	State Rule
Most common type of foreclosure process	Judicial. In the past, most foreclosures in Hawaii were nonjudicial. However, lenders have switched to judicial foreclosures in order to bypass Hawaii's Mortgage Foreclosure Dispute Resolution (MFDR) Program. This could change if the legislature amends the MFDR Program.
Notice of the foreclosure	Borrower has 20 days to respond after being served with summons and complaint. For judicial foreclosures, the foreclosing party must publish a notice of sale in a newspaper once each week for three consecutive weeks, with the sale taking place no sooner than 14 days after the date of the publication of the third public notice advertisement; or the Notice of Sale may be published not less than 28 days before the date of the public sale on a state website. (If the public notice is published on a website, the notice must also be published at least once in a newspaper not less than 14 days prior to the public sale.)
Reinstatement of loan before sale	Not available in a judicial foreclosure (except as permitted by the terms of the mortgage)
Redemption after sale	Not available
Special protections for foreclosures involving high-cost mortgages	None
Special state protections for service members	Protections similar to the federal Servicemembers Civil Relief Act provided for members of the state military forces, including the right to postpone legal proceedings and a prohibition on nonjudicial foreclosures. Haw. Rev. Stat. §§ 657D-1 to 657D-63
Deficiency judgments	Allowed for judicial foreclosures
Cash exempted in bankruptcy	None. Under federal bankruptcy exemptions, $13,100 for one person, $26,200 for a married couple.
Notice to leave after house is sold	In a judicial foreclosure, new owner must get a court order (write of possession) to remove former homeowner after the sale.
Foreclosure statutes	Haw. Rev. Stat. §§ 667-1 through 667-20.1 (judicial); §§ 667-21 through 667-41 (nonjudicial)

Idaho

Foreclosure laws change! Check for updates at www.nolo.com/legal-updates.

Topic	State Rule
Most common type of foreclosure process	Nonjudicial under power of sale in deed of trust
Notice of the foreclosure	Foreclosing party must mail homeowner a notice of default and a 120-day notice of sale before the date set for sale. Foreclosing party must also make attempt to personally serve occupant with notice of sale and post notice of sale on property at least 30 days before the sale, as well as publish notice of sale over four consecutive weeks at least 30 days before sale. The notice of default must be accompanied by a modification request form. The lender must respond to a request for modification within 45 days and may not proceed to a foreclosure sale until it has responded to the modification request.
Reinstatement of loan before sale	Available within 115 days after notice of default is filed with county recorder
Redemption after sale	Not available after a nonjudicial foreclosure
Special protections for foreclosures involving high-cost mortgages	None
Special state protections for service members	Idaho law extends protections of federal Servicemembers Civil Relief Act to national guard ordered to state active duty by governor in certain circumstances. Idaho Code § 46-409
Deficiency judgments	May be obtained in a lawsuit brought within three months after sale. Amount of deficiency is limited by fair market value at time of sale.
Cash exempted in bankruptcy	None
Notice to leave after house is sold	New owner is entitled to possession of the property on the tenth day following sale but must go to court to evict former owner. An eviction trial must be scheduled within 12 days after the filing of the complaint.
Foreclosure statutes	Idaho Code §§ 45-1505 to 45-1515

Illinois

Foreclosure laws change! Check for updates at www.nolo.com/legal-updates.

Topic	State Rule
Most common type of foreclosure process	Judicial
Notice of the foreclosure	Borrower has 30 days to respond after being served with summons and complaint. After court issues a judgment of foreclosure, a notice of sale must be published three times between 45 and seven days before sale. Notice of sale must be mailed to borrower at least ten business days before the sale.
Reinstatement of loan before sale	Available within 90 days after foreclosure complaint is served on borrower. Under High-Risk Home Loan Act, foreclosing party must serve notice of right to reinstate at least 30 days before starting foreclosure lawsuit.
Redemption after sale	Available for seven months after the complaint is served or three months after foreclosure judgment entered, whichever is later. If the mortgage holder is the purchaser at the sale, property sold below a certain value may be redeemed for 30 days after confirmation of sale by paying sales price plus costs and interest.
Special protections for foreclosures involving high-cost mortgages	Special defenses to foreclosure lawsuit. High-Risk Home Loan Act, 815 Ill. Comp. Stat. §§ 137/1 to 137/175
Special state protections for service members	Certain service members may apply to the court for a 90-day stay of foreclosure proceedings or, in some cases, a reduction in the monthly payments for up to 90 days. 735 Ill. Comp. Stat. §§ 5/15-1501.5, 5/15-1501.6. Court can postpone proceedings if state or federal military service directly results in failure to meet pre-service obligations. 330 Ill. Comp. Stat. § 60/5.1
Deficiency judgments	May be sought as part of the foreclosure lawsuit. Allowed only if borrower is served personally (unless borrower enters an appearance in the action).
Cash exempted in bankruptcy	Using the wildcard exemption, up to $4,000 for one person, $8,000 for a married couple.
Notice to leave after house is sold	Court may order homeowner removed 30 days after it confirms the sale. New owner must file a complaint for forcible entry and detainer to remove any occupant who wasn't personally named in the foreclosure case.
Foreclosure statutes	735 Ill. Comp. Stat §§ 5/15-1501 to 5/15-1605

Indiana

Foreclosure laws change! Check for updates at www.nolo.com/legal-updates.

Topic	State Rule
Most common type of foreclosure process	Judicial
Notice of the foreclosure	Foreclosing party must give borrower 30 days' notice before filing foreclosure complaint. Borrower generally gets 20 days to respond to complaint. After the complaint is filed, house can't be sold for three months (a waiting period) in most cases (longer for certain older mortgages). Foreclosing party must publish notice of sale once a week for three consecutive weeks with the first publication occurring at least 30 days before the scheduled sale, and mail a copy to homeowner at the time of the first advertisement. Notice of sale must also be posted at courthouse.
Reinstatement of loan before sale	If the borrower reinstates before the court enters judgment, the foreclosure must be dismissed. If the borrower reinstates after judgment, but prior to the sale, the foreclosure must be stayed (postponed). Reinstatement also available for high-cost home loans (defined in Ind. Code § 24-9-2-8) any time before title is transferred by means of foreclosure.
Redemption after sale	Not available after sale
Special protections for foreclosures involving high-cost mortgages	Borrower in foreclosure may raise violations of the high-cost home loan statute as a claim, counterclaim, or defense to foreclosure. Ind. Code § 24-9-5-1. Borrower may cure the default and reinstate a high cost home loan at any time until title is transferred by means of foreclosure. Ind. Code § 24-9-5-2
Special state protections for service members	Protections under the federal Servicemembers Civil Relief Act extended to national guard members ordered to state active duty for 30 or more consecutive days. Ind. Code § 10-16-7-23
Deficiency judgments	Allowed if borrower does not waive applicable waiting period. (Borrower may agree to waiver in exchange for lender's agreeing not to seek a deficiency judgment.)
Cash exempted in bankruptcy	$400 for one person, $800 for a married couple.
Notice to leave after house is sold	Foreclosing party (if it is the purchaser at the sale) may proceed with an eviction against the former owners as an extension of the foreclosure action.
Foreclosure statutes	Ind. Code §§ 32-30-10-1 to 32-30-10-14, 32-29-1-1 to 32-29-1-11, 32-29-7-1 to 32-29-7-14

Iowa

Foreclosure laws change! Check for updates at www.nolo.com/legal-updates.

Topic	State Rule
Most common type of foreclosure process	Judicial
Notice of the foreclosure	Foreclosing party must mail notice of default and right to cure (reinstate) to borrower at least 30 days before filing suit (or 45 days if the property is agricultural) and a demand for payment of the accelerated balance 14 days before filing suit, along with a notice about counseling and mediation. To officially start the foreclosure, the lender files a lawsuit in court and serves borrower a summons and complaint. Notice must be posted and published four weeks before date of sale.
Reinstatement of loan before sale	Available within 30 days after notice of default if the land is nonagricultural (or 45 days if the land is agricultural)
Redemption after sale	If foreclosure is judicial with redemption, the borrower can redeem the home within one year, six months (if the lender waives the deficiency in the foreclosure action and other criteria are met), or 60 days (if the borrower abandons the home and other criteria are met). If the lender elects to foreclose without redemption, the borrower can demand a delay of sale and redeem before the sale (no post-sale right of redemption). Post-sale redemption not available for alternative nonjudicial voluntary foreclosures.
Special protections for foreclosures involving high-cost mortgages	None
Special state protections for service members	If the service member entered into the mortgage to purchase real estate prior to military service, nonjudicial foreclosure is prohibited. Iowa Code § 29A.103
Deficiency judgments	Generally allowed, but prohibited under certain circumstances. (Consult with an attorney to find out if a deficiency judgment is permitted in your situation.)
Cash exempted in bankruptcy	Using the wildcard exemption, up to $1,000 for one person, $2,000 for a married couple.
Notice to leave after house is sold	If the foreclosure is judicial, the foreclosing party may generally include the eviction as part of the foreclosure action. If the foreclosure is nonjudicial, the new owner must file a separate eviction lawsuit.
Foreclosure statutes	Iowa Code §§ 654.1 to 654.26, 655A to 655A.9, 628.26, 628.27

Kansas

Foreclosure laws change! Check for updates at www.nolo.com/legal-updates.

Topic	State Rule
Most common type of foreclosure process	Judicial
Notice of the foreclosure	Borrower who is personally served with the complaint has 21 days to respond; if notice is only by publication in a local newspaper of general circulation, borrower has 41 days to respond. After court issues a foreclosure judgment, foreclosing party must publish a notice of sale at least three times; last publication must be between seven and 14 days before sale date.
Reinstatement of loan before sale	Not available (except as permitted by the terms of the mortgage)
Redemption after sale	Available for 12 months from the sale date (less if homeowner abandoned premises). Available for three months if borrower defaulted on mortgage before one-third of original debt was repaid. Court may extend three-month redemption period by another three months if homeowner loses his or her job after the sale and during the initial three-month period. Available for 12 months if all mortgage debt on property totals less than one-third of the house's market value.
Special protections for foreclosures involving high-cost mortgages	None
Special state protections for service members	None
Deficiency judgments	Allowed if court confirms that the price paid for property at sale is adequate compared to its fair market value. Sales price that covers foreclosing party's judgment, taxes, interest, and costs is considered adequate.
Cash exempted in bankruptcy	None
Notice to leave after house is sold	New owner does not have to send former owner a notice to terminate. After the redemption period, the new owner can get a writ of assistance as part of the foreclosure action commanding the sheriff to forcibly remove the former owner.
Foreclosure statute	Kan. Stat. Ann. §§ 60-2410, 60-2414, and 60-2415

Kentucky

Foreclosure laws change! Check for updates at www.nolo.com/legal-updates.

Topic	State Rule
Most common type of foreclosure process	Judicial
Notice of the foreclosure	Borrower has 20 days to respond after being served with the complaint. If court issues a foreclosure judgment, foreclosing party must post notice on courthouse door (and three other places) and publish notice in a newspaper.
Reinstatement of loan before sale	Generally, no right to reinstate (except as permitted by the terms of the mortgage). If loan is a high-cost home loan (under Ky. Rev. Stat. Ann. § 360.100), foreclosing party must provide a notice of default giving the borrower at least 30 days to reinstate before filing the foreclosure complaint.
Redemption after sale	Available six months after sale, if sale amount is less than two-thirds of property's appraised value.
Special protections for foreclosures involving high-cost mortgages	Before foreclosing a high-cost home loan, the foreclosing party must provide a notice of default to the borrower that gives 30 days to cure the default and reinstate the mortgage. Ky. Rev. Stat. Ann. § 360.100
Special state protections for service members	Protections under the federal Servicemembers Civil Relief Act extended to state national guard ordered to state active duty by governor for a period of 30 days or more. Ky. Rev. Stat. Ann. § 38.510
Deficiency judgments	Allowed (but not against a defendant who is constructively summoned, and who has not appeared in the action)
Cash exempted in bankruptcy	Using the wildcard exemption, up to $1,000 for one person, $2,000 for a married couple. Under federal bankruptcy exemptions, $13,100 for one person, $26,200 for a married couple.
Notice to leave after house is sold	New owner is entitled to possession upon ten days' notice. If former owner does not move out, purchaser can get a writ of possession issued by the court.
Foreclosure statutes	Ky. Rev. Stat. Ann. §§ 426.005, 426.200, 426.260, 426.530, 426.560

Louisiana

Foreclosure laws change! Check for updates at www.nolo.com/legal-updates.

Topic	State Rule
Most common type of foreclosure process	Judicial, but most common process is an "executory" proceeding. In the mortgage document, the borrower will typically have "confessed to judgment" in case of a default. Upon default the foreclosing party files a foreclosure petition with the mortgage attached, and the court summarily orders the property seized and sold unless the borrower appeals or brings a lawsuit asking the court to stop (enjoin) the proceeding.
Notice of the foreclosure	The sheriff must serve the borrower a written notice of seizure. Notice of sale is published at least twice and not less than three days after the debtor has been served with the notice of seizure.
Reinstatement of loan before sale	Not available (unless permitted by the terms of the mortgage)
Redemption after sale	Not available
Special protections for foreclosures involving high-cost mortgages	None
Special state protections for service members	None
Deficiency judgments	Allowed. Can be obtained in an ordinary proceeding or in a separate suit after an executory proceeding (or by converting executory proceeding into an ordinary proceeding) if the property was properly appraised.
Cash exempted in bankruptcy	None
Notice to leave after house is sold	New owner can get writ of possession from court and the sheriff will remove former owners from the premises.
Foreclosure statutes	La. Code Civ. Proc. Ann. Arts. 3721 to 3753, 2631 to 2772

Maine

Foreclosure laws change! Check for updates at www.nolo.com/legal-updates.

Topic	State Rule
Most common type of foreclosure process	Judicial
Notice of the foreclosure	Foreclosing party must send a notice of right to cure 35 days before starting foreclosure. Borrower has 20 days to respond after being served with summons and complaint. After the redemption period expires (see below), the foreclosing party must publish notice of public sale for three consecutive weeks. Sale must be held 30 to 45 days after date of first publication. Foreclosing party must also mail a notice of sale at least 30 days before sale date to all parties who appeared in the foreclosure action.
Reinstatement of loan before sale	Borrower has the right to reinstate within 35 days after receiving the notice of right to cure. Also, lender, in its sole discretion, may let borrower reinstate the loan any time before the sale.
Redemption after sale	Redemption period is 90 days from the date the foreclosure judgment is entered, unless borrower appeals.
Special protections for foreclosures involving high-cost mortgages	Creditor cannot charge a prepayment penalty and cannot engage in flipping. If the creditor violates the law, the borrower can get damages. Me. Rev. Stat. tit 9-A, § 8-506
Special state protections for service members	Certain military service members (including state military forces on active state service) get the opportunity to stay (postpone) court proceedings. Me. Rev. Stat. Ann. tit. 37-B, § 389-A
Deficiency judgments	Allowed, but limited to the difference between the fair market value of the property at the time of the sale and the total outstanding debt if the foreclosing party buys the home at the foreclosure sale.
Cash exempted in bankruptcy	Using the wildcard exemption, $6,400 for one person, $12,800 for a married couple.
Notice to leave after house is sold	Foreclosing party can get a writ of possession against the foreclosed homeowners as part of the foreclosure action.
Foreclosure statutes	Me. Rev. Stat. Ann. tit. 14, §§ 6101 to 6325

Maryland

Foreclosure laws change! Check for updates at www.nolo.com/legal-updates.

Topic	State Rule
Most common type of foreclosure process	Nonjudicial under power of sale in deed of trust, but a court must ratify the sale
Notice of the foreclosure	Foreclosing party must serve borrower with notice of intent to foreclose at least 45 days before starting foreclosure, along with mediation information if applicable. Service must be by first-class and certified mail, return receipt requested. The foreclosing party officially starts the foreclosure by filing an Order to Docket with the court and serving a copy to the borrower along with mediation information, if applicable. Foreclosing party must also publish notice for three consecutive weeks, with the last publication not more than one week before sale. In addition, person authorized to make the sale must serve (by certified mail, return receipt requested) a notice of sale on homeowner at least 10 days but not more than 30 days before sale.
Reinstatement of loan before sale	Available until one day before sale date
Redemption after sale	Redemption available until the court ratifies the sale
Special protections for foreclosures involving high-cost mortgages	None
Special state protections for service members	Protections provided under the federal Servicemembers Civil Relief Act extended to members of the National Guard or Maryland Defense Force ordered to state military duty for a period of 14 consecutive days or longer. Md. Code Ann. [Pub. Safety] § 13-704
Deficiency judgments	Foreclosing party may file a motion for a deficiency judgment within three years after ratification of the auditor's report.
Cash exempted in bankruptcy	Using the wildcard exemption, $6,000 for one person, $12,000 for a married couple.
Notice to leave after house is sold	After the court ratifies the sale, the new owner can obtain an order of possession from the court to evict the foreclosed homeowners.
Foreclosure statute	Md. Code Ann. [Real Prop.] §§ 7-105 to 7-105.8

Massachusetts

Foreclosure laws change! Check for updates at www.nolo.com/legal-updates.

Topic	State Rule
Most common type of foreclosure process	Nonjudicial under power of sale
Notice of the foreclosure	Prior to accelerating the loan and initiating foreclosure proceedings, the foreclosing party must mail (or serve) to the borrower a 90-day notice of the right to reinstate the mortgage and that borrower may be eligible for state agency assistance. After loan is accelerated, the foreclosing party must mail a notice of sale to homeowner at least 14 days before the sale date, and publish notice for three consecutive weeks before the sale date.
Reinstatement of loan before sale	90-day right to cure (the terms of the mortgage may provide additional time)
Redemption after sale	Not available after a nonjudicial foreclosure
Special protections for foreclosures involving high-cost mortgages	If the original lender (or its assignee) violates Massachusetts' high-cost home loan law, the borrower can rescind the loan and use rescission as a defense to the foreclosure. Mass. Gen. Laws ch. 183C §§ 18, 15. Lender is required to attempt to modify certain high-cost and predatory loans. Mass. Gen. Laws ch. 244 § 35B.
Special state protections for service members	The foreclosing party typically files a Servicemembers Civil Relief Act (SCRA) action with the land court separate from the actual foreclosure. The only purpose is to determine whether a borrower is entitled to the protections of the SCRA. The foreclosing party serves a copy of the complaint to the borrower, which gives the borrower the opportunity to file an answer if he or she is in the military.
Deficiency judgments	Can be obtained in separate lawsuit if a notice of intent to seek a deficiency is mailed to borrower at least 21 days before sale date.
Cash exempted in bankruptcy	$2,500 for one person, $5,000 for a married couple (plus an additional $6,000 using the wildcard exemption). Under federal bankruptcy exemptions, $13,100 for one person, $26,200 for a married couple.
Notice to leave after house is sold	The new owner must first give a notice to quit (leave) and then can begin eviction proceedings by filing a complaint in court.
Foreclosure statutes	Mass. Gen. Laws ch. 244, § 14, 17A, 17B, 18, 35A

Michigan

Foreclosure laws change! Check for updates at www.nolo.com/legal-updates.

Topic	State Rule
Most common type of foreclosure process	Nonjudicial under power of sale in a mortgage
Notice of the foreclosure	Foreclosing party must publish notice once a week for four consecutive weeks before sale and post a notice on property within at least 15 days of first publication. No notice need be mailed or served to borrower, however the mortgage contract may require the foreclosing party to mail a notice of default (typically giving 30 days to cure the default) prior to starting foreclosure proceedings.
Reinstatement of loan before sale	Not available (except as permitted by the terms of the mortgage)
Redemption after sale	If property is not abandoned and more than two-thirds of the original mortgage is still owed, redemption allowed for six months. If less than two-thirds is owed, the redemption period is one year. If the property is abandoned, redemption period is one month.
Special protections for foreclosures involving high-cost mortgages	None
Special state protections for service members	Michigan law provides special protections against foreclosure to certain military service members, including members of the Michigan national guard. So long as either the mortgagor entered into the mortgage before becoming a service member or the mortgagor is deployed in overseas service, lender cannot foreclose nonjudicially during the service member's period of military service (or within 6 months thereafter) unless a court ordered the sale or foreclosure. Mich. Comp. Laws § 600.3285
Deficiency judgments	Allowed, after a nonjudicial foreclosure, but if the mortgage holder buys the property at the foreclosure sale then borrower can contest the amount of the deficiency if the foreclosure sale price was substantially less than the fair market value of the property.
Cash exempted in bankruptcy	None. Under federal bankruptcy exemptions, $13,100 for one person, $26,200 for a married couple.
Notice to leave after house is sold	New owner may start court proceedings to evict the former owner after the redemption period expires, unless former owners unreasonably refuse to allow the new owner to inspect the home, cause damage, or damage is imminent during the redemption period. Then eviction proceedings can be started earlier.
Foreclosure statutes	Mich. Comp. Laws §§ 600.3101 to 600.3185, 600.3201 to 600.3285

Minnesota

Foreclosure laws change! Check for updates at www.nolo.com/legal-updates.

Topic	State Rule
Most common type of foreclosure process	Nonjudicial under power of sale in a mortgage
Notice of the foreclosure	In most cases, foreclosing party must mail the borrower a notice of default giving 30 days to cure before officially starting a foreclosure, along with a notice about foreclosure prevention counseling. Foreclosing party must serve notice of sale on the occupant of the home, along with a foreclosure advice notice, at least four weeks before the sale and must publish the notice six weeks before the sale.
Reinstatement of loan before sale	Available any time before the foreclosure sale
Redemption after sale	For most borrowers, available for six months after the sale. In some cases, redemption period is 12 months (for example, the amount due is less than two-thirds of the original principal amount of the loan) or five weeks (abandoned homes or if the borrower postpones the sale under Minn. Rev. Stat. § 580.07). Former owner may stay in the house during this period.
Special protections for foreclosures involving high-cost mortgages	None
Special state protections for service members	Protections under the federal Servicemembers Civil Relief Act extended to service members called to state active service. Minn. Stat. § 190.055
Deficiency judgments	Not allowed in nonjudicial foreclosure with six-month redemption period (most common type of foreclosure) or five-week redemption period (applicable to abandoned properties)
Cash exempted in bankruptcy	None. Under federal bankruptcy exemptions, $13,100 for one person, $26,200 for a married couple.
Notice to leave after house is sold	New owner may file an eviction lawsuit after the redemption period expires.
Foreclosure statutes	Minn. Stat. §§ 580.01 to 580.30 (nonjudicial foreclosures)

Mississippi

Foreclosure laws change! Check for updates at www.nolo.com/legal-updates.

Topic	State Rule
Most common type of foreclosure process	Nonjudicial under power of sale in deed of trust
Notice of the foreclosure	Foreclosing party must publish notice of sale three consecutive weeks before sale date and post notice on the courthouse door. No notice need be mailed to borrower under state law, though most deeds of trust require the foreclosing party to send a 30-day notice of default prior to acceleration.
Reinstatement of loan before sale	Available at any time before the sale
Redemption after sale	Not available
Special protections for foreclosures involving high-cost mortgages	None
Special state procedures for service members	None
Deficiency judgments	May be obtained if lawsuit filed within one year of the sale. To get a deficiency judgment, the winning bid at the foreclosure sale must be reasonable based on the fair market value of the property, particularly if the lender is the high bidder.
Cash exempted in bankruptcy	Using the wildcard exemption, $50,000 for one person aged 70 or older, $100,000 for a married couple aged 70 or older.
Notice to leave after house is sold	The new owner must go to court to get an eviction order, usually after making a demand for possession.
Foreclosure statutes	Miss. Code. Ann. §§ 89-1-55 to 89-1-59

Missouri

Foreclosure laws change! Check for updates at www.nolo.com/legal-updates.

Topic	State Rule
Most common type of foreclosure process	Nonjudicial under power of sale in deed of trust
Notice of the foreclosure	Foreclosing party must send a notice of sale by registered or certified mail to the borrower not less than 20 days before the sale and publish notice in a newspaper.
Reinstatement of loan before sale	Not available (except as permitted by the terms of the deed of trust)
Redemption after sale	Available for one year after sale if borrower gives a notice of intent to redeem at the sale or within ten days before sale, satisfies bond requirement, and the holder of the debt being foreclosed buys the property at foreclosure sale.
Special protections for foreclosures involving high-cost mortgages	None
Special state protections for service members	None
Deficiency judgments	May be obtained in a separate lawsuit
Cash exempted in bankruptcy	Using the wildcard exemption, $600 for one person, $1,200 for a married couple, $1,250 for head of family plus $350 per child.
Notice to leave after house is sold	New owner files an unlawful detainer (eviction) lawsuit against the foreclosed homeowner.
Foreclosure statutes	Mo. Rev. Stat. §§ 443.290 to 443.440

Montana

Foreclosure laws change! Check for updates at www.nolo.com/legal-updates.

Topic	State Rule
Most common type of foreclosure process	Nonjudicial under power of sale in deed of trust (a trust indenture under the Small Tract Financing Act of Montana)
Notice of the foreclosure	Under the Small Tract Financing Act, foreclosing party must mail a notice to the borrower at least 120 days before sale and publish in a newspaper prior to the sale.
Reinstatement of loan before sale	Any time prior to sale under the Small Tract Financing Act
Redemption after sale	No right of redemption after a nonjudicial foreclosure under the Small Tract Financing Act
Special protections for foreclosures involving high-cost mortgages	None
Special state protections for service members	Courts may stay civil proceedings related to a service member's nonpayment on a mortgage for their primary residence or adjust the payment due. Mont. Code Ann. § 10-1-903. Applicable to any member of the Montana army or air national guard serving on active duty ordered by the governor or full-time national guard duty. Mont. Code. Ann. § 10-1-902
Deficiency judgments	Not allowed under the Small Tract Financing Act
Cash exempted in bankruptcy	None
Notice to leave after house is sold	Under the Small Tract Financing Act, the purchaser at the trustee's sale is entitled to possession of the property on the 10th day following the sale. If the former owner does not leave, the purchaser may initiate a lawsuit to evict the former homeowner after giving notice to quit (leave).
Foreclosure statutes	Mont. Code Ann. §§ 71-1-221 to 71-1-235 and §§ 71-1-301 to 71-1-321

Nebraska

Foreclosure laws change! Check for updates at www.nolo.com/legal-updates.

Topic	State Rule
Most common type of foreclosure process	Nonjudicial under power of sale in deed of trust
Notice of the foreclosure	Foreclosing party must record a notice of default at least one month before giving notice of sale (two months if the property is agricultural) and, in most cases, mail a copy to the borrower within ten days after recordation, notice of sale is then published once a week for five consecutive weeks; the last publication must be made at least ten days but not more than 30 days prior to the sale. Notice of sale must also be sent to the borrower 20 days prior to sale (in most cases).
Reinstatement of loan before sale	Borrower may reinstate by paying amount due within one month after recordation of notice of default (two months if the property is agricultural).
Redemption after sale	Not available
Special protections for foreclosures involving high-cost mortgages	None
Special state protections for service members	None
Deficiency judgments	May be obtained by filing separate lawsuit within three months after foreclosure sale. Judgment cannot exceed the difference between the indebtedness and the property's fair market value or the difference between the indebtedness and the sale price, whichever is less.
Cash exempted in bankruptcy	Using the wildcard exemption, $2,500 for one person, $5,000 for a married couple.
Notice to leave after house is sold	New owner may begin an eviction action after the foreclosure sale.
Foreclosure statutes	Neb. Rev. Stat. §§ 76-1005 through 76-1018 (nonjudicial)

Nevada

Foreclosure laws change! Check for updates at www.nolo.com/legal-updates.

Topic	State Rule
Most common type of foreclosure process	Nonjudicial under power of sale in deed of trust
Notice of the foreclosure	Foreclosing party records a three-month notice of default and election to sell and mails a copy to the borrower. The notice of default must also be posted on the property. Foreclosing party must also serve a notice stating borrower is in danger of losing the home to foreclosure at least 60 days before sale, and mail a notice of sale at least 20 days before sale. Notice of sale must also be posted on the property, in several public places, and published.
Reinstatement of loan before sale	Borrower may reinstate up to five days prior to sale.
Redemption after sale	Not available after nonjudicial foreclosure
Special protections for foreclosures involving high-cost mortgages	For a mortgage loan on or after October 1, 2003, that is subject to the Home Ownership and Equity Protection Act of 1994 (HOEPA), Nevada law requires the lender to serve the borrower a notice at least 60 days prior to the foreclosure. Nev. Rev. Stat. § 107.85. Violations of high-cost home loan statutes support a defense to foreclosure. Nev. Rev. Stat. §§ 598D.110
Special state protections for service members	None
Deficiency judgments	Foreclosing party may obtain deficiency judgment by filing a separate lawsuit within six months of foreclosure sale, but not if: loan was made on or after October 1, 2009, lender is a financial institution, the property is a single-family home owned by the borrower at the time of sale, borrower has resided in home continuously, the borrower used the proceeds of the loan to purchase the property, and the borrower has not refinanced the loan. Amount of deficiency is limited to the lesser of the difference between the total debt and fair market value of the home, or the difference between the total debt and foreclosure sale price.
Cash exempted in bankruptcy	$1,000 for one person, $2,000 for a married couple.
Notice to leave after house is sold	New owner must give former owner a three-day notice to quit (leave) before filing an eviction lawsuit.
Foreclosure statute	Nev. Rev. Stat. §§ 107.0795 through 107.130; 40.451 through 40.463

New Hampshire

Foreclosure laws change! Check for updates at www.nolo.com/legal-updates.

Topic	State Rule
Most common type of foreclosure process	Nonjudicial under power of sale in a mortgage
Notice of the foreclosure	Foreclosing party must either personally serve borrower or mail notice 45 days (as of January 1, 2016) before the sale, and publish the notice once a week for three consecutive weeks, with the first publication at least 20 days before the sale.
Reinstatement of loan before sale	Not available (except as permitted by the terms of the mortgage contract)
Redemption after sale	Not available after a nonjudicial foreclosure
Special protections for foreclosures involving high-cost mortgages	None
Special state protections for service members	Federal Servicemembers Civil Relief Act protections extended to members of the state guard, or militia called to active duty by the governor for a period of 30 days or more. N.H. Rev. Stat. Ann. § 110-C2
Deficiency judgments	May be obtained by filing separate lawsuit after the foreclosure sale, provided lender exerts every reasonable effort to obtain a fair and reasonable price at the sale.
Cash exempted in bankruptcy	Using the wildcard exemption, up to $8,000 for one person, $16,000 for a married couple. Under federal bankruptcy exemptions, $13,100 for one person, $26,200 for a married couple.
Notice to leave after house is sold	New owner must give former owner a 30-day notice to quit (leave) before bringing an eviction lawsuit.
Foreclosure statute	N.H. Rev. Stat. Ann. § 479:25

New Jersey

Foreclosure laws change! Check for updates at www.nolo.com/legal-updates.

Topic	State Rule
Most common type of foreclosure process	Judicial
Notice of the foreclosure	Foreclosing party must send notice of intention to foreclose, by registered or certified mail, to borrower 30 days before filing a foreclosure lawsuit. Foreclosing party then serves borrower summons and complaint. The foreclosing party must mail the borrower a notice 14 days before applying for final judgment giving one final chance to cure the default. Borrower may then get an additional 45 days to cure the default if he or she responds to the notice. Notice of sale must be mailed to homeowner (and all parties who appeared in the action) at least ten days before sale, as well as posted on the property and in the sheriff's office, and published in two newspapers for four weeks.
Reinstatement of loan before sale	Available up to date of final judgment of foreclosure. Judgment may be delayed for 45 days if borrower needs extra time to reinstate.
Redemption after sale	Within the ten-day period after the sale, and up until the court issues an order confirming the sale if objections to the sale are filed. Also, if mortgage holder obtains a deficiency judgment, borrower can bring action for redemption within six months after deficiency judgment is entered. However, if you file an answer to the deficiency judgment lawsuit to dispute the deficiency, you lose the right to redeem.
Special protections for foreclosures involving high-cost mortgages	Foreclosure must be filed in court. Home Ownership Security Act, N.J. Stat. Ann. § 46:10B-26(k).
Special state protections for service members	New Jersey law provides protections similar to the federal Servicemembers Civil Relief Act. For example, a service member can potentially stay (postpone) court proceedings and the period of military service is not included in the redemption period. The law applies to service members on federal duty or in state military service pursuant to the governor's orders. N.J. Stat. Ann. §§ 38:23C-1 to 38:23C-26

New Jersey (continued)

Deficiency judgments	May be obtained by filing a separate lawsuit within three months of sale or, if confirmation of the sale is required, from the date of the confirmation of the sale; court can limit amount to difference between loan debt and fair market value.
Cash exempted in bankruptcy	$1,000 for one person, $2,000 for a married couple. Under federal bankruptcy exemptions, $13,100 for one person, $26,200 for a married couple.
Notice to leave after house is sold	If the foreclosed homeowners do not leave after the foreclosure, the new owner (usually the foreclosing party) applies for writ of possession from the court.
Foreclosure statutes	N.J. Stat. Ann. §§ 2A:50-1 to 2A:50-21, 2A:50-53 to 2A:50-63

New Mexico

Foreclosure laws change! Check for updates at www.nolo.com/legal-updates.

Topic	State Rule
Most common type of foreclosure process	Judicial, but nonjudicial foreclosures are also possible
Notice of the foreclosure	**Judicial:** Borrower has 30 days to respond after being served with summons and complaint. After the court issues a foreclosure judgment, sale may not occur for 30 days. Foreclosing party must publish notice of sale four consecutive weeks before sale in a newspaper and also post notices in six of the most public places in the county. **Nonjudicial:** Foreclosing party must record notice of sale at least 90 days before the sale date and mail a copy to the borrower within five days of recording. Foreclosing party must also publish notice in a newspaper.
Reinstatement of loan before sale	Borrower usually gets a 30-day opportunity to reinstate before the foreclosing party initiates foreclosure. Some borrowers may also reinstate at any time prior to the time title is transferred by means of foreclosure sale.
Redemption after sale	For both judicial and nonjudicial foreclosures, New Mexico law gives a borrower nine months to redeem the home after a foreclosure sale. However, the terms of the mortgage or deed of trust can reduce the redemption period to not less than one month. (Most mortgages and deeds of trust contain a provision stating that the redemption period will be one month.)
Special protections for foreclosures involving high-cost mortgages	Assignees of high-cost loans may be held responsible for acts of lenders and mortgage originators and violations may be used to defend against the foreclosure. Home Loan Protection Act, N.M. Stat. Ann. § 58-21A-1
Special state protections for service members	The rights, benefits, and protections of the federal Servicemembers Civil Relief Act extended to members of the national guard ordered to state active duty for a period of 30 or more consecutive state duty days or to any federally funded duty performed in an operational role for homeland security. N.M. Stat. Ann. § 20-4-7.1
Deficiency judgments	**Judicial:** Allowed. **Nonjudicial:** May be obtained by filing a separate lawsuit within six years of foreclosure sale; may not be recovered against a low-income household.

New Mexico (continued)

Cash exempted in bankruptcy	Using the wildcard exemption, up to $5,500 for one person, $11,000 for a married couple.
	Under federal bankruptcy exemptions, $13,100 for one person, $26,200 for a married couple.
Notice to leave after house is sold	New owner (usually the foreclosing party) can get a writ of assistance to evict the former owner as part of the foreclosure action (judicial foreclosures) or file a separate lawsuit (nonjudicial foreclosures).
Foreclosure statutes	N.M. Stat. Ann. §§ 48-7-1 to 48-7-24, 39-5-1 to 39-5-23 (judicial); 48-10-1 to 48-10-21 (nonjudicial)

New York

Foreclosure laws change! Check for updates at www.nolo.com/legal-updates.

Topic	State Rule
Most common type of foreclosure process	Judicial
Notice of the foreclosure	Foreclosing party must provide notice to borrower at least 90 days before filing foreclosure complaint. Complaint must be accompanied by notice regarding legal options and explanation of foreclosure procedure. Borrowers have 20 to 30 days to respond to the complaints, depending on whether they are served personally or by another method. Notice of sale must be published in a newspaper and posted publicly, in some cases.
Reinstatement of loan before sale	Available any time before final foreclosure judgment (foreclosure will be dismissed) and any time after judgment, but before sale (foreclosure will be stayed).
Redemption after sale	Not available
Special protections for foreclosures involving high-cost mortgages	If lender violated provisions that apply to high-cost loans, borrower may use this as a defense against foreclosure. N.Y. Banking Law § 6-l, N.Y. Real Prop. Acts. Law § 1302.
Special state protections for service members	New York has a law that is similar to the federal Servicemembers Civil Relief Act that applies to those on federal active duty or state duty pursuant to an order of the governor. Among other things, it provides that a service member may apply to the court for a stay of proceedings (postponement) in a foreclosure action under certain circumstances. N.Y. Mil. Law §§ 301 through 328.
Deficiency judgments	Allowed if borrower is personally served or appears in the lawsuit. The deficiency amount is the amount of the debt less the higher of the fair market value or the sales price.
Cash exempted in bankruptcy	$11,025 for one person, $22,050 for a married couple. Under federal bankruptcy exemptions, $13,100 for one person, $26,200 for a married couple.
Notice to leave after house is sold	New owner can evict by summary proceeding after giving a ten-day notice to leave or by getting an order of possession from the court as part of the foreclosure action.
Foreclosure statutes	N.Y. Real Prop. Acts Law §§ 1301 to 1391

North Carolina

Foreclosure laws change! Check for updates at www.nolo.com/legal-updates.

Topic	State Rule
Most common type of foreclosure process	Nonjudicial under power of sale in deed of trust. Property cannot be sold until the court clerk holds a hearing, reviews foreclosing party's paperwork, and certifies sale.
Notice of the foreclosure	A notice of hearing must be filed with the court to initiate the foreclosure. Foreclosing party must send borrower a notice including amount needed to cure the default and resources that are available to avoid foreclosure at least 45 days before filing a notice of hearing, as well as a notice of default 30 days before the date of the notice of hearing. After the notice of hearing is filed, it must be served to the borrower not less than ten days before the hearing (20 days if served by posting). The hearing may be continued (postponed) for up to 60 days if loss-mitigation efforts may help avoid foreclosure. If foreclosure approved at hearing, borrower must be mailed a notice of sale at least 20 days before the sale, which must also be published in a newspaper and posted publicly.
Reinstatement of loan before sale	Not available (except as permitted by the terms of the mortgage or deed of trust)
Redemption after sale	Available within ten days after the sale
Special protections for foreclosures involving high-cost mortgages	None
Special state protections for service members	Nonjudicial foreclosure prohibited during or within 90 days after a borrower's period of military service if the mortgage or deed of trust originated before the period of military service. N.C. Gen. Stat. §§ 45-21.12A, 45-21.16
Deficiency judgments	No deficiency judgment in nonjudicial foreclosures for purchase money (seller financed) mortgages and deeds of trust. Lender may also be barred from seeking a deficiency judgment if the mortgage is nontraditional (for example, pick-a-payment or option ARM loans) or is a rate spread home loan (where the annual percentage rate exceeds a certain threshold), and the mortgage secures borrower's principal residence.
Cash exempted in bankruptcy	Using the wildcard exemption, up to $5,500 for one person, $11,000 for a married couple.
Notice to leave after house is sold	New owner must give former owner a 10-day notice to quit (leave) before getting an order of possession from the court.
Foreclosure statutes	N.C. Gen. Stat. §§ 45-21.1 to 45-21.33, 45-100 to 47-107

North Dakota

Foreclosure laws change! Check for updates at www.nolo.com/legal-updates.

Topic	State Rule
Most common type of foreclosure process	Judicial
Notice of the foreclosure	Foreclosing party must serve (usually by mail) borrower with a notice at least 30 days and not more than 90 days before starting the foreclosure. Foreclosing party gives notice of the foreclosure lawsuit by serving the borrower with the complaint and summons. Borrower has 21 days to respond. Notice of sale must be published in a newspaper for three weeks, and, in some cases, mailed to interested parties.
Reinstatement of loan before sale	Available within 30 days after service of the notice before foreclosure
Redemption after sale	Available within 60 days after foreclosure sale
Special protections for foreclosures involving high-cost mortgages	None
Special state protections for service members	None
Deficiency judgments	Not allowed in foreclosures of residential property of four or fewer units, one of which is occupied by the owner as his or her primary residence, on up to 40 contiguous acres.
Cash exempted in bankruptcy	$3,750 for one person without dependents, $7,500 for the head of household, $10,000 for one person (cannot use the homestead exemption), $20,000 for a married couple (cannot use the homestead exemption).
Notice to leave after house is sold	Former owner can stay in the house until redemption period ends. After the redemption period expires, the court can order the former homeowner to give possession to the purchaser, which is typically the foreclosing party.
Foreclosure statutes	N.D. Cent. Code §§ 32-19-01 to 32-19-41

Ohio

Foreclosure laws change! Check for updates at www.nolo.com/legal-updates.

Topic	State Rule
Most common type of foreclosure process	Judicial
Notice of the foreclosure	After foreclosing party files lawsuit, borrower has 28 days to respond. After the court issues a foreclosure judgment, foreclosing party files the notice of sale with the court at least seven days prior to the sale and sends a copy to the debtor and parties who appeared in the action. Foreclosing party must publish notice of sale in a newspaper for three weeks before sale date.
Reinstatement of loan before sale	Not available (except as permitted by the terms of the mortgage)
Redemption after sale	Available until the court confirms the sale
Special protections for foreclosures involving high-cost mortgages	None
Special state protections for service members	Protections under the federal Servicemembers Civil Relief Act extended to national guard ordered by the governor into active duty or training. Ohio Rev. Code Ann. §§ 5919.29, 5923.12
Deficiency judgments	Allowed, but judgment is void two years after confirmation of the sale by the court. Property cannot be sold for less than 2/3 of appraised value at the foreclosure sale.
Cash exempted in bankruptcy	Using the wildcard exemption, up to $1,725 for one person, $3,450 for a married couple.
Notice to leave after house is sold	After the sale is confirmed, the new owner can ask the court for a writ of possession and have the sheriff remove the foreclosed homeowners from the home.
Foreclosure statutes	Ohio Rev. Code Ann. §§ 2323.07, 2329.26

Oklahoma

Foreclosure laws change! Check for updates at www.nolo.com/legal-updates.

Topic	State Rule
Most common type of foreclosure process	Judicial (the foreclosure can be nonjudicial if the mortgage contract includes a power of sale clause; however, the borrower can force the lender to foreclose judicially by taking certain steps)
Notice of the foreclosure	After foreclosing party files lawsuit, borrower usually has 20 days to respond. After the court issues a foreclosure judgment, foreclosing party must serve a notice of sale on borrower by mail and publish notice of sale in a newspaper at least 30 days before the sale.
Reinstatement of loan before sale	Not available (except as permitted by the terms of the mortgage)
Redemption after sale	Allowed until court confirms sale
Special protections for foreclosures involving high-cost mortgages	None
Special state protections for service members	Federal Servicemembers Civil Relief Act protections extended to members of the Oklahoma National Guard when ordered to state active duty or full-time National Guard duty. Okla. Stat. tit. 44, § 208.1
Deficiency judgments	Allowed, but limited to the difference between the total debt and the fair market value of the property, or the difference between the total debt and the foreclosure sale price, whichever is less. Lender must ask the court for deficiency judgment at the same time it makes a motion for an order confirming the foreclosure sale or within 90 days after sale.
Cash exempted in bankruptcy	None
Notice to leave after house is sold	If the foreclosed homeowners don't leave the home, the court may (in the order confirming the sale) order the clerk of the court to issue of a writ of assistance to the sheriff to give the purchaser possession of the home.
Foreclosure statutes	Okla. Stat. tit. 12, §§ 686, 764 to 765, 773; Okla. Stat. tit. 46, §§ 41 to 49

Oregon

Foreclosure laws change! Check for updates at www.nolo.com/legal-updates.

Topic	State Rule
Most common type of foreclosure process	Probably nonjudicial. In the past, most foreclosures in Oregon were nonjudicial. In 2012, lenders switched to judicial foreclosures for various reasons that are no longer applicable. Lenders are now typically using the nonjudicial process again.
Notice of the foreclosure	Before filing a notice of default, foreclosing party provides notice about a resolution conference (mediation) to the borrower. Foreclosing party must record a notice of default in the county records and serve a notice of sale on borrower 120 days before the sale, either by personal service or mail, along with a "danger" notice that warns of the impending foreclosure mailed on or before the date the notice of sale is served or mailed. Notice of sale must also be published in a newspaper for four weeks.
Reinstatement of loan before sale	Available up to five days before sale. The law limits the amount borrower can be charged in attorney or trustee fees.
Redemption after sale	Not available after a nonjudicial foreclosure
Special protections for foreclosures involving high-cost mortgages	None
Special state protections for service members	Violations of the Servicemembers Civil Relief Act are an unlawful practice under Oregon law. Or. Rev. Stat. §§ 646.605, 646.608(LLL). The lender can't initiate a suit to foreclose a mortgage if the land covered by the mortgage is owned by a service member called into active service during war. Or. Rev. Stat. § 408.440
Deficiency judgments	Not allowed after a nonjudicial foreclosure or a judicial foreclosure of a residential trust deed.
Cash exempted in bankruptcy	Using the wildcard exemption, $400 for one person, $800 for a married couple.
Notice to leave after house is sold	New owner entitled to possession ten days after the sale; after which the purchaser may start an eviction action to remove former owner from the home.
Foreclosure statutes	Or. Rev. Stat. §§ 86.726 to 86.815, 88.010-88.106

Pennsylvania

Foreclosure laws change! Check for updates at www.nolo.com/legal-updates.

Topic	State Rule
Most common type of foreclosure process	Judicial
Notice of the foreclosure	For most borrowers, at least 30 days before starting the foreclosure, foreclosing party must mail the borrower a notice of intention to foreclose and send a notice about financial assistance under the Homeowner's Emergency Mortgage Assistance Program. After foreclosing party files foreclosure lawsuit, homeowner borrower has up to 30 days to respond. A notice of sale must be posted on the property and served to the borrower at least 30 days before the sale, as well as published in a newspaper once a week for three weeks.
Reinstatement of loan before sale	Available until one hour before the bidding at the foreclosure sale, but a maximum of three times in one year
Redemption after sale	Not available
Special protections for foreclosures involving high-cost mortgages	None
Special state protections for service members	Pennsylvania National Guard members on active state service (and 30 days thereafter) are exempt from civil process. Pa. Cons. Stat. Ann. tit. 51, § 4105
Deficiency judgments	Allowed if foreclosing party files separate lawsuit within six months after sale. If the foreclosing party was the purchaser at the sale, the deficiency is limited by the fair market value of the property.
Cash exempted in bankruptcy	$300 for one person, $600 for a married couple. Under federal bankruptcy exemptions, $13,100 for one person, $26,200 for a married couple.
Notice to leave after house is sold	New owner may start a separate ejectment action after foreclosure to evict former owner from the premises.
Foreclosure statutes	Pa. Stat. Ann. tit. 35, §§ 1680.402c to 1680.409c; Pa. Stat. Ann. tit. 41, §§ 403 to 404; Pa. R. Civ. P. 1141-1150

Rhode Island

Foreclosure laws change! Check for updates at www.nolo.com/legal-updates.

Topic	State Rule
Most common type of foreclosure process	Nonjudicial under power of sale in mortgage
Notice of the foreclosure	Foreclosing party must provide a mediation notice to borrower prior to initiating foreclosure. Notice of sale must be mailed by certified mail to borrower at least 30 days before first publication and published in a newspaper for three consecutive weeks before sale.
Reinstatement of loan before sale	Not available (except as permitted by the terms of the mortgage)
Redemption after sale	Not available after a nonjudicial foreclosure
Special protections for foreclosures involving high-cost mortgages	Borrower can ask court to stop (enjoin) the foreclosure if the lender violated the Rhode Island Home Loan Protection Act, which forbids certain activities (such as balloon payments and negative amortization) related to high-cost home loans. R.I. Gen. Laws §§ 35-25.2-1 to 35-25.2-11
Special state protections for service members	Protections under the federal Servicemembers Civil Relief Act extended to all national guard members on state active duty for a continuous period over 90 days. R.I. Gen. Laws § 30-7-10
Deficiency judgments	Allowed if foreclosing party files separate lawsuit after sale.
Cash exempted in bankruptcy	Using the wildcard exemption, up to $6,500 for one person, $13,000 for a married couple.
	Under federal bankruptcy exemptions, $13,100 for one person, $26,200 for a married couple.
Notice to leave after house is sold	After foreclosure, the purchaser may send a notice to vacate (leave) and then file an eviction lawsuit.
Foreclosure statutes	R.I. Gen. Laws §§ 34-27-1 to 34-27-5; 34-25.2-1 to 34-25.2-15

South Carolina

Foreclosure laws change! Check for updates at www.nolo.com/legal-updates.

Topic	State Rule
Most common type of foreclosure process	Judicial
Notice of the foreclosure	After foreclosing party files lawsuit, borrower has 30 days to respond. After court issues a foreclosure judgment, foreclosing party must publish notice of sale in a newspaper and also post it in three public places three weeks before the sale.
Reinstatement of loan before sale	Not available (unless the mortgage terms allow reinstatement)
Redemption after sale	Not available (though borrower can make an upset bid during the 30-day period following sale, if lender demands a deficiency judgment)
Special protections for foreclosures involving high-cost mortgages	If the court finds a violation of the high-cost home loans statute, it may refuse to enforce the agreement, or the term or part that was unlawful, or it may rewrite the agreement to eliminate the unlawful part. In an action to collect a debt, a borrower may assert a violation of the statute as a matter of defense by recoupment or set-off in such action. S.C. Code Ann. § 37-23-50
Special state protections for service members	None
Deficiency judgments	Allowed as part of the foreclosure lawsuit
Cash exempted in bankruptcy	$5,900 for one person, $11,800 for a married couple.
Notice to leave after house is sold	The foreclosing party (typically the purchaser at the sale) may include an eviction as part of the foreclosure action and get a writ of assistance from the court.
Foreclosure statutes	S.C. Code Ann. §§ 15-39-610, 29-3-630 to 29-3-790

South Dakota

Foreclosure laws change! Check for updates at www.nolo.com/legal-updates.

Topic	State Rule
Most common type of foreclosure process	Nonjudicial under power of sale in a mortgage (but homeowner borrower may choose judicial foreclosure)
Notice of the foreclosure	Foreclosing party must publish notice of sale in a newspaper once a week for four weeks (including a statement about the right to insist on judicial foreclosure) and must serve borrower with written copy of the notice of foreclosure sale at least 21 days before sale.
Reinstatement of loan before sale	Not available in a nonjudicial foreclosure (unless allowed by the mortgage contract)
Redemption after sale	There is a 180-day redemption period after the purchaser records a certificate of sale in the land records.
Special protections for foreclosures involving high-cost mortgages	None
Special state protections for service members	State law extends legal protections under the federal Servicemembers Civil Relief Act to members of the South Dakota National Guard ordered to active duty service by the Governor or the President of the United States. S.D. Cod. Laws Ann. § 33A-2-9
Deficiency judgments	Allowed, but if mortgage holder buys property at foreclosure sale, amount of deficiency is limited to difference between house's actual market value at time of sale and amount still owing on mortgage.
Cash exempted in bankruptcy	$5,000 for one person (not head of family), $7,000 for head of family, $12,000 for married couple.
Notice to leave after house is sold	If the foreclosed homeowner doesn't leave the home after the redemption period, the purchaser must give a three-day notice to quit (leave) before initiating an eviction action.
Foreclosure statutes	S.D. Cod. Laws Ann. §§ 21-48-1 to 21-48-26, 21-47-1 to 21-47-25

Tennessee

Foreclosure laws change! Check for updates at www.nolo.com/legal-updates.

Topic	State Rule
Most common type of foreclosure process	Nonjudicial under power of sale in deed of trust
Notice of the foreclosure	Foreclosing party must publish notice of sale in a newspaper at least 20 days before sale or post notice in several public places 30 days before sale (if there is no newspaper in the county). Foreclosing party must mail the borrower a copy of the notice of sale on or before the first publication.
Reinstatement of loan before sale	Not available (except as permitted by the terms of the mortgage or deed of trust, or in the case of a high-cost home loan)
Redemption after sale	Available for up to two years after sale, unless redemption period is waived in mortgage or deed of trust
Special protections for foreclosures involving high-cost mortgages	In the case of a high-cost home loan, the lender must send a notice of right to cure to the borrower at least 30 days before publishing the notice of foreclosure. The borrower can reinstate prior to three business days before the sale by paying the amount due to the lender. This right to cure may be exercised only once in any 12-month period. Tenn. Code Ann. § 45-20-10
Special state protections for service members	If a member of a reserve or Tennessee national guard unit entered into a mortgage or deed of trust to purchase a home, and is subsequently called into active military service outside the U.S. during hostilities, the lender cannot foreclose until 90 days after the service member returns to the state. Tenn. Code Ann. § 26-1-111
Deficiency judgments	Allowed, but if the borrower proves that the foreclosed property sold for an amount materially less than fair market value, the court will limit the deficiency judgment to the difference between the outstanding mortgage debt and the fair market value of the property.
Cash exempted in bankruptcy	$10,000 for one person, $20,000 for a married couple
Notice to leave after house is sold	Former owner may be evicted through an ejectment procedure.
Foreclosure statutes	Tenn. Code Ann. §§ 35-5-101 to 35-5-111, 66-8-101 to 66-8-103

Texas

Foreclosure laws change! Check for updates at www.nolo.com/legal-updates.

Topic	State Rule
Most common type of foreclosure process	Nonjudicial under power of sale in deed of trust
Notice of the foreclosure	Foreclosing party must serve notice of default to borrower by certified mail 20 days before serving notice of sale. Notice of sale must be served (mailed) to borrower 21 days before sale. Foreclosing party must also post notice of sale on courthouse door and file it in the office of the county clerk.
Reinstatement of loan before sale	Available within 20 days after foreclosing party serves (mails) the notice of default
Redemption after sale	Not available
Special protections for foreclosures involving high-cost mortgages	None
Special state protections for service members	Statutes of limitations are tolled for those under a "legal disability" who are entitled to sue for the recovery of real property or entitled to make a defense based on the title to real property. (The definition of "legal disability" includes those serving in the United States Armed Forces during time of war.) Tex. Civ. Prac. & Rem. Code § 16.022
Deficiency judgments	Allowed after a nonjudicial foreclosure if foreclosing party brings separate lawsuit within two years of sale. Amount may be determined by fair market value of the property, if borrower requests it.
Cash exempted in bankruptcy	$50,000 for one person, $100,000 for a family.
	Under federal bankruptcy exemptions, $13,100 for one person, $26,200 for a married couple.
Notice to leave after house is sold	New owner must serve former owner with three-day notice to quit (leave) and then file eviction (forcible detainer) lawsuit.
Foreclosure statutes	Tex. Prop. Code Ann. §§ 51.002 to 51.003

Utah

Foreclosure laws change! Check for updates at www.nolo.com/legal-updates.

Topic	State Rule
Most common type of foreclosure process	Nonjudicial under power of sale in deed of trust
Notice of the foreclosure	Foreclosing party must mail a notice of intent to file a notice of default to the borrower giving 30 days to cure the default. Foreclosing party then records a notice of default at least three months before giving notice of sale and mails a copy to the borrower within ten days of recording. At least three months after the notice of default is recorded, the foreclosing party publishes a notice of sale in a newspaper for three weeks; the last date of publication must be at least ten days but not more than 30 days before the sale. The notice of sale must also be posted on the property and mailed to the borrower at least 20 days before the sale.
Reinstatement of loan before sale	Available for three months after notice of default is recorded
Redemption after sale	Not available after a nonjudicial foreclosure
Special protections for foreclosures involving high-cost mortgages	None
Special state protections for service members	Utah law extends protections similar to the federal Servicemembers Civil Relief Act to National Guard members serving full-time with a recognized military unit called into service by the governor for at least 30 days. Utah Code Ann. §§ 39-7-102, 39-7-115
Deficiency judgments	May be obtained in a separate lawsuit within three months after the sale. The amount is limited by the property's fair market value.
Cash exempted in bankruptcy	None
Notice to leave after house is sold	If the homeowner doesn't vacate the home after the sale, the purchaser must give the foreclosed homeowner a notice to quit (leave) before initiating an eviction action.
Foreclosure statutes	Utah Code Ann. §§ 57-1-19 through 57-1-34; 78B-6-901 through 78B-6-906.

Vermont

Foreclosure laws change! Check for updates at www.nolo.com/legal-updates.

Topic	State Rule
Most common type of foreclosure process	Judicial (strict foreclosure or by judicial sale)
Notice of the foreclosure	After foreclosing party files lawsuit, borrower generally has 20 days to respond. In a foreclosure by judicial sale, the lender must mail a notice of sale to the borrower no fewer than 30 days before the sale date and publish the notice in a newspaper no fewer than 21 days before the sale. When the court issues a foreclosure judgment in a strict foreclosure, it may also transfer ownership to foreclosing party without a sale so long as there isn't significant equity in the house.
Reinstatement of loan before sale	Available upon agreement before sale
Redemption after sale	In a strict foreclosure, available six months from date of foreclosure decree unless the judge orders (or the borrower and lender agreed upon) a shorter period. In a foreclosure by judicial sale, the redemption period is six months from the date of the foreclosure decree, unless the court orders a shorter time. Redemption is also available before the sale takes place, even if the initial redemption period expired.
Special protections for foreclosures involving high-cost mortgages	None
Special state protections for service members	Statute of limitations tolled for those who are in military or naval service of the United States or a member of the Vermont National Guard and ordered to state active duty, and at the time of entering such service or duty, had a cause of action against another person, or another person had a cause of action against him or her. Vt. Stat. Ann. tit. 12, § 553
Deficiency judgments	May be requested in the foreclosure complaint and is waived if not requested prior to the confirmation order (foreclosure by judicial sale), or in a separate lawsuit (strict foreclosure). If the mortgage holder buys the property, the amount of the deficiency is limited by the property's fair market value.
Cash exempted in bankruptcy	Using the wildcard exemption, up to $8,100 for one person, $16,200 for a married couple. Under federal bankruptcy exemptions, $13,100 for one person, $26,200 for a married couple.

Vermont (continued)

Notice to leave after house is sold	In a strict foreclosure, after the judgment is issued and the redemption period has ended, the court will issue a writ of possession. The writ of possession has the same force and effect and is executed in the same manner as a similar writ issued after an ejectment (eviction) proceeding.
Foreclosure statutes	Vt. Stat. Ann. tit. 12, ch. 172, §§ 4931 to 4954

Virginia

Foreclosure laws change! Check for updates at www.nolo.com/legal-updates.

Topic	State Rule
Most common type of foreclosure process	Nonjudicial under power of sale in deed of trust
Notice of the foreclosure	Foreclosing party must serve notice of sale on homeowner personally or by mail 14 days before the sale. Notice must be published in a local newspaper of general circulation once a week for four consecutive weeks or five days, unless deed of trust provides for a different interval (but not less than once a week for two weeks or once a day for three days). Sale can be held eight days after the first publication, and no more than 30 days after last publication.
Reinstatement of loan before sale	Not available (unless permitted by the loan documents)
Redemption after sale	Not available
Special protections for foreclosures involving high-cost mortgages	None
Special state protections for service members	Servicemembers Civil Relief Act protections extended to National Guard members called to state active duty by the governor for 30 or more consecutive days. Va. Code Ann. § 44-102.1
Deficiency judgments	May be obtained in a separate lawsuit after the sale.
Cash exempted in bankruptcy	$10,000 for one person, $15,000 for unmarried person 65 years of age or older, $20,000 for married couple. Additional amount available for disabled veteran.
Notice to leave after house is sold	New owner does not have to give former owner notice before filing eviction lawsuit, though foreclosed owner may receive a five-day notice to quit.
Foreclosure statutes	Va. Code Ann. §§ 55-59 to 55-66.6

Washington

Foreclosure laws change! Check for updates at www.nolo.com/legal-updates.

Topic	State Rule
Most common type of foreclosure process	Nonjudicial under power of sale in deed of trust
Notice of the foreclosure	Foreclosing party must contact (or meet the requirements for attempting to contact) borrower at least 30 days before issuing notice of default to inform him or her about the opportunity to meet with the lender to try to work out an alternative to the foreclosure. A notice of default must be served on borrower 30 days before notice of sale is recorded or served. The notice of default must be served by both first-class mail and by registered or certified mail, return receipt requested, and by either posting the notice on the premises in a prominent place or by personal service on borrower. Foreclosing party must mail a copy of the notice of sale to the borrower and post on the property (or serve the occupant a copy) at least 120 days (or 90 days in some cases) before sale date. The notice of sale must also be published in a newspaper. No sale may occur within 190 days after the date of default.
Reinstatement of loan before sale	Available up to 11 days before sale
Redemption after sale	Not available after a nonjudicial foreclosure
Special protections for foreclosures involving high-cost mortgages	None
Special state protections for service members	Similar to federal Servicemembers Civil Relief Act. Applies to any resident of Washington state who is a member of the national guard or member of a military reserve component. Wash. Rev. Code §§ 38.42.010 to 38.42.904
Deficiency judgments	Not allowed after a nonjudicial foreclosure
Cash exempted in bankruptcy	$2,000 (no doubling for a married couple). Under federal bankruptcy exemptions, $13,100 for one person, $26,200 for a married couple.
Notice to leave after house is sold	New owner entitled to possession on 20th day after purchase of the foreclosure sale and may then file eviction (unlawful detainer) lawsuit. The purchaser has a right to summary proceedings to obtain possession.
Foreclosure statutes	Wash. Rev. Code §§ 61.24.020 to 61.24.140

West Virginia

Foreclosure laws change! Check for updates at www.nolo.com/legal-updates.

Topic	State Rule
Most common type of foreclosure process	Nonjudicial under power of sale in deed of trust
Notice of the foreclosure	Notice of default must be given to the borrower, giving ten days to cure. Notice of sale must be sent to the borrower by certified mail, return receipt requested, a reasonable amount of time before the sale takes place and published in a newspaper, generally once a week for two weeks.
Reinstatement of loan before sale	Notice of default must give the borrower ten days to cure the default and reinstate the loan. The borrower loses the right to reinstate after three defaults.
Redemption after sale	Not available
Special protections for foreclosures involving high-cost mortgages	None
Special state protections for service members	None
Deficiency judgments	Allowed
Cash exempted in bankruptcy	Using the wildcard exemption, up to $25,800 for one person, $26,600 for a married couple.
Notice to leave after house is sold	After sending a notice to vacate, purchaser may initiate an unlawful detainer (eviction) lawsuit against the foreclosed homeowners to evict them from the property.
Foreclosure statutes	W.Va. Code §§ 38-1-3 to 38-1-15

Wisconsin

Foreclosure laws change! Check for updates at www.nolo.com/legal-updates.

Topic	State Rule
Most common type of foreclosure process	Judicial
Notice of the foreclosure	After foreclosing party files lawsuit, borrower has 20 days to respond. If foreclosure is granted, court issues judgment and order of sale. Sale can't be held until after the redemption period (see below). A notice of sale must be published in a newspaper (and online sometimes) and posted publicly for three weeks prior to sale.
Reinstatement of loan before sale	Available any time before judgment. Borrowers may reinstate after judgment, but if they subsequently default, the foreclosure will continue.
Redemption after sale	Not available after sale. In Wisconsin, the redemption period ranges from five weeks to 12 months depending on the circumstances and occurs prior to the sale. The property can be redeemed at any time during this period.
Special protections for foreclosures involving high-cost mortgages	Prohibition on certain things (such as interest rate increases after a default) for high-cost home loans. Wis. Stat. §§ 428.202 to 428.211
Special state protections for service members	Protections against foreclosure for members of the national guard or state defense force who are ordered into state active duty for 30 days or more. Lender cannot foreclose during or within 90 days after the service member's period of state active duty unless a court approves it before active duty and after the foreclosure. Applies to mortgages taken out prior to active duty. Wis. Stat. § 321.62
Deficiency judgments	Must be requested in the foreclosure complaint. The foreclosing lender will often waive the deficiency in order to shorten the redemption period.
Cash exempted in bankruptcy	$5,000 for one person, $10,000 for a married couple. Under federal bankruptcy exemptions, $13,100 for one person, $26,200 for a married couple.
Notice to leave after house is sold	Foreclosed homeowner may remain in possession through the redemption period up until the confirmation of the sale. The order confirming the sale may also include a writ of assistance, which is an order from the court directing the sheriff to remove the foreclosed homeowner from the home.
Foreclosure statutes	Wis. Stat. §§ 846.01 to 846.25

Wyoming

Foreclosure laws change! Check for updates at www.nolo.com/legal-updates.

Topic	State Rule
Most common type of foreclosure process	Nonjudicial under power of sale in a mortgage
Notice of the foreclosure	Foreclosing party must send a notice of intent to foreclose to homeowner by certified mail with return receipt at least ten days before first publication of the notice of sale. Notice of sale must be published in a newspaper once a week for four weeks. Also, prior to the first date of publication, a notice of sale must be sent to the homeowner by certified mail.
Reinstatement of loan before sale	Not available (except as permitted by the terms of the mortgage)
Redemption after sale	Available for three months after sale (12 months after sale if the property is agricultural)
Special protections for foreclosures involving high-cost mortgages	None
Special state protections for service members	Legal protections under the federal Servicemembers Civil Relief Act are extended to members of the Wyoming National Guard ordered to active state service by the state or federal government for a period of more than 30 consecutive days. Wyo. Stat. Ann. § 19-11-122
Deficiency judgments	Allowed
Cash exempted in bankruptcy	None
Notice to leave after house is sold	New owner must provide a notice to quit (leave) before filing an eviction lawsuit.
Foreclosure statutes	Wyo. Stat. Ann. §§ 34-4-101 to 34-4-113; 1-18-101 to 1-18-115

Index

⚖ NOLO *Online Legal Forms*

Nolo offers a large library of legal solutions and forms, created by Nolo's in-house legal staff. These reliable documents can be prepared in minutes.

Create a Document

- **Incorporation.** Incorporate your business in any state.
- **LLC Formations.** Gain asset protection and pass-through tax status in any state.
- **Wills.** Nolo has helped people make over 2 million wills. Is it time to make or revise yours?
- **Living Trust (avoid probate).** Plan now to save your family the cost, delays, and hassle of probate.
- **Trademark.** Protect the name of your business or product.
- **Provisional Patent.** Preserve your rights under patent law and claim "patent pending" status.

Download a Legal Form

Nolo.com has hundreds of top quality legal forms available for download—bills of sale, promissory notes, nondisclosure agreements, LLC operating agreements, corporate minutes, commercial lease and sublease, motor vehicle bill of sale, consignment agreements and many more.

Review Your Documents

Many lawyers in Nolo's consumer-friendly lawyer directory will review Nolo documents for a very reasonable fee. Check their detailed profiles at **Nolo.com/lawyers**.

On Nolo.com you'll also find:

Books & Software

Nolo publishes hundreds of great books and software programs for consumers and
business owners. Order a copy, or download an ebook version instantly, at Nolo.com.

Online Legal Documents

You can quickly and easily make a will or living trust, form an LLC or corporation, apply
for a trademark or provisional patent, or make hundreds of other forms—online.

Free Legal Information

Thousands of articles answer common questions about everyday legal issues
including wills, bankruptcy, small business formation, divorce, patents,
employment, and much more.

Plain-English Legal Dictionary

Stumped by jargon? Look it up in America's most up-to-date source for
definitions of legal terms, free at nolo.com.

Lawyer Directory

Nolo's consumer-friendly lawyer directory provides in-depth profiles of lawyers all
over America. You'll find all the information you need to choose the right lawyer.

FIFO6